To my parents, Robert E. and Alice R. Boston,
with love and gratitude

Contents

Preface and Acknowledgments

In a very real sense, the Religious Right forced me to write this book. In recent years aggressive Religious Right organizations have released a torrent of books, magazines, and pamphlets attacking the concept of separation of church and state. These publications promote a distorted history claiming that church-state separation was not the intention of the nation's founders. They assert that the Supreme Court invented the separation concept in the 1940s and that the United States was founded to forever be a "Christian" nation—"Christian" as they define the term.

The Religious Right charges that the Supreme Court, through a line of decisions designed to protect church-state separation and ensure the religious neutrality of the public school system, has "driven God out of the schools" or launched some type of vendetta against religion in public life.

I believe this propaganda is not only wrong, it is dangerous. Since so much of this Religious Right material is based on myths, half-truths, or distortions, I believe it is vital that someone set the record straight about how separation of church and state came about in the United States and what the principle means today. This book is designed to do just that.

At this juncture in our history—when church-state issues continue to capture headlines and engender public discourse—it is especially important that Americans not be duped by the Religious Right's campaigns of misinformation. Accordingly, I believe that those who favor the concept of separation of church and state must step up their efforts to publicly promote their viewpoint. If we do not, we are by default helping the anti-separationists define the terms of the debate. Nothing could be more tragic.

Anti-separationists are conducting a well organized campaign to discredit separation of church and state that goes far beyond distorted books and pamphlets. Letters denouncing separation appear regularly in daily and weekly newspapers across the country. The view is heard on evangelical radio networks and promoted in slick Religious Right magazines. Much of this propaganda leaks into the general population through secular radio and TV stations. In light of this campaign, I am confident there could not be a better time for a book reminding Americans of the value of separation of church and state.

The Religious Right's war against separation of church and state has had damaging effects. Thanks to a steady torrent of anti-separationist propaganda from the Religious Right, millions of Americans now believe that leaders like James Madison and Thomas Jefferson didn't really support separation of church and state; that the separation concept was invented by Communists; that separation is hostile to religion; that the Supreme Court has been stacked with atheists determined to drive religion out of American life.

My purpose is to counteract these falsehoods and others promoted by various anti-separationist forces, as well as give readers a solid understanding of how separation of church and state developed and how the courts have applied the principle.

I acknowledge a debt of gratitude of those who have come before me. However, I do see one critical shortcoming in those previous efforts: Much of the pro-separation material that has been written in the past few years, while excellent, has reached a limited audience or has been geared more toward those working in academia. In this volume, I hope to state the separationist position in clear, simple language that is easily understandable to the man and woman on the street, the believer in the pew and the activist in the community. I hope to take the very strategy that has worked so well for the Religious Right and turn it against them.

In taking on the Religious Right's falsehoods, I will also review the history of American church-state relations and the key court rulings in this area. In that sense, readers can consider this book a primer on the separation of church and state, Church and State 101 if you prefer. It is designed for the layperson, the non-lawyer or non-academician, who seeks a better understanding of what religious freedom means and how the concept of separation of church and state evolved in the United States.

In the spirit of total disclosure, I must hold out a few caveats to the reader. First of all and of primary importance, this book will unabashedly and proudly speak in favor of separation of church and state. As I have noted, the separation principle has come under increasing attack in recent times—from politicians, scholars and even some religious leaders. I consider this trend deplorable. Indeed, it is my contention that meaningful religious liberty cannot exist without a separation of church and state.

Given that, I will argue that the concept of a "wall of separation," first articulated so well by Thomas Jefferson nearly two hundred years ago, is as vital and meaningful for Americans today as it was during the post-colonial period—perhaps even more so in this age as the country struggles to accommodate new religious groups on a regular basis.

It is proper to call this book a manifesto. I am convinced that the concept of separation of church and state stands in grave peril today, thanks primarily to the Religious Right's propaganda war. The gravity of the situation cannot be overstated. We are dangerously close to demolishing Jefferson's wall.

My purpose, then, is to call for a return to this bedrock principle—complete religious freedom for all through the total separation of church and state. This is my view, and I am not ashamed of it. Those who oppose separation, whose minds are closed to the value of Jefferson's wonderful metaphor, would be well advised to stop reading here.

For everyone else, I offer a short, but I hope compelling, look at the history behind the separation concept and contemporary issues in church-state relations.

The book's approach will be non-technical. I will begin by setting the stage by reviewing some key developments in the relationship between church and state in world history that pre-date the existence of the United States.

From there, I will examine U.S. colonial history and take a look at the events leading up to the passage of the First Amendment to the Bill of Rights. I will continue on, following the course of U.S. church-state relations through the 18th and 19th centuries into the modern age. I will then look at some of today's controversies in this field. Throughout I will challenge the misguided notions of those who criticize the principle of separation of church and state and point out where the Religious Right and the "accommodationists," who argue in favor of a closer legal relationship between church and state, have got it wrong.

I will wrap up with some reflections on the importance of church-state separation. By then, I hope to have proved my assertion that without separation of church and state, the United States cannot remain a free nation.

I approach this task with no particular theological or sectarian axe to grind and seek to remain neutral on questions of religious belief. I contend that separation of church and state is the best policy for *all* Americans—religious and non-religious, conservative and liberal, Catholic, Protestant and Jew.

One other point needs to be made: In this book I will often speak forcefully when I deal with the Religious Right. This volume defines that term as that segment of the American religious community that is theologically conservative *and* active in the movement to abolish separation of church and state in the United States. While I do not take issue with theological conservatism, I must acknowledge that today, unfortunately, it often (but not always) goes hand in hand with attacks on church-state separation.

I do not hesitate to take the Religious Right to task in these pages, and many of my views about this movement are strongly worded. I make no apology for this and maintain that it reflects no bias on my part. The Religious Right started this fight by attacking the concept of separation of church and state. I am merely returning fire with similar spirit and vigor. This is entirely appropriate. I am convinced that the defense of separation of church and state deserves nothing less than a full-fledged commitment.

I am indebted to many fine scholars who have done important and more in-depth research in this area. Many of their works are listed in Appendix 4, "Suggestions for Further Reading," and I enthusiastically direct readers interested in further research to them. Primary sources include *Church, State and Freedom*, by Leo Pfeffer; *The Establishment Clause*, by Leonard Levy; *Toward Benevolent Neutrality*, by Ronald B. Flowers and Robert T. Miller and *Religious Liberty and the Secular State*, by John Swomley. Also useful were two standard world histories: *People and Nations* and *The Columbia History of the World* as well as *A Pocket History of the United States*, by Allan Nevins and Henry Steele Commager.

In addition, I am indebted to Professor Edwin S. Gaustad, emeritus history professor at the University of California, Riverside, for his excellent research on the Northwest Ordinance, which appears in chapter 4. I also owe a debt of thanks to the staff of Americans United for Separation of Church and State, whose church-state files were invaluable during my research. Special thanks go to Joe Conn of Americans United; under his careful guidance I first began to study separation of church and state. Special thanks also to Paula Wiley, who for years has provided expert computer technical assistance to both Joe and me. I also thank Steven K. Green, Americans United's staff attorney, whose comments improved the manuscript.

Lastly, I would like to thank my wife, Carol, whose support, encouragement and counsel were vital throughout the project.

Rob Boston,
June 1993

Introduction

Just as there are two clauses about religion in the First Amendment to the U.S. Constitution, the erosion of religious liberty in our nation can come from two directions. Governments can interfere directly with the "free exercise" of religion by passing laws or enacting regulations that impede the practice of one's faith. On the other hand, by passing laws "respecting an establishment of religion," government can give preferential support to some religions over others, or religion generally over individuals and institutions that subscribe to no religious faith.

The first danger is more obvious. When a government restricts the practices in which a religious adherent can participate, it is readily noticeable. Most people recognize that when meddlesome bureaucrats forbid a church to change the arrangement of its altar because of historical landmark laws, a violation of fundamental rights has occurred. Most people would find it objectionable. The same goes for efforts of a municipal fire department to ban candlelight Easter services because of a purely speculative fire hazard. Many of these conflicts have a way of working themselves out because of public outcry against what seems to be overreacting and insensitivity by government bureaucrats.

Admittedly, conciliation is not always the result, particularly if the religious group is relatively new or extremely small and the religious practice seems out of the mainstream. The sacrifice of animals in religious rituals in same areas of Florida has been forbidden (even though, ironically, most people don't think twice about eating animals), and the use of hallucinogenic cactus by Native Americans is even more controversial. Generally in these cases (although a recent Supreme Court case has complicated this) the right of the religious person is balanced against whether a "compelling" interest of the government outweighs it.

The other threat to religious liberty is more insidious and often far less visible. It comes when religious groups seek to have government promote their activities either directly or indirectly. Obviously, if one religious group convinces government to accept a narrow sectarian view about some subject, it is likely that adherents of other beliefs or none at all will find their lives made more difficult. Similarly, if one group persuades government to erect symbols of its faith on government property, it is likely that others will be made to feel like second-class citizens in their own communities. Finally, if one group gets heavy government subsidies to promote its programs (its schools, for example), that group will have distinct advantages in its efforts to proselytize for new members.

It is from this direction that the greatest threats to religious freedom currently arise. Extremely powerful and well-funded groups, ranging from the so-called "Religious Right" to the Roman Catholic hierarchy, have set up an agenda that seeks to find more creative ways to persuade government to adopt their views, promote their goals, and support their schools and other institutions. They are playing in every arena imaginable.

The Religious Right, primarily through Pat Robertson's Christian Coalition, is seeking to take over America's public schools. In school board elections they have been remarkably successful in electing "Christian" candidates (Christian as they narrowly define it). They often run what have been described as "stealth" campaigns, not generally acknowledging who their candidates are, with political advertising limited only to certain churches with specific ideological bents. In other areas, the stealth nature of the campaign is to hide the full range of radical change that is sought by the candidate, focusing instead on only one or two areas. "Hiding your light under a bushel" in American politics is dishonorable. Democracy depends on having voters hear what candidates really think about the range of matters that will come before them.

New legal organizations, such as the American Center for Law and Justice (another Pat Robertson-related group) and the Rutherford Institute are also trying to stand constitutional principles on their heads. For example, they send out a variety of threatening and misleading letters to school boards purporting to "explain" the rights of students to engage in religious activity in public schools. In fact, these missives are designed to intimidate school officials with threats of lawsuits, while the legal "advice" they contain is really designed to circumvent Supreme Court decisions on issues like state-sponsored prayer in public schools.

State legislators are also being besieged by a variety of religious groups demanding more and more state-funded services for their private schools. Although tax dollars should never be used to promote any religious activity, the public trough has seemed like a good feeding zone for schools unwilling to be satisfied with raising funds from members of their sponsoring religious body and from the voluntary choices of parents who want their children to attend those schools. One of the ploys now being promoted to secure state subsidies for religious schools is the voucher system, in which parents can take a voucher to any school in which their child is enrolled with the state treasury (our tax dollars) then being used to redeem the vouchers. This would provide, of course, direct government funding of religious schools. So far these schemes have been rejected by state lawmakers and by the public through ballot referenda, but advocates of parochial school aid keep trying new plans to keep the idea alive.

The irony of all these efforts at subterfuge and worse is that they are so often based on a total misunderstanding of history and constitutional principles. The Rev. Jerry Falwell once said the whole principle of separation of church and state is "bogus." He's wrong. What *is* "bogus" is the idea that the framers of our Constitution didn't understand the need for separation of church and state and didn't try to implement that principle. Supreme Court Justice Hugo Black articulated the view held by most of the Framers when he warned that "a union of government and religion tends to destroy government and degrade religion."

Our nation has the highest rate of church attendance in the world. As a minister, I realize that one of the most powerful reasons for this is that we are a freely worshipping people. Religion in America flourishes or perishes without the support or opposition of government. That is as it was intended, as it should be, and as it must continue if genuine religious liberty is to be preserved.

This book is an effort to clear the air of some of the historical nonsense being promoted by those who seek special privileges and governmental support for their religious beliefs and practices. When the truth about our heritage is made readily available, we can hope that the danger to our religious future will be lessened.

The Rev. Barry W. Lynn
Executive Director
Americans United for Separation of Church and State

1

Why So Many Church-State Problems?

It isn't always easy to stand up for what you believe in. Just ask Daniel Weisman. In 1989 the Providence, Rhode Island, resident and his family protested the inclusion of sectarian prayers at a public middle school graduation ceremony. Weisman, whose daughter Deborah was enrolled in the school at the time, had attended a graduation ceremony three years earlier for his older daughter, Merith, during which a fundamentalist Christian preacher recited a very sectarian prayer ending "in Jesus' name." For the Weismans, who are Jewish, it just didn't seem right that they should be asked to honor Jesus at a government-sponsored, public event.

Weisman took his concerns to officials at Nathan Bishop Middle School. Though sympathetic, school officials refused to drop the invocation. They did tell Weisman, however, that a rabbi would deliver that year's prayer.

The Weisman family didn't care what type of religious official was delivering the prayer. They believe that *any* type of state-sponsored religious exercise at public schools is inappropriate. The family has nothing against religion; they simply believe in separation of church and state.

Backed by the American Civil Liberties Union, Weisman filed suit in federal court to stop the prayers as an unconstitutional government endorsement of religion.

That's when the trouble started.

As soon as news of the lawsuit broke, Weisman's phone began ringing. Night and day the family was harassed by nasty phone calls. Some were obscene, others virulently anti-Semitic. In a few days, hate mail started arriving.

"The phone just kept ringing and ringing around the clock," Weisman remembers. "Many of the calls were abusive, some threatening—like people saying there's a bomb in the house."

The mail was even worse. "The ones that were against us were really nasty—swastikas and all that," says Weisman.

One local right-wing radio talk show host was so incensed over the family's lawsuit that he read their telephone number over the air and encouraged listeners to give them a call and tell the Weismans what they thought of the legal action.

There's no doubt about it: Church-state disputes can bring out the worst in people!

Many people, when they read about a case like the Weismans' in the newspaper, may think it's much ado about nothing. What's the big deal if a minister says a prayer at graduation? Who does it hurt if the city council puts a nativity scene on the steps of the courthouse at Christmas? Why all the fuss? Why are there so many church-state problems?

The last question is a good one, and this opening chapter will give some answers for it. It is important, as the tone is set for this book, to look beyond the superficial appearance of church-state disputes and go deeper. When people take the time to do that, they can better understand the powerful forces that motivate a family like the Weismans to take such an unpopular stand.

Many Support Separation

To begin with, it must be made clear that church-state matters *are* a big deal to lots of people, and it's not always a case of Christians vs. Jews or minorities vs. majorities. Scores of people in the United States, many of them quite devout, simply believe that separation of church and state has been a good policy for the country over the past two hundred years. They are offended when the government appropriates religion for *any* reason—even a seemingly small and innocuous one.

Many of the people who feel this way are members of the clergy. They see it as their role to spread religious messages and promote sectarian ideas and are disturbed when functionaries of the state try to usurp that authority.

Some people are fiercely protective of their own beliefs and don't want to support any other religions, directly or indirectly. Like Thomas Jefferson, they contend that it is "sinful and tyrannical" for the government to force citizens to give material support or public acknowledgement to religions in which they disbelieve. Accordingly, these people demand that they never be taxed to support any church or church-related institution, such as parochial schools, or be asked to take part in religious events against their will.

Others are motivated by self-interest. If the government can sponsor my religion today, they argue, it can just as easily denounce it tomorrow and sponsor someone else's. It's better, they say, to keep the government neutral toward religion, thus placing every faith on the same footing.

Some approach the subject of church and state with an amusing form of cynicism. The government, they say, has screwed up everything it has been involved in over the last few years. Why on earth would we want to let it meddle with religion? If there's one thing that will destroy religion in the United States, they argue, it's letting the government have a say in it.

It's clear that Americans support separation of church and state for a variety of reasons. Religious Right groups try to say only atheists support church-state separation or that support for separation is always motivated by an anti-religion bias. They're wrong.

Sure, lots of atheists do support separation of church and state. So what? So do lots of Methodists, Baptists, Presbyterians, Congregationalists, Episcopalians, Unitarians, Jews, Catholics, Buddhists, Quakers, Muslims, Lutherans, and so on.

Telling the Whole Story

One of the reasons some people get the idea that church-state cases are fueled by hostility toward religion is that the media often fails to tell the whole story behind these cases. In the dispute involving the Weisman family, for example, many newspapers, magazines, and television stations that covered the case, which went all the way to the Supreme Court, never bothered to report that the Weisman family had been offended by the fundamentalist Christian minister's invocation in 1986. As a result, many people who read about the case wondered why the family became so upset over a "non-sectarian" prayer offered by a rabbi.

Plaintiffs in a church-state case sponsored by Americans United for Separation of Church and State, a religious liberty organization based in the Washington, D.C., suburb of Silver Spring, Maryland, encountered similar problems in 1989 when they challenged public funding of the Rev. Jerry Falwell's Liberty University.

Facing financial woes, Falwell asked the Lynchburg, Virginia, Industrial Development Authority to grant the school $60 million in tax-free revenue bonds. Falwell hoped to use the bonds to finance new construction at the university and consolidate the school's debt.

There was one catch: State law in Virginia does not allow these types of bonds to go to "pervasively sectarian" institutions. Three Lynchburg residents, Haynie Kabler, Nick Habel and Jeff Somers, got wind of what Falwell was up to and decided to try to stop him. (See chapter 6 for more on this controversy.)

After negotiations with the city council proved fruitless, the three residents filed suit. Although a low-level state judge approved the aid, the case was appealed to the Virginia Supreme Court by Americans United. The result was a unanimous ruling from the state high court blocking issuance of the bonds to Liberty University. Falwell was outraged and accused Kabler, Habel, and Somers of harboring some type of prejudice against Liberty or Christianity in general.

No one was more surprised by these charges than Habel, a former Baptist minister. Habel is both devoutly religious and deeply pro-separationist. His actions were in no way motivated by any malice toward

Liberty University. In fact, during the court proceedings he and his wife prayed nightly for the well-being of the university!

"It's not my purpose to downgrade the university or to hurt anybody," Habel told Americans United's *Church & State* magazine. "I just want Jerry Falwell to live by the Constitution and recognize what's been good for all of us."[1]

Continued Habel, "I'm not a Falwell basher. I'm a pro-American constitutional separationist."

Attacks by the Religious Right

The dispute over Liberty University underscored one salient feature of church-state conflict: All too often when a church-state controversy erupts, the Religious Right finds it easier to launch personal attacks against those who bring the complaint rather than give thoughtful analysis to the issue or even admit that in a diverse society differences of opinion will exist. After all, why enter into a rational dialogue when you can label those who disagree with you "secular humanists," "enemies of Christ," or "tools of Satan"?

In the New Orleans area, several concerned public school parents have been involved in a long-running court battle to block state programs that unconstitutionally funnel tax aid to sectarian schools, mostly Roman Catholic secondary institutions.

The parents' actions were at first motivated by practical concerns. As parents whose children attend public schools, they were angered to see huge amounts of state money flow to private schools instead of the ailing public system. As the litigation dragged on over the years, however, the parents—Neva Helms and Marie Schneider—came to have a better understanding of and appreciation for the concept of separation of church and state.

But often when citizens challenge government aid to parochial schools in court they are accused of "anti-Catholicism." Roman Catholic bishops often foster this view. For example, in 1988 Cardinal John J. O'Connor of New York told the National Catholic Educational Association that the government's refusal to extend public aid to Catholic schools is due to anti-Catholicism.

Pleaded the cardinal, "Why can't we simply admit that and stop *creating* constitutional and other problems that are too often smoke screens for prejudice?"[2]

We can't admit it because it isn't true. In the New Orleans lawsuit, the charge is especially off the mark. Schneider, one of the lead plaintiffs in the case, is a devout Roman Catholic whose seven children once attended Catholic schools.

"Believe me, I know my faith," asserts Schneider. "And nothing I've studied makes what I'm doing wrong. I go to mass every week, never miss. Nothing in the public schools prevents that in any way."[3]

The parochial school aid lawsuits demonstrate once again how anti-separationists are too willing to substitute name calling and baseless charges of bias for a reasoned debate of the issues. Such an attitude can only serve to inflame what are already highly controversial issues. The charges add nothing positive to the ongoing public dialogue and only serve as a platform for further polarization, making the job of the courts all the more difficult.

Unfounded Allegations

Such an attitude only serves to makes church-state disputes ugly. Instead of learning the art of compromise, or simply accepting the limitations of our Constitution, the anti-separationists are rebuffed by the courts and in their anger go on to press further unfounded allegations of bigotry and discrimination.

Representatives of the Religious Right will never forthrightly admit, "We sought favored status and special financial support from the government, but the courts turned us down." Instead they say something like, "The courts have launched an all-out war against Christianity and refused to uphold the moral foundation of our nation, paving the way for a secular humanist takeover."

Indeed, the misinformation, the distortions and sometimes outright lies of anti-separationist groups are a chief reason why there seems to be so many church-state disputes. The Religious Right is fond of forcing the hand of the separationists. They believe these types of actions further their agenda. They think that if the American people are told often enough that the courts are hostile to religion they will eventually come to believe it. Many of the incidents the Religious Right provokes could be settled by reasoned dialogue and an understanding that in this nation people of many different faiths are struggling to live together in peace. Instead these disputes end up in the sterile world of the judiciary to be adjudicated according to impersonal legal formulas.

What Is the Religious Right?

Because the Religious Right features so prominently in today's church-state disputes and is discussed extensively in this book, it is important to take a few minutes here to properly set the stage by discussing what the term "Religious Right" means when used in these pages.

First, as has already been stated, theological conservatism alone does not make an individual or a religious denomination a member of the Religious Right. Many Christian denominations are conservative but not affiliated with this movement—the Seventh-day Adventists and Jehovah's Witnesses are two examples.

The Religious Right is marked by theological conservatism—generally meaning a belief that the Bible is inerrant—*and* a political outlook that is tied to far-right positions on a variety of social issues, including an overt hostility to separation of church and state.

Although movements fitting this definition have popped up at different points in American history, in this book, the term "Religious Right" refers to the movement that began, generally speaking, around 1980 with the rise of the Rev. Jerry Falwell's Moral Majority. Falwell, goaded by very conservative political strategists, ushered in this era by calling for a return to the Bible—as he interpreted it along fundamentalist lines—and demanding that believers of his persuasion step up their activity in the political sphere. (See appendix 2 for a short history of the Religious Right.) Today the Religious Right is primarily a Protestant phenomenon, but it also includes far-right traditionalist Roman Catholics and even anti-separationist Orthodox Jews.

The growth and expansion of the Religious Right is undoubtedly a key reason why church-state conflict is on the rise today. As the movement grew, it spawned political pressure groups. These groups eventually become quite aggressive and began filing church-state lawsuits.

The Role of the Media

Increased activity by Religious Right groups feeds into yet another reason why there seems to be an inordinate amount of church-state conflict in American life these days—the nature of the modern mass media. Church-state issues are always controversial, and there are few things reporters like better than controversy. Regional stories about relatively minor church-state flaps spawned by local units of national Religious Right groups can be picked up by news services and sent all over the country, dramatically increasing their perceived importance. Because church-state conflict makes good copy, it is more readily brought to the public's attention than other types of news.

And, as indicated, the Religious Right has also greatly contributed to the number of church-state cases in the courts. Several Religious Right "legal aid" groups now exist, and they file lawsuits all over the country. In some cases, minor problems are blown out of proportion or exaggerated for fundraising purposes before being rushed into court.

Religious Right groups do not hesitate to file church-state lawsuits they know cannot be won in court. In 1991 an attorney affiliated with a Virginia-based group called the Rutherford Institute filed suit on behalf of a California public school biology teacher in Mission Viejo who sought the right to teach "creation science" to his students, even though school officials had ordered him not to.

Putting the validity of the teacher's views on creationism aside for a moment, consider what it would have taken for a judge to uphold this claim: a finding that public school teachers are completely autonomous in the classroom and are under absolutely no obligation to follow the dictates of their superiors or the curriculum guidelines.

No judge in this country, no matter how politically motivated, is going to buy into such reasoning. Sure enough, a U.S. District Court judge threw out the lawsuit, declaring that the teacher has "no right to conduct himself as a loose cannon in his classroom . . . and teach theories of his own choosing, despite the fact that they are not authorized by and are prohibited by the state Board of Education curriculum."[4]

The Rutherford Institute, apparently believing that it had not wasted enough of the taxpayers' money or the court system's time, appealed.

Likewise, the Institute for Justice, a pro-voucher organization in Washington, D.C., filed legal action in mid-1992 on behalf of inner-city parents in Los Angeles and Chicago seeking to force state authorities to provide the parents with $2,500 vouchers to be used to offset the cost of education in parochial and other private schools. Institute for Justice attorneys said the state had to provide vouchers because public education in the inner city had failed.

Legal experts agreed that the cases would be tossed out of court in a matter of months, and indeed they were. The lawsuits were not filed as serious legal actions but rather as a political ploy designed to advance the pro-voucher public policy agenda of the Institute for Justice and to capture newspaper headlines.

At a time when our courts are clogged with pressing civil and criminal matters, such frivolous lawsuits do more than simply contribute to the public's confusion over separation of church and state. They add to the growing litigation crisis that threatens to eventually cripple America's judicial system.

The Religious Right Gets Excited

At different times over the past several years, many Religious Right organizations became convinced that the country was on the verge of major changes in church-state relations. In some cases they filed litigation to try to speed that change along. In other instances, groups of adults, working through public school students, have tried to disrupt the religious neutrality of the public school system, leading to still more court battles.

This is not to suggest that *every* lawsuit filed by a Religious Right group is without merit. But in those rare instances where a Religious Right group does have a valid point to make, it seems to be more interested in rushing into court and using the incident to gain media attention than entering into a dialogue that might lead to resolution.

Why does the Religious Right have such eagerness to shoot from the hip? Remember, the number of Religious Right groups has increased dramatically over the past fifteen years. Since the number of Americans who actually agree with this viewpoint is fixed (and nowhere near a majority) these groups are all chasing the same dollars. Those that do not appear to be aggressive enough in taking on the "liberals and humanists" will not survive. By exploiting problems that take place in public schools, always a favorite target of Religious Right groups, these organizations feed on the often paranoid views of their members and keep themselves afloat by ensuring that the dollars roll in.

Public Schools: The Big Bogeyman

These organizations have led their followers to believe that public schools are moral wastelands where all manner of perversions take place. Many of those who follow the Religious Right really believe that all public schools are handing out condoms to fourth graders on a daily basis and that a truly voluntary prayer can get a student expelled. Kids read textbooks written by Satan himself and receive all their classroom instruction from members of the ACLU, NOW, and the Gay/Lesbian Caucus.

Having built up this tower of lies, the Religious Right must then keep the myth alive with more and more outrageous tales of debauchery from the public school system. The quest for funds and new members leads them to send out hysterical fundraising appeals that have little connection to reality. As a result, millions of Americans who have had no contact with the public school system for decades believe they know exactly what goes on behind the schoolhouse doors, and they don't like it one bit.

In a climate like this, is it any wonder the United States is plagued with church-state conflict?

The Humanist Myth

The Religious Right claims that so much church-state conflict exists because "secular humanists," "pagans," or other, similarly vague forces are working to undermine Christianity in the United States by expelling it from public life. In reality, the conflict has been brought about primarily by the actions of aggressive Religious Right groups.

Like many of their claims, the Religious Right's charge of an atheist/humanist/pagan cabal is simply dead wrong, as a quick glance at some basic statistical data proves. Over the years, Gallup and Roper polls and research conducted by the Princeton Religion Research Center and other organizations have shown the United States to be the most religious of the Western nations. A summary of some of the polls' findings reveals some very interesting things:

- 90 percent of Americans polled say they do not doubt the existence of God.
- 58 percent of Americans say religion is "very important" to them.
- 42 percent say they have attended a religious service within the previous seven days.
- 59 percent agree that religion can answer all or most of today's problems.
- Only 2 percent of those polled say they are atheists; another 2 percent say they are agnostics.
- 77 percent say prayer is an important part of their daily lives.[5]

Most recently, a 1992 survey conducted by the Barna Research Group found 56 percent of Americans agreeing with the statement, "The Bible is the written word of God and is totally accurate in all that it teaches." Only 9 percent strongly disagreed with that statement.

Barna also asked respondents if the Ten Commandments are outdated. Sixty-four percent said they are not. Only 10 percent said they are. Asked if the notion of sin is outdated, 56 percent said no, 10 percent yes.

Furthermore, Barna asked respondents if they believe in the power of prayer. Again an overwhelming majority—71 percent—said they strongly or somewhat agree that prayers have the power to change circumstances.[6]

The atheist/humanist/pagan cabal is obviously asleep at the wheel! Despite the hysterical claims of the Religious Right, religion is alive and well in the United States.

The real problem, as far as the Religious Right sees it, is that many Americans stubbornly continue to believe they can be religious without believing in the theologies espoused by various camps of the fundamentalist world. Many Americans are both very devout and unaffiliated with any denomination. This offends the Religious Right because many leaders in this community persist in believing that only those who believe *exactly as they do* are really "serious" about religion. Most Religious Right leaders won't admit to holding this view, but sometimes the more radical ones admit it.

In 1988, Rousas John Rushdoony, a leader in the Christian Reconstructionist movement, a group of fundamentalist extremists who seek to impose Old Testament law on the United States (see chapter 8) told *Church & State* magazine, "Most church members today are practical humanists. God does not have a priority in their lives. They believe in Jesus Christ as the world's great fire and life insurance agent."[7]

In other words, to Rushdoony and other Religious Right leaders, one either believes just as they do or is branded a humanist! It would come as quite a surprise to most Catholics, Methodists, Presbyterians, Baptists, Christian Scientists, etc. to learn that they are really secular humanists. Rushdoony's sneering arrogance is deplorable.

The Religious Right needs the cloak of creeping humanism to shift attention away from its own radical agenda, an agenda most Americans reject outright. So far their ploy is not working. In 1992 Gallup conducted an interesting poll that asked respondents if they were concerned over the influence of two philosophies on society: secular humanism and religious fundamentalism. Of the respondents, 36 percent said they were concerned about secular humanism, but *50 percent* said they were concerned with religious fundamentalism.[8]

The Religious Right knows that Americans fear fundamentalism more than humanism, so it spreads distortion in a desperate effort to change that equation. In the process, the Religious Right adds to the country's church-state turmoil. Will their tactics work? Probably not. The number of Americans who identify themselves as "secular humanists" is so small it doesn't even register on opinion poll surveys.

In short, most Americans have never met a bona fide secular humanist. But most Americans have met far-right fundamentalists. They have fought their attempts to ban books in public schools. They have defeated them in political campaigns. They have argued with them in newspaper columns. Americans see the threat posed by fundamentalism and know it is real, unlike the bogeyman of humanism.

To succeed, the Religious Right must convince Americans that millions of their neighbors, friends, and associates—people who may claim to be Baptists, Seventh-day Adventists, Jews, Roman Catholics, Mormons, Lutherans, Episcopalians, and the like—are really closet humanists seeking to destroy religion in America and force atheism on everyone. Given the active presence of religion in American society, this cynical plan stands no chance of succeeding. Its continued propagation, however, adds to public confusion over the church-state issue.

Religious Pluralism

There is another reason why the number of church-state conflicts seem to be increasing, and this one has little to do with the Religious Right. Quite simply, religious pluralism in America is expanding. New religions regularly appear in America. Some are old faiths brought to the United States for the first time by immigrants. Others are offshoots of existing religions created by disputes over theology or doctrine. Some simply evolve over time, generated by the ideas of thinkers or philosophers.

Adherents of these new faiths expect the same free exercise rights as the members of mainline denominations, and in most cases they have few difficulties claiming those rights. But occasionally religious groups will appear on the American scene that engage in unusual or unlawful practices, leading to conflicts with secular authorities.

A good example of this phenomenon unfolded in south Florida while this book was being written. There, members of an Afro-Cuban religion known as Santeria went to court to fight for the right to engage in animal sacrifice.

Members of the Church of the Lukumi Babalu Aye say animal

sacrifice is an integral feature of their belief system. Priests of the church, which has an estimated 50,000 followers in south Florida, say the sacrifice rituals occur most commonly to mark rites of passage. (See chapter 7 for more on this dispute.)

When officials in the Miami suburb of Hialeah learned that the group was practicing animal sacrifice, they quickly passed a series of laws designed to outlaw the rituals. Frustrated, members of the church took the matter to court. Although they lost the first two rounds, the dispute went all the way to the U.S. Supreme Court, which ruled unanimously in favor of the church.

Remarked Ernesto Pichardo, a Santeria priest, "We're dealing with ritual offerings, an ancient practice. Nobody wants to do this hiding in their houses. All we want are the proper facilities to practice our religion."[9]

Obviously not every dispute raised by a new religion ends up at the Supreme Court or captures as much media attention as the Santeria case. But the Florida dispute exemplifies a trend: The United States is constantly struggling to accommodate new religions. In a nation that seeks to maximize religious freedom for all, new religions will continue to jockey for power as they seek the rights they believe are rightfully theirs. This perfectly understandable attitude adds to our country's volume of church-state strife.

The "Incorporation" Doctrine

There is a final reason why church-state conflict has increased in recent years that is also not connected to the Religious Right. This reason deals with the nature of our country's court system and the way the Supreme Court interprets the Constitution. In 1940 the high court, deciding the case *Cantwell v. Connecticut*, made it clear that the Constitution's Fourteenth Amendment means that the Bill of Rights is binding on the states, a doctrine known as "incorporation."

Prior to incorporation, many church-state disputes were settled in state courts. When church-state controversies were exhausted in those courts, that was as far as they could go. Incorporation changed that, making it possible for some of these cases to be heard in the federal courts for the first time. This naturally increased the volume of church-state cases in the federal courts, sparking a trend that continues until this day.

The doctrine of incorporation was a major step forward for civil liberties. The principle clearly forbids states from suppressing religious freedom, establishing churches or engaging in other activities that are unconstitutional under the First Amendment. But there is no denying that an unintended side effect of the doctrine has been an increase in the caseload of the federal courts.

In summary, then, church-state conflict stems most often not from a desire to squelch religion but merely from efforts to maintain the healthy distance between the two institutions. Egged on by misinformation from the Religious Right, however, many Americans have come to believe in the myth of a systematic war against religion waged by some sort of sinister cabal or band of atheists who have infiltrated our schools, courts, government and other public institutions.

To understand the church-state issue better and see why the Religious Right is wrong, it is necessary to take a step back and look at religious freedom in history—in the United States and other nations. The next chapter begins this brief historical survey.

Notes

1. Joseph L. Conn, "Don't Buy Liberty Bonds!" *Church & State* 43 (March 1990): 4-6.

2. Robert L. Maddox, "Air, Prayer, Holy Water—And Tax Dollars?" *Church & State* 41(June 1988): 23.

3. Joseph L. Conn, "The Louisiana Purchase," *Church & State* 42(October 1989): 4-7.

4. "Creationist Teacher Can't Be 'Loose Cannon,' Court Rules," *Church & State* 45(March 1992): 3.

5. "Religion Here And Abroad," *The American Enterprise Public Opinion and Demographic Report* 3(November-December 1992): 93-97.

6. Barna Research Group press release, Glendale, Calif., 1992.

7. Rob Boston, "Thy Kingdom Come," *Church & State* 41(September 1988): 6–12.

8. "Survey: Americans Don't Believe In Absolutes," Religious News Service (March 30, 1992).

9. Rob Boston, "Blood Feud," *Church & State* 45 (May 1992): 7–11.

2

Church-State Relations in the Middle Ages

Religion has always been a prominent aspect of human life, predating the development of the first governments. When people began to live together in organized societies thousands of years ago, it was inevitable that these two institutions, religion and government, would interact.

Unfortunately, that interaction has too often taken on a negative cast. For as nearly as long as humans have been participating in religion, be it monotheism, polytheism, or something else, governments have assumed the power to regulate, suppress, foster, or otherwise control aspects of this relationship. State-sponsored religion existed alongside the earliest forms of government and has persisted to the present day in many parts of the globe.

The birth of the United States as a political unit saw the rise of a radical experiment in government and religion—the concept of the separation of church and state. The ratification of the U.S. Constitution marked the first time any nation had dared to put a formal distance between these two institutions.

Like any other great notion, separation of church and state did not rise in a political vacuum. The men who wrote and ratified the Constitution were astute observers of the political scene of their times. They had seen the dangers of church-state unions in both Europe and colonial America. Having witnessed state-sponsored religious persecution up close, they were determined that unions of church and state would find no safe haven in the new country.

But placed in the perspective of world history, the United States is a relatively young country with a short history. Civilizations flourished in Western Europe, Asia, and Africa long before the settlement of North America by Europeans. These nations had their own experiences with religion and state—and again the interaction was all too often negative.

(Before going any further I should point out that this chapter is not intended to be a complete review of church-state relations in the ancient world and Middle Ages. Instead, this chapter touches on some of the key conflicts between church and state during this period, with the aim of showing how destructive these conflicts were to both church and state and how they damaged religious freedom. The story of religion and state in early history is fascinating, and readers interested in a more complete treatment should visit a local library.)

Early Church-State Relationships

Ancient Egypt, for example, saw conflicts between religion and government, often brought about by that society's powerful priests. Ancient Egyptian society was polytheistic, meaning the people worshipped many gods. An attempt by the pharaoh Amenhotep in 1379 B.C. to force the people to accept monotheism and worship one god—the Sun god— greatly destabilized society.

There were occasional instances of more enlightened thinking. In 270 B.C. Asoka, one of the greatest rulers of the Maurya Empire of what is now India, accepted Buddhism and encouraged his followers to do the same. Though Asoka became a devout believer in Buddhism and sent missionaries to nearby lands, he insisted on religious toleration for everyone. Spurred by his beliefs, he urged his followers to show greater charity toward their fellow citizens.[1]

The spread of Islam in the Middle East around A.D. 600 also demonstrated some fairly progressive thinking on religious toleration. Many early Muslims were warriors who lived to win new lands, but most did not force conversion on those they conquered. People living in areas conquered by Arab armies were given the option to either accept Islam or keep their current religion and pay an annual tax.

Sadly, however, these types of events are the minority. More commonly, early history is filled with stories of religiously based persecution and forced conversion. In the year 800, for instance, the emperor of what is today China, alarmed by the growing wealth and power of Buddhist priests, launched a program of persecution against Buddhists. Nearly 5,000 monasteries were destroyed, and more than 250,000 monks and other religious figures were forced to renounce their vows. In 988 Vladimir, emperor of Kiev Rus, the germ of the Russian Empire that later became the Soviet Union, converted to Christianity, ordered all pagan statues destroyed and commanded all of his subjects to accept Christian baptism.

Church and State in Europe

These early struggles between religion and government, while interesting, are sidelights to our story. To understand what took place in the United States and why it took place, it is necessary to look more closely at the experience of medieval Europe, the power of the papacy, and the Protestant Reformation. Developments that unfolded during this period eventually led to the creation of the church-state arrangement put into effect in the fledgling United States.

First, it is important to know a little of what life was like for the average person of the Middle Ages. The life of the common citizen in Western Europe during this period was dominated by his or her relationship to the land. The vast majority of people were peasants, farmers who worked the fields daily from sunup until sundown to carve out a meager living.

Europe during the 700s and 800s was fragmented and consisted of various fiefdoms ruled by often aggressive lords who were frequently at war with their neighbors. The thirst for expansion was great.

A huge chasm separated the peasants from the wealthy; there was no middle class. The Roman Catholic Church was a powerful force that often held monopoly power over the affairs of the government, and popes such as Leo III frequently intervened in governmental affairs. For instance, the church during this era claimed that it had the right to crown and depose kings, pointing to an incident in 754 when a pope proclaimed Pepin the Short "king by the grace of God."

The relationship between church and state cut both ways—dependency was often mutual. Kings needed the power and prestige of the church to hold office. The church, militarily weak at its headquarters in Rome, needed the armies of the state for its defense. Since the popes believed they had the authority to install kings, they did not hesitate to call on them for assistance. If, for example, a region of Europe were facing invasion by an outside army, the pope might demand that the king send troops to defend the region.

Despite the fierce competition between rulers, some leaders did attempt to unify Europe. One of these was Charlemagne, who ruled the Frankish kingdom of what is today France and Austria from 768 to 814. The deeply religious king pushed the boundaries of his empire southeast into what is today Italy as well as north and southwest.

Charlemagne eventually controlled much of Western Europe. On Christmas Day in the year 800, Pope Leo III proclaimed him "Emperor of the Romans," referring to the glory that had once been the Holy Roman Empire.

To the south of Charlemagne's empire, Muslim armies ruled, but in Western Europe, there was no other religious force except Catholicism. The Protestant Reformation was still hundreds of years away, and, while there were certainly people testing the boundaries of the church, no formalized religious opposition existed.

Charlemagne was an aggressive proponent of Christianity. He often forced people in the areas he conquered to accept baptism or be killed. After Charlemagne's death in 814, the great empire he had created splintered and chaos ensued as Muslim raiders from the south and fierce Vikings from the north swept across Europe.

Surprisingly, these invasions by various forces did not create a great degree of instability for the common peasant. Land fell under the sway of one group or another, but peasants usually remained on their farms. Their masters simply forwarded taxes to the new rulers.

The Influence of the Roman Catholic Church

Against this backdrop of frequent confusion, the Roman Catholic Church was the one stable force everyone could rely on to remain the same. By the 1100s, the church had formalized its hierarchical structure, from parish priest to pope. (The same structure remains intact today.) The church by this time had also fully developed its seven sacraments. These rituals, most of which occurred at points where a peasant's life underwent change—marriage, childbirth, death—meant that the church touched nearly everyone's life at one time or another. The church was seen as universal, unchanging, and infallible—a truly catholic movement.

Because of the church's overwhelming presence and formalized rituals, it in many ways took on the functions of local government to the peasants who were close to the land, and perhaps geographically far away from the king's seat of power. For instance, the church ran charities and provided various social services. Church officials even collected taxes and maintained a court system that had the power to levy fines.

Popes were well aware of the great power of their church. Most issued decrees stating flatly that all governments had a duty to submit to the church and its teachings. The church's power was enhanced because of its extreme wealth in the form of land holdings. For example, the church controlled a region called the Papal States, located in what is today Italy. This region existed for hundreds of years.

Because the political power of Catholicism was so great, it was inevitable that the popes would come into conflict with civil rulers. Indeed, there was a constant struggle for power between the church and the state spanning hundreds of years in the Middle Ages. Some kings sought to place curbs on the church's power, thus gaining more power for themselves.

Popes vs. Kings

For instance, King Henry II of England tried to limit church power in the mid-1100s. Henry had a keen interest in the law and established a traveling court system to deal with legal matters throughout the country. (His reforms led to the jury system still used in the United States today.)

But Henry II made one mistake. He sought to transfer some court functions from the Roman Catholic Church to the state. Henry believed, for instance, that some clergy members who were accused of misconduct should be tried in secular courts, probably reasoning that church leaders were more likely to get an unbiased hearing there.

Thomas Becket, the archbishop of Canterbury, strongly opposed the proposal. The disagreement made the two men bitter enemies. Word of the feud spread, and one day four of Henry's knights decided to take matters into their own hands. They entered Becket's cathedral and murdered him. The knights might have thought they were doing Henry a favor, but their action had negative fallout. Henry, facing the threat of excommunication by the pope, had to abandon his court reform.

Church-state conflict also ravaged Germany and parts of Italy. Here the state often came out on top in the struggle for power with the church. In the mid-900s Pope John XII proclaimed King Otto I "Emperor of the Romans" in appreciation for Otto's providing military assistance that John had sought. Sensing that John XII was a weak church leader, Otto used the relationship to his advantage. When John died, Otto proclaimed one of his assistants pope. A pattern was thus set, and for the next four decades German kings chose the popes.

The papacy during this period was often in a state of confusion, and the close tie between church and state only made matters worse. Henry III, a German leader who lived after Otto I, regarded the church as a tool of the state. At one point, three men each claimed to be pope, giving Henry III an opportunity to intervene. The king solved the dispute by ordering all three men dismissed and installing his own candidate as pope. Henry continued selecting popes for years.

Then the situation reversed, and the church gained the upper hand. Henry IV assumed the German throne after his father died in 1056. At this time the intelligent, crafty Pope Gregory VII was in office, and he quickly seized the opportunity to restore the church's lost power. Henry IV resisted these efforts, and his dispute with Gregory VII escalated to such a degree that the pope eventually excommunicated the king.

A weak leader, Henry IV was forced to travel to Italy to beg the pope for forgiveness and readmission into the church. When Henry arrived at the pope's winter castle at Canossa in the Italian Alps, Gregory kept him waiting in the cold rain and snow for three days before granting him an audience. It was a humiliating defeat for the king.

Despite Gregory VII's triumph, clashes between church and state persisted in Germany after both men were dead. Key to the dispute was the issue of who had the power to appoint bishops—kings or popes. Finally in 1122 leaders of church and state met in the German city of Worms in an attempt to resolve the matter. The resulting Concordat of Worms gave church leaders the right to appoint bishops but allowed kings control over certain secular duties of the clergy. The Concordat, while a well intentioned effort, did little in reality to ease the struggle between church and state during this period. Leaders from both institutions continued to meddle in the affairs of the other.

In 1198 another very powerful pope, Innocent III, came to power. Innocent insisted that the church have control over all kings, whom he regarded as simply servants of the church. Innocent achieved great success by using two powerful weapons of the papacy: excommunication of political leaders who disagreed with him, and interdiction, a practice whereby a pope excommunicated an entire country or region.

Interdiction was Innocent's greatest tool. Denying an entire nation the services of the church greatly increased the pressure on the country's leader. Peasants saw the church as the only path to Heaven, and interdiction condemned everyone to the fires of eternal Hell. People clamored for a speedy return to the church.

At one point Innocent III placed all of England under interdict and forced the king to agree to pay him a yearly fee before lifting the decree. Innocent also used his powers to dispose of leaders in Italy and Germany and put his own supporters on those thrones. He was perhaps the most powerful pope the world has ever known. Innocent III died in 1216.

Later popes had mixed success in dealing with the state. In 1294 Boniface VIII took issue with a plan by French King Philip IV to tax the clergy. When the two met in 1302 to try to resolve the matter, Philip ordered Boniface imprisoned. Boniface was quickly released but died soon thereafter. The power and influence of the papacy decreased.[2]

In 1378 the Catholic Church suffered a serious schism brought about by secular officials. During the period immediately preceding the schism, French kings controlled the papacy. Philip IV had even moved the papacy's headquarters from Rome to Avignon, a city in southern France.

People in Rome demanded an Italian pope, but naturally French leaders balked at this request. Eventually, two men—one French and one Italian—claimed to be pope. For the next forty years popes reigned in both Rome and Avignon, and secular rulers sided with the pope of their choosing, usually for political, not spiritual, reasons. In 1414 a church council began working on a plan to heal the schism, leading to a single pope in office at Rome three years later.

Church Over State and State Over Church

So it went, a back-and-forth struggle between church and state that sometimes resulted in church over state but just as often state over church. In any case, neither institution was truly free, and neither was untainted by corruption.

Against this backdrop occurred events such as the sporadic Christian Crusades of the 1100s and 1200s, whereby Christians attempted to wrest control of Middle Eastern holy lands from the Muslims. The Crusades were often instigated by popes and led by kings ostensibly in the name of Christianity, but the real goal of these forays was secular—to achieve better trade routes and commercial arrangements for business. None was very successful.

The situation remained much like this—a see-saw type battle for power between church and state—throughout the Middle Ages. Since the Roman Catholic Church had no competition, its power continued to solidify. Periodic church councils were held to determine questions of doctrine and faith. Those who strayed from church dogma were often dealt with harshly, especially during the first Inquisition of the 1200s. Many were accused of heresy against the church and burned at the stake.

Early Rumblings of Dissent

Despite the severe penalties that could be levied for heresy, some brave thinkers continued to disagree with church doctrine. Even though the Catholic Church's power seemed all-pervasive, dissenters gradually grew in number. In time, the voice of the dissenters became too loud and powerful for the church to ignore or squelch.

Critics began publishing broadsides that took the Catholic Church to task. In 1324 two priests, Marsilius of Padua and John of Jandun wrote a book called *Defender of the Peace* that claimed that popes should hold only spiritual, not civil, power. An English priest named John Wycliffe adopted these ideas and began preaching that persons could be saved by appealing to God directly, without the aid of a priest. This was in direct conflict with church teachings.

Although other critics clamored for reform, little was done. The church simply persecuted those who disagreed with it or excommunicated them. The seeds for change had been sowed, however, and dissatisfaction with the church would rise again.

The Protestant Reformation

What is known today as the Protestant Reformation began in the 1500s, when church critics began to increase in numbers and solidify their arguments against the church. Their dissatisfaction with Catholicism was multi-faceted, and Reformation leaders joined the call for reform for different reasons. In general, though, many felt that the Catholic Church had become obsessed with wealth and power and had thus strayed from its role as God's church on Earth. Reformers sought to bring the faith back to the people and re-emphasize personal salvation and piety.

An example of the church's emphasis on money, many reformers said, was the practice of selling indulgences, or a pardon from sin. The sale of indulgences had originally been limited only to those who engaged in extremely pious acts, but by the 1500s popes had taken to selling them simply to raise money.

The Reformation sparked first in Germany, with the ideas of Martin Luther, a Catholic monk. Luther's study of the Bible led him to conclude that the Catholic Church's heavy emphasis on ceremony was misguided. All that mattered, Luther argued, was that the sinner sincerely seek forgiveness. God would take care of the rest.

Luther was incensed when in 1517 a Dominican friar arrived in Wittenberg, where Luther resided, to sell indulgences. The friar had been ordered by Pope Leo X to raise money for the rebuilding of St. Peter's Church in Rome. The friar told the poor that for every coin they dropped into his box, a soul would depart purgatory and fly into heaven.

Later that year Luther executed a bold plan of action: At the door of the Catholic church in Wittenberg he posted the 95 Theses, a document that strongly attacked the sale of indulgences. Luther did not intend his action to amount to a formal break with the church and did not think of himself as a reformer, but his actions had severe consequences. Church leaders could not let such a brazen challenge go unanswered. They began to attack Luther and the reforms he suggested. The battle was under way.

Luther took advantage of the printing press, a relatively new invention, to spread his ideas through a series of pamphlets that summarized his thinking. He continued to argue strongly that people did not need priests or other intermediaries to communicate with God. Catholic Church leaders were infuriated. In 1520, Pope Leo X excommunicated Luther. Luther responded by burning the decree in public.

A special church council was convened to condemn Luther and ban the sale of his writings. Luther's life was in danger, but because Germany lacked a strong central government he was able to flee to the Saxony region, where he sought protection from its ruler. While there, Luther continued to spread his ideas and write pamphlets.

Luther worked feverishly to translate the Bible into German. Until this time, most common people had never actually read the Bible, since most peasants could not read in their own language, let alone the Latin of the Catholic Church. Luther's translation meant that Germans who could read would have access to the Bible for the first time.

The religion that became known as Lutheranism began to spread. Eventually, Luther officially formed a new church, which he believed was in keeping with biblical edicts concerning religion.

Leaders in some parts of Germany began to accept Lutheranism and even establish it as a state religion. One leader, Charles V, attempted to crush Lutheranism through military action but failed. The 1555 Peace of Augsburg that ended the conflict guaranteed each German ruler the right to choose a state religion.

While Luther's ideas and the chain of events he set into motion are crucial to world history, it is important to keep in mind that Luther, as important as he is to the development of religious liberty hundreds of years later across the sea in North America, did have faults. For instance, Luther did not believe in religious liberty as we understand the concept today. Although he sought the freedom to interpret the Bible in a way that differed from the view of the Catholic Church, Luther then assumed that his interpretation was the only correct one and persecuted those who disagreed. He was convinced that those who took issue with his views were inspired by Satan and called the pope the Anti-Christ. Luther was also a virulent anti-Semite who wanted to exterminate the Jews. Like so many early dissenters from established churches, Luther sought freedom only for himself and those who believed exactly as he did. Despite these faults, however, the actions that Luther took were a crucial bridge to events that were to unfold later. In that respect, he may properly be called a hero of religious liberty.

In the wake of Luther's success, other reformers sprang up. Many new Christian denominations took shape and began to grow. In many cases, groups of people simply gathered in houses for informal worship without forming an official church.

The English Reformation

Although Luther's ideas did spread to England, they had little impact there. The Reformation in England was sparked by a wholly different chain of events. King Henry VIII, who had a reputation as a strong defender of the Roman Catholic Church, brought about change for largely personal reasons. Seeking a male heir to his throne, Henry VIII wanted to divorce his wife, Catherine of Aragon, and marry Anne Boleyn, an attendant to the queen.

Pope Clement VII refused to grant Henry an annulment of his marriage to Catherine, mostly for political reasons. Clement feared the power of Catherine's nephew, Charles V of Spain, whose forces had attacked and sacked Rome in 1527.

Enraged, Henry VIII disestablished Catholicism in England and set up his own church, the Anglican Church, or the Church of England. (It is known in the United States today as the Episcopal Church.) The archbishop of Canterbury became the highest religious authority in the land, and Henry VIII quickly received his divorce. In fact, he married five more times.

Not satisfied with disestablishing the Roman Catholic Church, Henry set out to make England a purely Anglican nation. He launched a reign of terror against Catholics that soon spread to Lutherans and Anabaptists (the precursors of today's Baptists). One of Henry VIII's favorite tactics for disposing of heretics was death by fire. Two pyres were set side by side; a Catholic was burned on one, an Anabaptist or a Lutheran on the other. It was a startling change for a king who had once been proclaimed "defender of the faith" by the pope.

After Henry's death confusion reigned in religious matters for England's citizens. Henry's successor, Edward VI, retained Anglicanism and persecuted Catholics, but following his reign Queen Mary reestablished Catholicism for five years, in turn persecuting Protestants. Mary's reign was marked by such great religious persecution that history knows her as "Bloody Mary." Finally, under Elizabeth I, England returned to Anglicanism, which remains the country's state church today.

Calvin's Geneva

In what is today Switzerland, Reformation leader John Calvin founded a Protestant church based on a rigid code of beliefs he spelled out in a 1536 work titled *The Institutes of the Christian Religion*. Calvin and his followers eventually took over the city of Geneva and established Calvinism there.

Unfortunately, Calvin had absolutely no understanding of the concept of religious liberty. Calvin's Geneva was a harsh theocracy where the clergy controlled all aspects of the lives of the citizens. Laws prohibiting dancing and gambling, for example, were strictly enforced, and violations brought swift punishment. Calvin's enforcers closed down the theaters and tried to rid the city of its taverns. One unfortunate man, Michael Servetus, who held Unitarian-style beliefs, was burned at the stake by Calvin's henchmen because he disagreed with Calvin's interpretation of the Trinity. The world still had a long way to go before anything resembling true religious freedom came into being.

Despite the heavy-handed flavor of Calvin's ideas, his thinking spread to other countries, notably France, where the presence of Calvinists among the heavily Catholic population resulted in bloody conflict. Calvin's religious ideas also caught on and spread in Scotland and the Netherlands. The thinking of Calvin was eventually embraced by some in England as well, where the faith went by the name of Puritanism. This strand of Calvinism was exported to North America in the 1660s.

New Religions Take Hold

Although leaders of the Catholic Church launched attempts to reverse the effects of the Reformation by initiating a series of internal changes, their actions simply came too late. The church called councils to clarify Catholic doctrine and took active steps to stamp out what was considered heresy within the church, but to no avail. Protestant religions continued to spread.

The Catholic Church certainly remained an important influence in Europe and later in many other parts of the world, but it now had to accept a future of sharing that influence with a variety of Protestant denominations.

Some new Christian denominations died out quickly but others survived and exist until this day. They include Baptists, Quakers, Congregationalists, and Presbyterians. And the Reformation, which spawned a multitude of new denominations, had a direct impact on events that were to unfold in the United States 250 years after Martin Luther took his hammer to a church door in Wittenberg.

Notes

1. Anatole G. Mazour and John M. Peoples, *World History: People and Nations* (Orlando: Harcourt Brace Jovanovich, 1990): 62.
2. Ibid., 269.

3

The Evolution of Church-State Separation in the United States

Americans can be fuzzy on their history. Every schoolchild knows that Columbus "discovered" the new world and that some years later colonists from England began to settle in North America. After that, the details get hazy for a lot of folks.

Proof of this occurs every year around Thanksgiving. In many small towns you can still pick up newspapers at that time of year and see ads run by local supermarkets or other businesses depicting black-hatted pilgrims toting muskets and perhaps dragging turkeys. The ad text speaks of the importance of American liberties.

The hat, musket, and turkey might be historically accurate, but the rest, unfortunately, is a lot of pseudo-patriotic hot air. Pilgrims and Puritans had absolutely no interest in promoting "liberties" or freedom for anyone but themselves. It's true that they came to America from England seeking religious freedom. But it is important to remember that they sought that religious freedom *only for themselves*. Once on these shores, they set up harsh theocracies where every aspect of religious life was regulated and a state-imposed orthodoxy was strictly enforced.

Pilgrims and Puritans

As we review this period, it is helpful to keep in mind the distinction between Pilgrims and Puritans. Both groups broke with the Church of England and came to America, but each had different ideas about the type of religious state they would establish.

Pilgrims founded Plymouth Bay Colony in 1620. They were separatists who broke completely with the Church of England. They believed that the church was so corrupt and had strayed so far from the true faith that the only way to set things right was to start all over again from scratch.

Puritans established Massachusetts Bay Colony in 1630. They never broke with the Church of England, hoping instead to purify the church (hence their name) and return it to what they considered to be the right course.

Of the two, Pilgrims were slightly more open-minded about religious toleration. Unfortunately, their colony struggled from day one to eke out even a meager survival and was eventually absorbed by the nearby Puritan colony.

The Puritans had no use for religious liberty as we understand the concept today. By their thinking you either agreed with them on religious matters or left town. Church and state were melded into one. By law, only members of the Puritan church, which ultimately became the Congregationalists, could vote or serve in the state assembly. Heavily influenced by John Calvin, Puritan leaders looked to the civil leaders of the government to enforce religious dictates. They argued that if government did not curb sin, society would fall apart.

The colony's General Court levied a tax on all citizens to support religion and the clergy. If you didn't pay, you went straight to jail. No questions asked. Church leaders also kept a tight rein on ministers. Since ministers were paid by the government, any who rebelled were quickly cut off and replaced.

Fortunately, the Puritan theocracy of Massachusetts was not duplicated in other colonies. Remember, not everyone who settled in the colonies did so for religious reasons. Some were entrepreneurs who came seeking business opportunities. Others, such as craftsmen and artisans, were lured by colonists in need of their special skills. Still others came simply for adventure or to make a fresh start in a new land. Thus, it is a misnomer to suggest that most of our forefathers came to America in search of religious liberty; relatively few of them did.

Naturally, not everyone who came to America had Puritan leanings. Baptists, Quakers, Deists, even a small number of Catholics and Jews eventually arrived on the scene. Some tried to settle in Massachusetts, but, finding themselves unwelcome and weary of fighting the powers that be, simply wandered off to other colonies to settle. Others stayed behind to fight.

Roger Williams and the Rhode Island Colony

One settler who was not about to roll over or voluntarily depart was the iconoclastic preacher Roger Williams. Williams began making trouble for religious authorities of Massachusetts almost as soon as he arrived in Boston.

Williams was an unusual character for the times. A devout Christian, he was absolutely convinced that his views on religion were correct and that any rational being would in time come around and agree with him once the facts were laid bare. But Williams insisted with equal force that the state should have no business in enforcing orthodoxy. A person's understanding of religion and truth, Williams insisted, must come from within. He argued for complete freedom of conscience, a concept he called "soul liberty."

Wrote Williams, "I must profess, while Heaven and Earth lasts, that no one Tenet that either London, England, or the World doth harbor, is so heretical, blasphemous, seditious, and dangerous to the corporal, to the spiritual, to the present, to the Eternal Good of Men, as the bloody Tenet . . . of persecution for cause of Conscience."[1]

Because Williams absolutely railed against the church-state union of Massachusetts, he soon came to the attention of the state's ecclesiastical and civil authorities. When the General Court decided that every member of the colony should take a loyalty oath to the governor ending in the phrase, "So help me, God," Williams went on the warpath.

"A magistrate ought not to tender an oath to an unregenerate man," wrote Williams, because it would cause the oath taker "to take the name of God in vain."[2]

By 1635 the Puritan leaders had had enough of Williams. The General Court found him guilty of "disseminating new and dangerous opinions" and banished him from the colony. Williams was ordered to return to England.

Accompanied by a small band of dedicated followers, Williams fled and headed south to what is today Rhode Island and founded the city of Providence. He announced that all who chose to live there would enjoy full religious and political freedom. Williams's proclamation proved the sincerity of his beliefs, as he soon had to suffer many religious views he personally found distasteful. For example, Williams detested Quakers and often blasted them in his writings. Yet in Rhode Island Quakers worshipped unmolested, at least during the years of Williams' oversight.

It was Williams who coined the phrase that may have been the grandfather to Thomas Jefferson's famous metaphor of the "wall of separation" between church and state. Williams spoke of the desirability of a "hedge of separation between the garden of the church and the wilderness of the world." A decent distance between church and state, he maintained, would keep the purity of the church intact and safe from the corrupting influence of government.

It should be pointed out, however, that Williams' Rhode Island was no paradise where multiple religious groups lived in harmony. In fact, the colony got off to a raucous start. The citizens argued among themselves frequently, despite Williams' pleas that they put aside their differences and work together for the good of the new community. Eventually, the squabbling did die down, and Rhode Island prospered.

Another early dissenter against the Puritan church-state union was Anne Hutchinson, a renegade would-be religious reformer who dared to hold unauthorized religious meetings in her home. Hutchinson was expelled from the colony by Gov. John Winthrop in 1638 and fled to Rhode Island where she settled for a while before moving on to New York, where she died at the hands of the Indians. When told of her death, Winthrop remarked, "God's hand is the more apparently seen therein, to pick out this woeful woman to make her, and those belonging to her, an unheard of heavy example of [the Indians'] cruelty."[3]

Other Colonies

Experiences in other colonies varied, but none matched the level of religious freedom found in Rhode Island. In many states, citizens were taxed to support the Protestant denomination of their choosing, a practice known as "multiple establishment." In other states, a single church was established.

There were sporadic attempts at increasing religious liberty in some colonies. Pennsylvania, for example, was founded by William Penn, a Quaker who embraced religious toleration. Penn and the other Quakers had been cruelly persecuted throughout the colonies, and every colony (save Rhode Island) had laws banning their worship. In Massachusetts, a band of Quakers who had been exiled from Boston dared to return and were promptly hanged.

Under Penn's Great Law of 1682, all persons who believed in one God and agreed to live peacefully in the colony were welcomed. Unfortunately, in practice toleration was extended primarily to Protestants, and Sunday religious observances were required by law. Still, some groups found the atmosphere in Pennsylvania liberating. Roman Catholics, for example, enjoyed more freedom in the colony than they had anywhere else, and by the time of the Revolution, Pennsylvania was the only colony where Catholics could hold public services.

The Calvert family, which settled Maryland, were converts to Catholicism who founded the colony as a haven for members of that often-persecuted group. The colony's Act of Toleration of 1649 extended religious liberty to all Christians. But the colony never had a Catholic majority, and in time the act was repealed after Protestants came to power in Maryland and established the Church of England. (Maryland was also subject to periodic raids by neighboring Protestants in Virginia, who feared their Catholic neighbors.)

In short, religious liberty as we understand the concept today existed nowhere in colonial America outside of Williams' Rhode Island. Citizens were usually taxed to support religion. Strict Sunday laws were rigidly enforced. Blasphemy was a capital offense. Some colonies were flat-out theocracies; others came very close to it.

Undoubtedly the harshest colony remained Massachusetts, where the dangers of church-state union were vividly illustrated in an outbreak of witch trials in 1692. As the hysteria spread, nineteen accused "witches" —mostly women—near Salem were executed by civil authorities working in conjunction with church leaders. Eighteen were hanged and one crushed to death with stones. The incident, which appalled leaders in some of the other colonies, went a long way to demonstrate the dangers of a church state.

The Beginnings of Separation

Eventually even the harshness of Massachusetts' church-state union began to fade. Why did things change? To answer that question, it is necessary to look with greater detail at the experience of one key state, Virginia, and two of its most famous sons, Thomas Jefferson and James Madison.

Virginia, like many of the original colonies, was founded primarily for economic reasons. But there was a religious component, too. Captain John Smith, founder of the colony, declared it the duty of all Virginians to "preach, baptise into the Christian religion and by the propagation of the Gospel to recover out of the arms of the devil, a number of poor and miserable souls wrapt up unto death in almost invincible ignorance."[4] (He was referring to Native Americans.)

The Anglican Church was established as Virginia's state church, and a series of religiously inspired laws were quickly laid down. Blasphemy was punishable by death. Those who spoke "in disrespect" to any minster could be flogged. The punishment for non-attendance at church services was a monetary fine for the first offense, whipping for subsequent offenses.

These harsh rules, published in 1612, were later softened. Non-attendance at church, for example, was made punishable only by monetary fines. Still, this was no period of liberalization. Quakers and Catholics were flatly barred from the colony, and parents could be fined for failing to have their children baptized. Denial of the Trinity could lead to a three-year jail sentence.

In addition, all Virginia residents were forced to support Anglicanism through taxation, whether they believed in the tenets of the church or not. Every taxpayer was required to turn over a bushel of corn and ten pounds of tobacco to support the church. In 1632, the legislature upped the mandatory contribution, requiring all taxpayers to also contribute their twentieth calf, goat, and pig.[5]

Laws like this, common in many southern colonies where Anglicanism was the established religion, angered a number of colonists and helped spur revolutionary fervor. By the mid-1700s, Anglicanism was a minority religion in the southern colonies, yet all residents were forced to pay taxes to support Anglican ministers. Feelings of discontent over this system began to grow.

It is important to note here that state-supported religion did little to encourage piety in colonial America. Church historian Robert R. Handy estimates that by 1800 only 10 percent of the population were church members. Handy says there was an "overwhelming indifference to religion." Two other scholars, Roger Finke and Rodney Stark, put the number of "religious adherents" in 1776 a little higher at 17 percent. In any case, church membership did not begin to take off in America until after the adoption of the First Amendment, which gave the country true religious freedom through the separation of church and state. Today U.S. church membership stands at nearly 50 percent, and the vast majority of Americans, church members or not, say religion is important to them.

A general spirit of intolerance toward other religions fueled discontent. In colonies like Virginia other religions were permitted to exist but were restricted in many ways, especially in evangelical activity. Baptists had an especially tough time. From 1768 to 1774, a period known as the "Great Persecution," Baptists were frequently imprisoned or publicly whipped. In the town of Fredericksburg, several Baptist ministers were thrown in jail for refusing to pay a licensing fee imposed on "dissident" clergy.

James Madison

Here is where James Madison enters the story. In 1774 he witnessed a shocking sight: Five or six men in the adjoining county had been imprisoned for publishing religious views at odds with the state's orthodoxy. Madison was incensed. In a letter to his friend William Bradford Jr. he called the men "well meaning" and spoke on their behalf.

"That diabolical, hell-conceived principle of persecution rages among some and to their eternal infamy the clergy can furnish their quota of imps for such business," Madison wrote. "This vexes me the worst of anything whatever. . . . I have neither patience to hear, talk, or think of anything relative to this matter; for I have squabbled and scolded, abused and ridiculed, so long about it to so little purpose, that I am without common patience. So I leave you to pity me and pray for liberty of conscience to revive among us."[6]

Naturally Madison was not the only man in the colonies who understood the importance of religious liberty. As the colonies grew, the idea germinated among others in the population. What the movement needed was leaders to take the cause forth. Men like Madison and Jefferson later played that role.

Looking back on the situation today, Madison seems an odd choice to fill the role of great advocate of religious liberty. As a young man he was frail and frequently of poor health. Small in stature, he was once described by a contemporary as a "withered little applejohn." Even Madison himself did not expect to live long. Ironically, he lived into his mid 80s.

Madison and other forward thinkers of his time had been influenced by the writings of various European philosophers, notably John Locke. An early advocate of religious freedom, Locke argued that government should exist only to protect the inalienable rights of the people. Church and state, Locke argued, served distinctly different functions in society and should be separate. Churches, he said, are voluntary associations that must be supported without coercion from the state. Locke's *Letter on Toleration* laid down these ideas powerfully.

Though keenly interested in new ideas such as Locke's, young Madison was unsure of what to do with his life. Like many young men of his day, he studied theology, taking a degree at the College of New Jersey, today known as Princeton University. Madison studied there until 1772, when he returned to his Virginia home in Orange County.

In 1776 Madison was elected to the Virginia Convention, a sort of rough government operating outside of British authority. Madison was only 25 at the time and on the verge of assuming a great role in American history.

As a convention member, Madison worked with fellow Virginian George Mason in writing a declaration of rights and a body of laws that would guide Virginia once independence was declared. Mason shared Madison's interest in religious liberty and drafted language that would guarantee religious toleration. Suspicious that the concept of mere toleration did not go far enough, Madison suggested substitute language guaranteeing that "all men are equally entitled to the full and free exercise of religion." In time the language was adopted. Madison also sought to add language disestablishing the Anglican Church in Virginia, but the convention rejected it.

The Virginia Convention declared independence and adjourned in July. Shortly thereafter Madison was elected to the newly created House of Delegates. In October he returned to Williamsburg, the colonial capital, for the body's first session.

Madison was assigned to the Committee on Religion, and began working with Jefferson on another attempt to end church establishment in Virginia. Madison may have been influenced by an appeal from Presbyterians in Prince Edward County. Members of that religious group petitioned the House of Delegates to deliver them from "a long night of Ecclesiastical bondage" and asked that "without delay, all Church establishments . . . be pulled down, and every tax upon conscience and private judgment be abolished" so that Virginia might become an "asylum for free inquiry, knowledge, and the virtuous of every denomination."[7]

Madison worked with Jefferson in an effort to comply with the Presbyterians' request by proposing legislation disestablishing the Anglican Church in Virginia. The move turned out to be premature, and it was blocked by powerful legislators, such as Edmund Pendleton, who favored retaining church establishment. Despite the failure, Madison and Jefferson had advanced the idea of church-state separation and laid the groundwork for a future success.

During the waning years of the Revolution, Madison was chosen to be a delegate to the Continental Congress, a body charged with formulating policy for the soon-to-be independent United States. With a peace treaty signed with Great Britain, Madison returned home to Orange County in 1784 and again won a seat in the Virginia House of Delegates.

Almost immediately Madison became involved in a battle over separation of church and state. Patrick Henry, the patriot best known for uttering the phrase, "Give me liberty or give me death," introduced a bill that would levy a general assessment on all state citizens to support ministers of Christian religions.

Henry's "Bill Establishing a Provision for Teachers of the Christian Religion" is quite severe by today's standards. It required all persons "to pay a moderate tax or contribution annually for the support of the Christian religion, or of some Christian church, denomination or communion of Christians, or for some form of Christian worship."[8]

Henry's bill was actually more tolerant than previous colonial establishment provisions. Under it, Christians in Virginina would have at least had the freedom to choose which church to support instead of being required to back one denomination. But Madison, ever the forward thinker, still found the measure full of shortcomings.

The assessments bill, Madison argued, was "obnoxious on account of its dishonorable principle and dangerous tendency."[9]

Henry sincerely believed that his proposal would safeguard the morality of the population. The bill was nothing new; versions of it had come up before in the Virginia legislature. As before, opposition from religious minorities was swift and angry, with Baptists leading the charge.

The politics of the post-colonial period was not so different from today, and Madison was able to use procedural moves to delay consideration of the bill until late in 1785—almost a year after the measure was introduced. In the interim period, a bill establishing the Episcopal Church in Virginia was introduced in the House of Delegates.

The establishment bill was a result of fallout from the Revolution. In the post-Revolution period, it hardly seemed appropriate to continue the establishment of the Church of England in the newly born United States. Some legislators, seeking to clarify the status of the church, backed the establishment bill.

Madison abhorred the idea of established churches, of course, but even he threw his weight behind the measure and voted for establishment. Madison saw no way he could successfully fight both that measure and Henry's general assessment bill. Since Madison considered the Henry bill much more dangerous to religious freedom, he decided to concentrate his energies on defeating it.

Madison's move illustrated his shrewd political maneuvering. An established church, Madison realized, was no longer what the people of Virginia wanted. If the establishment bill should pass, he figured, it would not last long. Madison was correct. Two years after its passage, the bill establishing the Episcopal Church in Virginia was repealed.

Madison used the eleven-month period before consideration of the Henry general assessment bill wisely. At Mason's urging, he penned what is today regarded as one of the classics of religious freedom— the "Memorial and Remonstrance against Religious Assessments."

The "Memorial and Remonstrance" is a list of fifteen reasons why Henry's bill should be rejected. The document was circulated widely throughout Virginia in the interim period and had a powerful influence on all who read it. Opposition to the Henry measure poured in from counties around the state, and thousands of opposition letters flooded the lawmakers' chambers.

Asserting that, "It is proper to take alarm at the first experiment on our liberties," the "Memorial and Remonstrance" observed in part, "Who does not see that the same authority which can establish Christianity, in exclusion of all other Religions, may establish with the same ease any particular sect of Christians, in exclusion of all other Sects? That the same authority which can force a citizen to contribute three pence only of his property for the support of any one establishment, may force him to conform to any other establishment in all cases whatsoever?"[10]

Elsewhere in the document Madison asserts, "If Religion be not within the cognizance of Civil Government how can its legal establishment be necessary to Civil Government? What influence in fact have ecclesiastical establishments had on Civil Society? In some instances they have been seen to erect a spiritual tyranny on the ruins of the Civil authority; in many instances they have been seen upholding the thrones of political tyranny; in no instance have they been seen the guardians of the liberties of the people."[11]

Madison's strategy worked. In the interim election, many supporters of the assessment bill lost their seats. When the Virginia legislature reconvened in the fall of 1785, the mood of the new body was clearly running against the Henry bill. No doubt many lawmakers were influenced by a stack of letters and petitions denouncing the bill that had poured into the legislature from all over Virginia. Henry himself had been elected governor of Virginia (partly with Madison's help), where he could no longer speak on behalf of his bill from the floor of the legislature. This sealed the measure's fate. It was soundly defeated.

Thomas Jefferson's Religious Freedom Bill

Madison decided to press his victory to its limits by resurrecting Thomas Jefferson's 1777 "Bill for Religious Freedom." Jefferson's measure, which declared that, "No man shall be compelled to frequent or support any religious worship, place, or ministry whatsoever," had gotten nowhere when originally introduced. On the heels of the defeat of the Henry general assessments bill, Madison believed the time was right to push it through.

At the time Jefferson was in Paris representing the interests of the U.S. government in France. He kept in close communication with Madison on the developments concerning his religious freedom bill.

Jefferson's bill was passed by a 60-27 vote in January 1786. Calling it "sinful and tyrannical to compel a man to furnish contributions for the propagation of opinions which he disbelieves and abhors," the measure takes a strong stand against state-supported religion and guarantees religious free exercise.

Reads the bill, "Be it therefore enacted by the General Assembly of Virginia that no man shall be compelled to frequent or support any religious worship, place or ministry whatsoever, nor shall be enforced, restrained, molested or burdened in his body or goods, nor shall otherwise suffer on account of his religious opinions or beliefs; but that all men shall be free to profess, and by argument to maintain, their opinions in matters of religion, and that the same shall in no wise diminish, enlarge or affect their civil capacities."[12]

Jefferson insisted that his bill was designed to protect *all* religious practitioners. He took great pride in noting that efforts to amend the measure by limiting its protections to Christians only were rejected. In his autobiography, Jefferson noted, "The insertion was rejected by a great majority, in proof that they meant to comprehend, within the mantle of its protection, the Jew and the Gentile, the Christian and Mahometan, the Hindoo, the infidel of every denomination."[13]

Thanks to the efforts of Jefferson and Madison, Virginia, in the space of a few years, went from state-established religion to a system that offered complete religious freedom to Christians, Jews, Muslims, believers and non-believers alike. This is a remarkable accomplishment.

The Bill of Rights

Madison's next achievement concerned the Bill of Rights. Many Americans may be surprised to learn that the Bill of Rights was actually a kind of constitutional afterthought. The Constitution was originally written without one. Indeed, many framers saw no need for a Bill of Rights. Madison himself was originally in this camp.

Certainly Madison did not oppose a Bill of Rights because he feared the concept of civil liberties. He held a view not uncommon in his day that insisted that by listing the rights of citizens in the Constitution, the government was implying that *only* those rights were to be granted to the American people. Madison thus feared that the enumeration of rights would serve as a natural limitation on freedom.

This is not to imply, however, that religious freedom was not discussed at the original Constitutional Convention of 1787. Indeed, Charles Pinckney, a young South Carolina delegate, proposed language stating that, "The Legislature of the United States shall pass no law on the subject of religion."[14]

Although convention delegates did not see this as necessary, they did adopt another of Pinckney's proposals forbidding religious tests for federal office. The prohibition is found in Article Six and reads, "[N]o religious test shall ever be required as a qualification to any office or public trust under the United States."

The Constitution fashioned in 1787 is a secular document. There is no mention of God, Jesus Christ, or a supreme being anywhere in the document. A minority faction of delegates pressed for some type of recognition of Christianity in the Constitution, but their views were rejected.

Contrary to common belief, convention delegates did not even lead off their deliberations with prayer. Although Benjamin Franklin made such a suggestion a month into the proceedings, the convention adjourned rather than vote on the measure, and did not take it up again after reconvening.

The omission of God in the Constitution was not intended as a slight. Although the action angered some religious leaders, Madison insisted that the move was for the best. He worried about what such God talk could lead to, insisting that the Constitution had created not even "a shadow of right in the general government to intermeddle with religion."[15]

(Incidentally, the omission of God in the Constitution has served to vex today's Religious Right activists, who insist that the United States was founded as a "Christian nation." Since Madison's statement and the omission serve as a great embarrassment to them, some have taken to asserting that the document recognizes Jesus Christ at the end, where the date contains the phrase "in the year of our Lord"!)

Despite the convention's work, it soon became apparent that legislators in some states, notably North Carolina and Rhode Island, would not ratify the Constitution lacking a Bill of Rights. Accordingly, debate began on a series of amendments in 1789.

By the time work began Madison had changed his mind, maintaining that he now favored an amendment to guarantee "all essential rights, particularly the rights of Conscience in the fullest latitude, the freedom of the press, trial by jury, security against general warrants, etc."

Jefferson too advocated a Bill of Rights. Writing to Madison from

France he insisted "[A] bill of rights is what the people are entitled to against every government on earth." He insisted that freedom of religion be among those rights.

The First Amendment Takes Shape

Madison was charged with the assignment of drafting what eventually became the First Amendment. His first effort is quite different from what was eventually settled on, but contains much of the spirit of the religious freedom guarantee we know today. It reads, "The civil rights of none shall be abridged on account of religious belief, nor shall any national religion be established, nor shall the full and equal rights of conscience in any manner or on any pretext be infringed."[16]

Much has been made by today's accommodationists of Madison's use of the word "national" in this version. They argue that all Madison intended to do was prevent the government from establishing a national church, not provide for church-state separation.

This weak argument has been thoroughly demolished by respected constitutional scholar Leonard W. Levy in his excellent book, *The Establishment Clause: Religion and the First Amendment.* Levy points out that at the time the First Amendment was drafted, it was intended to apply only to the federal government. The word "national" was added, he writes, in order to make it clear to the states that the prohibition was limited to Congress. (States retaining established churches wanted an assurance that they could keep them.) And, as Levy points out, the word was quickly removed during debate over the language of the amendment. Madison himself added that he believed the people feared that one religious denomination might assume prominence in the United States or perhaps two powerful groups would join together to establish a religion to which they would compel others to conform. He saw adding the word "national" as one way of making it clear that the amendment would specifically prevent this from happening.[17]

An eleven-member House committee, which included Madison, began working on the language and soon rewrote it to read, "No religion shall be established by law, nor shall the equal rights of conscience be infringed." A second committee-approved proposal read, "No state shall infringe the equal rights of conscience."[18]

The proposals were then referred to the full House of Representatives. For a time the House favored a version reading, "Congress shall make no laws touching religion, or infringing the rights of conscience." But the House ultimately adopted a version put forth by Fisher Ames of Massachusetts. It read, "Congress shall make no law establishing religion, or to prevent the free exercise thereof, or to infringe the rights of conscience."[19]

The amendment then moved to the Senate. The Senate considered and rejected three alternative versions:

- "Congress shall make no law establishing one religious sect or society in preference to others."
- "Congress shall not make any law infringing the rights of conscience, or establishing any religious sect or society."
- "Congress shall make no law establishing any particular denomination of religion in preference to another."[20]

The fact that these versions were defeated clearly indicates that today's accommodationists are wrong in stating that all the First Amendment was intended to do was ban the establishment of a national church. Were that the case, the third version above would have sufficed. Obviously, the Senate had something more far-reaching in mind.

After a short recess the Senate took up the matter of the religion clauses again. The record of these deliberations is sketchy, but we do know that the Senate eventually emerged with the following language: "Congress shall make no law establishing articles of faith or a mode of worship, or prohibiting the free exercise of religion."[21]

House members, however, refused to accept the Senate's version of the religion clauses. A joint conference committee was appointed to resolve the matter. Madison played a key role in these negotiations, and on September 24 the final wording of the religion clauses was announced: "Congress shall make no law respecting an establishment of religion, or prohibiting the free exercise thereof."

As Levy points out, the Constitution grants the government limited powers. The First Amendment was carefully drafted to tell the government what it may *not* do in matters of religion. Today's accommodationists, who assert that the amendment somehow grants government the right to give non-preferential aid to religion, stand on crumbling ground. The legislative history of the religion clauses proves exactly the opposite. The First Amendment is a command to government to keep its hands off religion—neither aiding nor hindering it—to the fullest extent possible.

State legislatures began passing the Bill of Rights, some rather quickly, others taking their time. By the end of 1791, the Bill of Rights had been ratified by a majority of the states and was an official part of the Constitution of the new country.

Jefferson and the "Wall of Separation"

Ten years later a group of Baptists in Danbury, Connecticut, wrote to President Thomas Jefferson to express their thoughts on religious liberty. At this time Congregationalism was still the established church of Connecticut. Baptists in the state chafed under this system, outraged that government officials were so presumptuous as to collect church taxes and regulate religious expression. Connecticut allowed tax money to be used to support churches that were approved by the majority in each town. Those who could prove they were adherents of another faith were technically exempt from paying the church tax. However, Baptists at the time were a rather despised minority, and some communities made it difficult for them to certify their membership.

Connecticut Baptists knew of Jefferson's reputation as a champion of religious freedom and were heartened by his election. They hoped Jefferson's view of religious freedom would be adopted in Connecticut and wrote to tell him so.

In his reply Jefferson described the First Amendment as building a "wall of separation between church and state."[22]

Although Jefferson was in France at the time the First Amendment was deliberated, he kept in close contact with Madison and followed the proceedings with keen interest. Madison was in many ways Jefferson's protege; the two men had nearly identical outlooks on religious liberty, and Madison had engineered Jefferson's religious freedom bill through the Virginia legislature.

Any allegation, therefore, that Jefferson was somehow unqualified to speak on the meaning of the First Amendment is not simply foolish. It is also offensive to the memory of this great American.

Jefferson responded to the Danbury Baptists' letter in 1802. Contrary to the assertions of today's anti-separationists, Jefferson's reply was not a hastily written note designed simply to curry favor with a political constituency. Jefferson well knew that he was making a major pronouncement on an issue of deep importance.

Before sending the missive, Jefferson asked Levi Lincoln, his attorney general, to review it. In an attached note Jefferson wrote, "Averse to receive addresses (letters), yet unable to prevent them, I have generally endeavored to . . . [make] them the occasion, by way of answer, of sowing useful truths and principles among the people, which might germinate and become rooted among their political tenets. . . . The Baptist address . . . furnished an occasion, too, which I have long wished to find, of saying why I do not proclaim fastings and thanksgivings, as my predecessors did."[23]

The care that Jefferson took in drafting his response to the Danbury Baptists clearly proves that he did not view this letter as a hasty reply to a bothersome constituency so that he could get on to more important business. He used his reply to the Danbury Baptists to make a major policy statement.

Observed Jefferson in the letter, "I contemplate with sovereign reverence that act of the whole American people which declared that their legislature should 'make no law respecting an establishment of religion, or prohibiting the free exercise thereof,' thus building a wall of separation between Church and State."[24]

It is important to remember that at the time Jefferson composed his response he was under fire from conservative religious elements who disagreed with his stand in favor of full religious liberty. Jefferson saw his response as an opportunity to explain his thinking on church-state relations. Far from being a mere courtesy, the letter represented a summary of Jefferson's thinking on the purpose and effect of the First Amendment's religion clauses.

False Stories about "the Wall"

Led primarily by Religious Right propagandist David Barton, some Religious Right activists have asserted that Jefferson later claimed that his wall was meant to be "one-directional" and designed only to protect the church from incursions by the state.[25] This is a fabrication. No such claim appears anywhere in Jefferson's writings. The assertion flies in the face of the entire body of Jefferson's thinking on church-state relations.

During the 1992 election, the Colorado branch of Pat Robertson's Christian Coalition circulated a document claiming that Jefferson called his wall "one-dimensional" and went on to say that the United States government should be based on "Christian principles." The Coalition also incorrectly claimed that Jefferson made the "wall" comment in an 1801 speech.[26]

The group is wrong on three counts. As history indicates, Jefferson first used the metaphor in an 1802 letter that says nothing about the wall being "one-directional" or "one-dimensional" and certainly says nothing about the U.S. government being based on Christian principles. Jefferson clearly believed no such thing. But rather than go to a public library and check their facts, the Christian Coalition and other Religious Right groups have simply continued to spread this distortion. They are either abysmally ignorant or engaging in an outright deception.

In fact, Jefferson's views on Christianity's relationship to government are clear and can be easily uncovered with a little bit of research. In an 1824 letter to John Cartwright, Jefferson expressed anger at judges who had based rulings on their belief that Christianity is part of the common law. Cartwright had written a book critical of these judges, and Jefferson was glad to see it.

Observed Jefferson, "The proof of the contrary, which you have adduced, is controvertible; to wit, that the common law existed while the Anglo-Saxons were yet pagans, at a time when they had never yet heard the name of Christ pronounced, or knew that such a character had ever existed."

Jefferson challenged "the best-read lawyer to produce another script of authority for this judicial forgery" and concluded, "What a conspiracy this, between Church and State!"[27]

Unfortunately for the Christian Coalition, even a cursory glance at Jefferson's record unmasks the group's deceptions. As president, Jefferson put his wall of separation theory into practice. For example, he refused to issue proclamations calling for days of prayer and fasting, holding that they violate the First Amendment. Jefferson considered explaining his opinion on the matter of proclamations in his letter to the Danbury Baptists. His original draft of the letter contained a sentence reading, "Congress thus inhibited from acts respecting religion, and the Executive authorized only to execute their acts, I have refrained from prescribing even occasional performances of devotion."[28]

Jefferson removed the sentence at the urging of Attorney General Lincoln, who believed it would hurt the president politically in New England. Jefferson took the advice but wanted to make his views clear. In the draft of the letter Jefferson wrote in the margin, "This paragraph was omitted on the suggestion that it might give uneasiness to some of our republican friends in the eastern states where the proclamation of thanksgivings etc. by their Executive is . . . [a] habit and is respected."[29]

A Few Inconsistencies

As strict a separationist as Jefferson was, however, he did backslide occasionally. For example, Jefferson approved treaties with Indian tribes that underwrote religious education for them, approving expenses to "propagate the Gospel among the Heathen." Again, Religious Right activists have tried to make the most of this and have claimed that Jefferson must not have favored strict separation since he took this action.

The Religious Right overlooks a few points, however. First, the early U.S. government considered Indian tribes foreign nations, and it is likely that Jefferson believed the First Amendment had no weight in the government's dealing with them. Secondly, Jefferson believed that religion would "civilize" Native Americans and improve relations between the tribes and settlers pushing westward. Finally, in many places, Christian missionaries had already established amicable relationships with the

Indians and were providing various humanitarian services. Instead of duplicating these efforts, the government employed the religious agencies to accomplish their secular goals. Like politicians today, Jefferson was willing to set aside a vital constitutional principle for the interests of national security.

The latter explanation may even be too hard on Jefferson. Keep in mind that the Bill of Rights was a radical idea. It would have been a miracle if it were applied without a hitch. And indeed it was not always smoothly applied. There were plenty of bumps along the way. For example, just a few years after the Bill of Rights was approved, Congress passed the Sedition Act, legislation that flew directly in the face of the First Amendment's free speech clause by punishing anyone who made "false, scandalous, or malicious" statements about the government. Many newspaper editors were prosecuted under the law.

Also, despite the Eighth Amendment's prohibition of "cruel and unusual punishment," whipping, branding, and public flogging remained common forms of sanctions used against criminals during this period.

Madison Under Attack

Religious Right advocates and accommodationists have made similar attempts to discredit Madison's credentials as a separationist. But once again their arguments persuade only the uninformed. For example, accommodationists like to point out that early in his career Madison approved of the concept of congressional chaplains paid for with public funds. What they omit is Madison's later thinking, in which he reversed his position and came out solidly in opposition to state-paid chaplains, writing, "The establishment of the chaplainship to Congress is a palpable violation of equal rights, as well as of Constitutional principles."[30]

Likewise, Religious Right activists point to an early piece of legislation Madison introduced in the Virginia legislature that would have punished sabbath breakers. The history surrounding this bill is fuzzy at best, and it's quite possible Madison sponsored it for political reasons (just as he voted for the Anglican Church establishment bill). Or Madison might simply have wanted to give the government some mechanism for punishing those who disrupted church services (a problem in some colonies). Madison may also have introduced it as part of a package of legislation providing a penal code for Virginia in the wake of the Revolution, intending to update it and remove the antiquated portions later. If this were the case, the law would still reflect pre-Revolution measures protecting the Church of England. Lastly, the bill could have been a youthful mistake taken before Madison's thinking on religious freedom jelled.

Whatever the case, this incident is a minor blotch on Madison's otherwise impeccable credentials as a separationist. It has been blown out of proportion by the Religious Right, but despite their wild allegations it cannot be used to blacken Madison's achievements in pioneering the concept of religious liberty.

Lastly, anti-separationists point out that Madison during his presidency issued proclamations calling for days of prayer and fasting. Again they tell only half of the story. Later in life Madison concluded that his actions had been unconstitutional and in a document known as the "Detached Memoranda" listed five reasons why presidents should not issue such proclamations. Madison noted that his own proclamations were written in such a way as to "deaded as much as possible any claim of political right to enjoin religious observances by resting these expressly on the voluntary compliance of individuals, and even by limiting the recommendation to such as wished simultaneous as well as voluntary performance of a religious act on the occasion."[31]

Madison excused his actions by noting that he served during a time of war (the War of 1812) and pointed out in an 1822 letter to Edward Livingston that, "I was always careful to make the Proclamation absolutely indiscriminate, and merely recommendatory."[32]

Like Jefferson, Madison's credentials as a separationist are well established in his personal writings. In an 1819 letter to Robert Walsh he wrote, "The civil government, though bereft of everything like an associated hierarchy, possesses the requisite stability and performs its functions with complete success whilst the number, the industry and the morality of the priesthood, and the devotion of the people have been manifestly increased *by the total separation of the church from the state.*"[33] (Emphasis mine.)

Also, in an undated essay that historians believe was written in the early 1800s, Madison wrote, "Strongly guarded . . . is the separation between Religion and Government in the Constitution of the United States."[34]

In 1833 Madison responded to a letter sent to him by Jasper Adams, president of the College of Charleston. Adams had written a pamphlet titled "The Relations of Christianity to Civil Government in the United States," which attempted to prove that the United States was founded as a Christian nation. He asked Madison for some comments about the piece.

Madison gently but firmly rejected Adams's ideas, pointing out that the question to be settled centers on whether Christianity is best served by government support or voluntary contributions. Madison made it clear that he believed the latter, writing, "In the Papal system, government and religion are in a manner consolidated, and that is found to be the worst of government."

Madison continued, "In most of the governments of the old world, the legal establishment of a particular religion and without or with very little toleration of others makes a part of the political and civil organization and there are few of the most enlightened judges who will maintain that the system has been favorable to either religion or to government. . . .

"The tendency to a usurpation on one side or the other, or to a corrupting coalition or alliance between them, will be best guarded against by an entire abstinence of the government from interference in any way whatever, beyond the necessity of preserving public order, and protecting each sect against trespass on its legal rights by others." The American experience, Madison concluded, would be the "decisive test."[35]

Adams sent his pamphlet to other influential figures of the day, including Supreme Court Justice Joseph Story, who enthusiastically endorsed its ideas and said the United States should align itself with Christianity. Religious Right activists claim that Madison must have endorsed the Christian nation concept himself, since he had appointed Story to the high court. Again they either don't know or won't tell the whole story. The truth is, Madison appointed Story to the Supreme Court with clear reluctance and offered him the position only after four others had turned it down. (The Supreme Court at that time was considered a low prestige, hardship post.)

What is rarely pointed out is that Story's church-state views were quite extreme, even by the standards of today's Religious Right. He defended Massachusetts' harsh system of church establishment all of his life and advocated strict enforcement of blasphemy laws and religious tests for public office, all clear violations of the Constitution. Tragically, Story is regarded as a hero by today's Religious Right while Madison and Jefferson are either ignored, defamed or lied about.

As president, Madison had opportunities to put his separationist philosophy into action. He vetoed two bills he believed would violate church-state separation. The first was an act incorporating the Episcopal Church in the District of Columbia that gave the church the authority to care for the poor. The second was a proposed land grant to a Baptist church in Mississippi. Had Madison believed that all the First Amendment was intended to do was bar setting up a state church, he would have approved these bills. Instead, he vetoed both, insisting that they ran afoul of the First Amendment.

Madison was so strict a separationist that in 1790 he expressed concern that a census he had proposed could lead to church-state entanglement if it attempted to count the number of ministers in the country. Madison proposed leaving a count of the professional classes out of the census, saying, "As to those who are employed in teaching and inculcating the duties of religion, there may be some indelicacy in singling them out, as the general government is proscribed from interfering, in any manner whatever, in matters respecting religion; and it may be thought to do this, in ascertaining who and who are not ministers of the gospel."[36]

According to Madison biographer Ralph Ketcham, one of the reasons Madison opposed the creation of a national bank is that he feared it would be granted the power to incorporate religious denominations, leading to church-state entanglement.[37]

Finally, evidence proves that Madison, like Jefferson, was confident that separation of church and state would protect the institutions of both government and religion. Late in his life Madison wrote to a Luthern minister about this matter, declaring, "A due distinction . . . between what is due to Caesar and what is due to God, best promotes the discharge of *both* obligations. . . . A mutal independence is found most friendly to practical religion, to social harmony, and to political prosperity."[38]

Again, these examples do not sound like the views of a man who believed that the First Amendment was intended only to bar a Church of the United States.

Inventing History

To be perfectly frank, accommodationists, unable to find support for their views in the historical record, have simply invented a new "history" by selectively culling material from the writings, speeches, and actions of certain framers. One of their favorite tricks is to point to the many speeches several framers made discussing the importance of religion to good government. These comments certainly do exist, but they say more about the Framers' views on religion then they do church-state separation. Many of the framers were quite devout and believed religion was necessary for government to function, but that did not preclude them in any way from being separationists.

Jefferson, for example, frequently spoke highly of the morals of Jesus Christ as recorded in the Bible's New Testament. Jefferson even recommended using the Bible in schools to teach morality to youngsters. But Jefferson also believed that the Bible could be used in a "non-sectarian" fashion, in a manner that would impart Jesus' moral teachings without fostering sectarianism. This is a far cry from the goals of today's Religious Right, which seeks to impose its narrow interpretation of the Scriptures on the public schools.

Religious Right groups often claim Jefferson as an ally in their crusade, a highly ironic move considering his personal religious views. Jefferson had grave doubts about the divinity of Jesus and even rewrote the Bible, removing all references to miracles and claims by Jesus to be the Son of God.

Similar attempts by the Religious Right to claim Madison as a theological compatriot are equally ludicrous. According to Madison biographer Ketcham, much of Madison's schooling was Christian but "relatively perfunctory, and he seems never to have been an ardent believer himself."[39] Ketcham even refers to Madison as a "deist."

Another favorite trick of many Religious Right activists is to quote Patrick Henry, who often made comments about the necessity of Christianity for good government. Henry was clearly an advocate of church-state union, but, as the Virginia experience proves, his views failed to carry the day. When the Religious Right quotes Henry, they are quoting the losing side as well as endorsing the views of a man who pushed incessantly for church taxes. Henry's comments, while interesting historically, tell us little about the church-state view that eventually prevailed.

In other cases, anti-separationists have simply downplayed the role of some Framers. Religious Right activists who aren't trying to adopt Jefferson as one of their own attempt instead to write him off entirely. Other Religious Right groups simply minimize the important contributions of great Americans and point enthusiastically to language endorsing Christianity found in the Mayflower Compact, as if the theocratic state that document inspired is a good model for today's society. Tragically, their well-orchestrated campaign of misinformation has had results. Today millions of Americans believe that Jefferson's wall of separation is a myth and that all the Framers sought to do was bar forever a Church of the United States.

I opened this chapter by pointing out that Americans have always been weak on their history. Even those who ought to know better sometimes fall into this trap. In his 1985 dissent to a Supreme Court ruling on school prayer, William H. Rehnquist, now chief justice of the United States, regurgitated the entire Religious Right's pseudo-historical line, discounted Jefferson, and said the government could aid religion as long as no one denomination were preferred over others.

Although this view has been soundly shown to be erroneous by numerous scholars since then, Rehnquist is sticking with it. He has concluded that he knows more about religious liberty than Jefferson and Madison and flatly stated, "The 'wall of separation between church and state' is a metaphor based on bad history, a metaphor that has proved useless as a guide to judging. It should be frankly and explicitly abandoned."[40]

Deep in the heart of the Virginia countryside, Jefferson and Madison must be spinning like tops in their graves.

Notes

1. Edwin S. Gaustad, *Liberty of Conscience: Roger Williams in America* (Grand Rapids, MI: Eerdmans, 1991), 85.

2. Edmund S. Morgan, *Roger Williams: The Church and the State* (New York: Harcourt, Brace and World, 1967), 31-32.

3. Leo Pfeffer, *Church, State, and Freedom* (Boston: Beacon Press, 1953), 67.

4. Ibid., 68.

5. Allan Nevins and Henry Steele Commager, *A Pocket History of the United States* (New York: Simon & Schuster, 1981), 19.

6. Norman Cousins, *In God We Trust* (New York: Harper, 1958), 299.

7. Ralph Ketcham, *James Madison: A Biography* (Charlottesville, VA: University Press of Virginia, 1971), 57.

8. Pfeffer, 98.

9. Ketcham, 162.

10. William Lee Miller, *The First Liberty: Religion and the American Republic* (New York: Alfred A. Knopf, 1985), 360.

11. Ibid., 362.

12. Ibid., 357.

13. Pfeffer, 102.

14. Ibid., 110.

15. Ibid., 110.

16. John M. Swomley, *Religious Liberty and the Secular State* (Buffalo: Prometheus Books, 1987), 45.

17. Leonard W. Levy, *The Establishment Clause: Religion and the First Amendment* (New York: MacMillan Publishing, 1986), 97–100.

18. Swomley, 47.

19. Ibid., 46.

20. Ibid., 47.

21. Ibid., 48-49.

22. Charles C. Haynes, *Religion in American History: What to Teach and How* (Alexandria, VA: ASCD, 1990), 48.

23. Pfeffer, 120.

24. Haynes, 48.

25. David Barton, *The Myth of Separation* (Aledo, TX: WallBuilders Press, 1989), 42.

26. Christian Coalition flyer, undated.

27. Pfeffer, 214.

28. Haynes, 52.

29. Ibid., 52.

30. Pfeffer, 215.

31. Robert S. Alley, *James Madison on Religious Liberty* (Buffalo: Prometheus Books, 1985), 94.

32. Anson Phelps Stokes and Leo Pfeffer, *Church and State in the United States* (New York: Harper and Row, 1950), 89.

33. Alley, 80-81.

34. Ibid., 89-94.

35. Cousins, 322-325.

36. Bernard Schwartz, *The New Right And The Constitution: Turning Back The Legal Clock* (Boston: Northeastern University Press, 1990), 32.

37. Ketcham, 165.

38. Ibid., 167.

39. Ibid., 46.

40. *Wallace v. Jaffree,* 105 S.Ct. 2479 (1985).

4

The De Facto Protestant Establishment in 19th-Century America

As the last chapter indicated, Religious Right activists have worked feverishly to try to discredit Thomas Jefferson, James Madison and other leading figures who helped pioneer church-state separation in the United States.

Unable to blacken the characters of these great Americans, the anti-separationists have zeroed in on minor inconsistencies in the records of both men in an effort to show that they did not intend to instill separation of church and state.

It just doesn't work. Looked at in whole, the records of Jefferson and Madison prove beyond a doubt that both were ardent separationists who knew full well the extent of the new political order they helped create. Of course, as we have seen, this does not mean at all that the men were opposed to religion. Jefferson had a keen interest in Christianity and the teachings of Jesus and undoubtedly believed that religion was necessary for good government. But that belief, also held by Madison, says nothing about the two's support for church-state separation. Supporting separation and being religious are not mutually exclusive, despite the Religious Right's attempt to claim otherwise.

Jefferson was attacked frequently in his day by conservative religious elements who disagreed with his stand for full religious liberty for all.

They often branded him an infidel. Today, Religious Right leaders like Tim LaHaye continue this attack by calling Jefferson an atheist, despite his Deistic beliefs and frequent praise for the moral teachings of Jesus.

Searching for "Christian America"

When they are not working to discredit Jefferson and Madison, the Religious Right is waxing nostalgically for a return to the days when the United States was a "Christian nation."

Although Religious Right activists often assert that a Christian nation was the original intent of the Framers, as the review in the last chapter clearly shows, this simply is not true. Had a Christian republic been the Framers' desire, they were certainly capable of stating that forthrightly in the Constitution. That they did not is a devastating blow to the Religious Right.

Many Religious Right boosters are also unaware that officials of the early U.S. government at least once explicitly denied that the United States was founded on Christian principles. Article 11 of the Treaty of Tripoli, an agreement signed between the United States and the Muslim region of North Africa in 1797 after negotiations conducted under George Washington, bluntly states, "As the Government of the United States is not, in any sense, founded on the Christian religion; as it has in itself no character of enmity against the law, religion or tranquility of Musselmen [Muslims]; and as the states never have entered into any war or act of hostility against any Mohometan nation, it is declared by the parties that no pretext arising from religious opinion shall ever produce an interruption of harmony existing between the two countries."[1]

Historian Morton Borden points out that Joel Barlow, a government official who served as counsel to Algiers, translated the Arabic version of the treaty into English. Barlow, a big advocate of secular government, apparently added the language found in Article 11 on his own.

Religious Right activists today argue that since Barlow took the action unilaterally, the statement found in Article 11 does not accurately reflect the sentiments of the U.S. government. Again, that is a distortion of the truth. The true story behind the treaty leads to the opposite conclusion.

The treaty as amended by Barlow was forwarded to high government officials for approval in 1797. Timothy Pickering, the secretary of state, endorsed it and President John Adams concurred, sending the document on to the Senate. The Senate in turn approved the treaty without one word of objection. All during this multi-layered review process, Article 11 never raised an eyebrow. Obviously, the various government officials who examined the treaty saw the wording of Article 11 as non-controversial and believed that it accurately reflected the tenets of the new U.S. government. Had they believed differently or been convinced that the United States was founded on Christian principles, they never would have approved the document as written by Barlow.

Article 11 remained in the trade agreement for eight years until the treaty was renegotiated. Perhaps by then U.S. officials felt the Muslims had been convinced of the new country's secular nature.

Unable to find support for the "Christian nation" concept in post-Revolutionary War America, members of the Religious Right look to a different period of history as their model for a Christian republic, a period that began just before the Civil War and that lasted well into the 20th century.

The Religious Right looks so fondly on this period because the country at this time was dominated by white male Protestants. These times were not so great for others, especially racial minorities, Roman Catholics, Jews, other religious minorities, and women—but this is of little concern to those who harbor dreams of theocracy.

The Northwest Ordinance

Before examining this period in a little more detail, it is important to look at one more accomplishment from the 18th century—the Northwest Ordinance. The Ordinance is often cited by anti-separationists who argue that the Framers did not mean to separate religion and government. The case they make is superficial at best but, due to the myth's persistence it must be debunked here. (In examining this document, I want to acknowledge a debt to scholar Edwin S. Gaustad, emeritus history professor at the University of California, Riverside, who has researched this area extensively.)

Thomas Jefferson wrote the Northwest Ordinance in the 1780s to help outline the United States' long-range policy for settling the "west" (then basically anything west of the Appalachian Mountains). The U.S. government had acquired new territories after the Revolution, and brave settlers were penetrating these rugged lands to create new settlements. Some type of policy was need to guide these pioneers in the hope that new states would eventually be added to the growing union.

Jefferson's first draft of the Ordinance was secular and contained no references to religion. In 1785 Jefferson's draft fell into the hands of a congressional committee for revision. The committee agreed that education would be important to every township settled under the ordinance, and accordingly it mandated that the central section of each township be reserved for the support of education.

A proposal was then made that a section of each township north of the area reserved for educational purposes be earmarked for religion. Several members of the committee, notably Charles Pinckney of South Carolina, were nervous over this suggestion. Pinckney recommended amending it to say the land would be used for the "support of religion and charitable uses."

But some members of the committee were unwilling to go along with that. A suggestion was made that the land be reserved simply for "charitable purposes." This too could not gain support of the majority. A stalemate ensued.

As is often the case in politics, a compromise was struck. The third article of the Ordinance was drafted to read, "Religion, Morality and knowledge being necessary to good government and the happiness of mankind, schools and the means of education shall be forever encouraged."

Had the committee wanted to endorse religion, Gaustad points out, the article would have ended, ". . . schools *and churches* shall forever be encouraged." But there was no way legislators, ever mindful of separation of church and state, were going to go that far. Thus, the watered-down language that the Religious Right sees as devastating to the separation of church and state actually underscores the concept, once the full history behind it is explained.

Gaustad observes, "A single sentence in the Northwest Ordinance thus summarizes the nature of a people divided on the question of what their government could or should do concerning religion in general or Christianity in particular. Religion and morality were necessary to good government and human happiness. Therefore. . . , what? Responsible authorities found themselves trapped in a cruel dilemma, or traveling down a passage that offered no exit."[2]

As the congressional committee's debate over the Northwest Ordinance shows, the debate over the need to keep church and state separate was still very much alive in the fledgling U.S. government. It didn't take long, however, for the importance of that principle to fade in the eyes of governmental leaders. As the 1800s progressed, the nation began to drift slowly from the principles laid down by Jefferson and Madison.

19th-Century Generic Protestantism

Despite the Constitution's pronouncement that church and state should be separate, the political and social reality of American life by the mid-19th century is that the two institutions often worked hand in hand.

The United States of this period was an overwhelmingly Protestant country. More often than not, its laws in the 19th century reflected general Protestant religious doctrines. It should also be noted that most laws were local in origin and as such reflected regional religious attitudes and biases. Blasphemy was a crime in most parts of the country, Sunday laws were strictly enforced, and public education reflected an overtly Protestant flavor.

Just as today, political leaders of the time talked a good line about American religious freedoms and the great measure of liberty offered to the country's citizens. But the unpleasant truth is that 19th century America was a mild form of Protestant theocracy. In this period, Protestantism was the America's *de facto* established religion.

This statement can even be qualified by adding "mainstream" before Protestant. The large Protestant groups—Methodists, Baptists, Presbyterians, Episcopalians, Congregationalists, and so on—held power and influenced government. Small Protestant groups that sprang up during the 19 century—Mormons, Seventh-day Adventists and Christian Scientists—were branded cults and written out of the power base. In many cases, they had to fight for their religious freedoms. Other non-Protestant minorities, such as Jews and Catholics, were tolerated only to the extent that they did not rock the boat. When members of these groups finally did begin to assert their rights, violence often ensued, as the burning of a Boston convent in 1834 and Philadelphia's "Bible War" so sadly attest. (See chapter 5 for full discussion of the "Bible War.")

The *de facto* Protestant establishment was made possible because most Americans were Protestant and because the federal courts rarely involved themselves in church-state matters. Therefore, there was little to stop lawmakers from passing and enforcing laws that had religious veneers. At this time, the First Amendment and the Bill of Rights was not seen as binding on the states. Although the Fourteenth Amendment was passed following the Civil War, it was not interpreted as applying the Bill of Rights to the states until 1940.

State Court Rulings

Church-state matters, then, were left chiefly to state legislators, and disputes, if they occurred at all, were resolved by state courts. Judges at this level were often appointed under political patronage systems or to fulfill campaign debts. In many cases, upholding the law was not their prime interest. They seemed to make many of their decisions based on public opinion, not constitutional commands. As a result, volumes of court decisions emerged from the states that today are seen as at odds with religious freedom and separation of church and state. It did not take the country long to stray from the Jeffersonian/Madisonian construct.

Religious Right activists often try to use these court rulings to prove that America is a "Christian nation." They do not point out that these rulings were aberrations that emerged during a period of intolerance and religious persecution. This era is something to be ashamed of; it is hardly an appropriate model to look toward for today's church-state relationship.

To be sure, many state courts in the 19th century did refer to the United States as a "Christian nation" or implied that Christianity should receive some type of special protection from the state. James Kent, a New York Supreme Court justice, declared in an 1811 blasphemy case, "[T]he people of this state, in common with the people of this country, profess the general principles of Christianity as the rule of their faith and practice; and to scandalize the author of these doctrines is not only in a religious point of view, extremely impious, but even in respect to the obligations due to society, is a gross violation of decency and good order."[3] (Kent later partially retracted these views.)

In 1822 the Pennsylvania Supreme Court, in another blasphemy case, wrote, "Christianity, general Christianity, is and always has been a part of the common law . . . not Christianity founded on any particular religious tenet; not Christianity with an established church, and tithes, and spiritual courts, but Christianity with liberty of conscience to all men."[4]

The fact that these statements occurred within the context of blasphemy trials indicates how quickly the church-state separation principle had deteriorated. Early American leaders were wary of blasphemy statutes. John Adams, the nation's second president, told Thomas Jefferson, "I think such laws a great embarrassment, great obstructions to the improvement of the human mind. . . . I wish they were repealed."[5]

Jefferson echoed those sentiments and insisted that the government refrain from setting itself up as a guardian of religious orthodoxy. He once observed, "It does me no injury for my neighbor to say there are twenty gods or no god. It neither picks my pocket nor breaks my leg."[6]

Nevertheless, prosecutions for blasphemy were a serious problem in 19th century America. In 1836 the Massachusetts Supreme Court upheld the conviction of Abner Kneeland, a freethinker who had been found guilty of publishing articles that questioned the biblical account of Jesus' life. Kneeland served 60 days in jail. By law, he could have received a public whipping or been sent to the pillory.

Likewise, the New York and Pennsylvania cases mentioned earlier both resulted in convictions.

The Holy Trinity Case

The U.S. Supreme Court even fell victim to the "Christian nation" mentality from time to time. Religious Right activists frequently cite 1892's *Holy Trinity Church v. United States* decision as proof that the high court considered the United States a "Christian nation." But as usual, they don't tell the whole story.

In the ruling, Justice David Brewer flatly declared, "This is a Christian nation." To this day, historians debate what Brewer meant by the term. It is unclear whether he meant to say the country's laws should reflect Christianity or was simply acknowledging the fact that most Americans are Christians.

A strong case can be made for the latter proposition by examining a case that came along five years after the *Holy Trinity* ruling. The dispute centered on legalized prostitution in New Orleans. A Methodist church challenged a city ordinance allowing prostitution in one area of the city. The church argued that prostitution should be illegal everywhere in New Orleans, and said the activity was inconsistent with Christianity "which the Supreme Court of the United States says is the foundation of our government."

Writing for a unanimous court, Brewer completely ignored the church's argument and upheld the New Orleans policy. Brewer's bypass in this case suggests that he did not mean to imply in *Holy Trinity* that the United States should enforce the dictates of Christianity by law. Had that been Brewer's intention, he surely would have upheld the Methodists' claim.

Since his phrase was being taken out of context and used by organizations seeking to amend the Constitution to include an endorsement of Christianity, Brewer felt compelled to explain himself. In 1905 he published a short book titled *The United States: A Christian Nation.* What Brewer has to say in this book is very interesting, and needless to say, never quoted by the Religious Right since it is completely at odds with their view.

"But in what sense can [the United States] be called a Christian nation?" asked Brewer. "Not in the sense that Christianity is the established religion or the people are compelled in any manner to support it. On the contrary, the Constitution specifically provides that 'Congress shall make no law respecting an establishment of religion or prohibiting the free exercise thereof.' Neither is it Christian in the sense that all its citizens are either in fact or in name Christians. On the contrary, all religions have free scope within its borders. Numbers of our people profess other religions, and many reject all."

Continued Brewer, "Nor is it Christian in the sense that a profession of Christianity is a condition of holding office or otherwise engaging in public service, or essential to recognition either politically or socially. In fact, the government as a legal organization is independent of all religions."[7]

The passage strongly suggests that Brewer simply meant that the United States is "Christian" in the sense that many of its people belong to Christian denominations and many of the country's customs and traditions have roots in Christianity. Brewer expounds on this theme for the rest of his ninety-eight page book, predicting that Christianity will one day unify the American masses and make the United States a leader in world affairs.

Whatever Brewer's views about the United States as a Christian nation, it is important to realize that the concept has never been fully embraced by the Supreme Court. The *Holy Trinity* ruling, for example, is something of a legal anomaly that has been cited favorably only once by the Supreme Court since it was handed down. It is an obscure ruling that has no bearing on the type of church-state relationship the Framers intended for this nation. *Holy Trinity* and an entire string of bizarre 19th century high court rulings—including one that decreed that women could be barred from practicing law and others that struck down laws designed to end the national scandal of child labor—cannot seriously be considered today as appropriate guidelines for American society. They are products of their time, and most have been relegated to forgotten volumes of legal history—where they belong.

"Christian Nation" Amendments

Not satisfied with the *de facto* establishment of Christianity in the U.S. government, precursors to today's Religious Right organizations pushed incessantly during the 19th century for a constitutional amendment that would add some type of endorsement of Christianity to the Constitution.

The movement was spearheaded by the National Reform Association, a coalition formed in 1863 by representatives from eleven Protestant denominations. One of the group's stated goals was "to secure such an amendment to the Constitution of the United States as will declare the nation's allegiance to Jesus Christ and its acceptance of the moral laws of the Christian religion, and so indicate that this is a Christian nation."

In 1864 the group petitioned Congress to amend the Preamble of the Constitution to read,

> We, the people of the United States, humbly acknowledging Almighty God as the source of all authority and power in civil government, the Lord Jesus Christ as the Ruler among the nations, His revealed will as the supreme law of the land, in order to constitute a Christian government, and in order to form a more perfect union, establish justice, insure domestic tranquility, provide for the common defense, promote the general welfare, and secure the inalienable rights and blessings of life, liberty, and the pursuit of happiness to ourselves, our posterity and all the people, do ordain and establish this Constitution of the United States of America.[8]

The amendment languished in Congress for years, occasionally being reintroduced. Finally in 1874 the House Judiciary Committee voted against its adoption. The committee said it took the action "in full realization of the dangers which the union between church and state had imposed upon so many nations of the Old World, with great unanimity that it was inexpedient to put anything into the Constitution or frame of government which might be construed to be a reference to any religious creed or doctrine."[9] The Christian nation amendment was introduced in Congress again in 1882, but this time it died in committee.

(Another "Christian America" amendment resurfaced nearly one hundred years later, when similar proposals were introduced in Congress in 1961, 1963, and 1965. The proposed addition to the Constitution would have had the United States "devoutly" recognize "the authority and law of Jesus Christ, savior and ruler of nations, through whom are bestowed the blessings of almighty God." One of the measure's sponsors was Illinois congressman John Anderson, who ran for president as an independent in 1980. During that campaign, Anderson dismissed the effort as a foolish move from a young congressman, saying, "It was a dumb thing to do, and I should not have introduced it.")[10]

Alongside the activities of the National Reform Association, religiously conservative ministers attacked the Constitution from the pulpit, usually because it lacks reference to God. In 1845 the Rev. D.X. Junkin wrote, "It (the Constitution) is negatively *atheistical,* for no God is appealed to at all. In framing many of our public formularies, greater care seems to have been taken to adapt them to the prejudices of the INFIDEL FEW, than to the consciences of the Christian millions."[11]

Junkin's words merely echoed previous attacks on the Constitution that had been delivered from pulpits all over the country since the ratification of the document. In 1793 the Rev. John M. Mason of New York called the lack of references to God in the Constitution "an omission which no pretext whatever can palliate." Much like today's Religious Right extremists, Mason was certain divine retribution would soon rain down upon the country and said God's vengeance would "overturn from its foundations the fabric we have been rearing, and crush us to atoms in the wreck."[12]

In 1811 the Rev. Samuel Austin told his congregation that the Constitution "is entirely disconnected from Christianity." Austin said this "one capital defect" would lead "inevitably to its destruction."[13]

These early attacks on the Constitution underscore how conservative religious forces have varied their rhetoric against the First Amendment over the years. In the 19th century, fundamentalist clerics acknowledged the secular nature of the Constitution and called for amending it to include references to God or Christianity. Most Religious Right activists today have abandoned this strategy and in the face of all available evidence insist that the Constitution was somehow written to afford special protection to Christianity.

The most extreme elements of the Religious Right are more honest, however. Christian Reconstructionist Gary North (see chapter 9) has brazenly called the Constitution a "secular humanist" document and called for scrapping it outright in favor of a new governing document based explicitly on the Bible—or at least his interpretation of the Bible.[14]

Censorship of the Arts

Christian amendment or not, many states continued passing and enforcing laws implicitly based on Protestant Christian principles. The arts were often targets of severe state regulation, and a type of religiously based censorship was widely imposed.

A good case study of the result of the *de facto* Protestant establishment on the arts in 19th century America is found in Alan Nielsen's excellent book, *The Great Victorian Sacrilege*. The volume tells the story of Salmi Morse, an eccentric Jewish entrepreneur who attempted to stage a theatrical version of the passion of Jesus Christ in the late 1800s in San Francisco and New York.

Outraged preachers and newspaper editors inflamed public opinion against the play, arguing that it was sinful to depict the life of Christ on the stage. (Many ministers of that day frequently preached against all forms of theater.) In San Francisco, the city Board of Supervisors passed a hastily written ordinance to ban performances of the play.

Morse's attempt to fight the ordinance in court was unsuccessful. As Nielsen relates, Judge Robert F. Morrison, upholding the ban on the play, ruled in effect that Morse's play offended Christianity, and that since Christianity required protection from the government, nothing could stop the state from squelching the performance.

Wrote Morrison, "The Board of Supervisors has seen fit to prohibit the exhibition in question because such exhibition is, in their opinion, against good morals, because it is calculated to bring religion, which is the foundation of all morality, into ridicule and contempt, and because the sacred mysteries of the passion and death of the Redeemer upon the cross are too solemn and sacred to be made the subject of a theatrical exhibition."[15]

The story was much the same in "enlightened" New York City. A young crusading newspaper editor, Harrison Grey Fiske, made a name for himself by repeatedly attacking the play and egging on the city's conservative religious establishment. Spurred by the hysteria, the city's Board of Aldermen held a special session to discuss Morse's play. Although one alderman recommended caution, saying a law banning the play would "introduce a religious element into the Board, which all of us should deprecate," the board overwhelmingly favored action.[16]

Just the threat of legal action scared off the play's backers, and the performance was canceled. Three years later, when Morse finally succeeded in briefly staging the passion in New York City, a state senator hurriedly prepared "An Act to prevent any attempt to personate or represent Jesus Christ, the Saviour of Mankind, in any exhibition, show, play, dramatic or other theatrical performance." As the bill speeded toward passage in the New York legislature, municipal officials in New York City used technicalities to shut the play down. Morse's passion play was finished in New York.

Compare the controversy over Morse's passion with the 1988 flap over the movie *The Last Temptation of Christ*. The Universal Studios film, which attempted to depict the human side of Jesus, was denounced by fundamentalists and labeled "blasphemous" from coast to coast. Boycotts against Universal were launched, but all legal efforts to stop the film from being shown failed outright.

In Escambia County, Florida, the county commissioners voted 4-1 to ban the film after a theater owner in Pensacola announced plans to show it. Almost immediately legal action was filed, and a federal judge declared the ordinance unconstitutional.

In a separate incident, a group of outraged fundamentalists filed a lawsuit in federal court arguing that the movie somehow infringed on their right to freely practice their religion. No federal court took the case seriously. The suit was rejected all the way up the federal court system and ultimately by the Supreme Court as well.

Unlike 1892, in 1988 there was a general understanding that the state should have no say in matters of religious orthodoxy. It simply is not the role of the government to determine what view of Jesus is correct and to censor any views that don't fit into the state's picture. It is difficult to imagine a more dangerous role for the government to take on.

Sunday-Closing Laws

Aside from blasphemy, a second issue that underscores the *de facto* establishment of Protestanitsm in the 19th century is the proliferation of mandatory Sunday closing laws, also known as "blue laws." These laws, which restricted commercial and sometimes leisure activity on Sunday, were always religiously motivated. The thinking of the Protestant majority was that Sunday, which most Protestants honor as the Sabbath, was in need of special protection by the government.

The laws were particularly vexing for Jews and Seventh-day Adventists, two groups that chose to worship on Saturdays. For Jewish shopkeepers, the laws served as an economic penalty. Devout Jews felt compelled to close their shops on Saturday. On Sunday, a day when they might have made up business lost on Saturday, they were forbidden to open under state laws. In some states, Seventh-day Adventists spent time in jail because they were caught working on Sundays.

Eventually, this situation became the basis for a lawsuit challenging blue laws at the Supreme Court, a case that will be looked at more closely in chapter 8.

Returning to Separation

The *de facto* Protestant establishment was a throwback, but it did not last. Eventually an attitude reflecting the proper relationship between church and state, which was pioneered in the post-Revolutionary War period and lay neglected for nearly one hundred years, re-emerged. Following the Civil War, courts became increasingly reluctant to look for religious justifications to uphold laws. Steven K. Green, an attorney for Americans United for Separation of Church and State who has researched the Christian nation concept extensively, reports that after 1860 courts began turning to secular justifications to uphold blasphemy statutes or school Bible-reading laws. In other cases, judges rejected the laws outright.

By the mid-20th century, church-state cases became more common at the Supreme Court, especially after the high court ruled in 1940 that the Fourteenth Amendment makes the Bill of Rights binding on the states. Eventually a line of decisions was spawned that laid down the church-state relationship still with us today.

Many of the high court's rulings have focused on two controversial issues, both related to education—religion in public schools and public aid to sectarian schools—as well as issues over free exercise. Of course, the Supreme Court has examined many other church-state issues such as religious symbols on public property, mandatory Sunday closing laws, and taxation of churches.

The next several chapters will look at some of these controversies in depth.

Notes

1. Morton Borden, *Jews, Turks and Infidels* (Chapel Hill, NC: University of North Carolina Press, 1984), 76-79.

2. Edwin S. Gaustad, "Religious Tests, Constitutions, and Christian Nation," unpublished paper.

3. *People v. Ruggles,* 8 Johns. (N.Y.) 290 (1811).

4. *Updegraph v. Commonwealth,* 11 Serg. & Rawle, Pa. (1822).

5. Joseph L. Conn, "Blasphemy Laws In America: 'A Great Embarrassment,' " *Church & State* 42(April 1989): 9.

6. Saul K. Padover, *Thomas Jefferson on Democracy* (New York: Mentor, 1946), 109.

7. David J. Brewer, *The United States: A Christian Nation* (Philadelphia: The John C. Winston Company, 1905), 12.

8. Leo Pfeffer, *Church, State, and Freedom* (Boston: Beacon Press, 1953), 209.

9. Ibid., 210.

10. "The Candidates, The Platforms, And Church-State Issues," *Church & State* 33(September 1980): 6-10.

11. Borden, 60.

12. Ibid., 59.

13. Ibid., 59.

14. Gary North, *Tools of Dominion* (Tyler, TX: Institute for Christian Economics, 1990), 1190-1216.

15. Alan Nielsen, *The Great Victorian Sacrilege: Preachers, Politics and The Passion, 1879-1884* (Jefferson, N.C.: McFarland & Co., 1991), 114.
16. Ibid., 159.

5

The Issue that Won't Go Away: Religion in Public Schools

In May 1992 a major American newspaper published an editorial cartoon by a Pulitzer Prize-winning cartoonist depicting a public school student being threatened in class by a fellow classmate wielding a handgun. The student was down on his knees begging for his life, and the teacher was saying something like, "What are you doing? You know you can't pray in here!"

The cartoon illustrates that even some members of the media, who by all rights ought to know better, are hopelessly confused by the school prayer issue and the controversy over religion in public schools generally. If public opinion polls are any indication, this is one issue where confusion reigns in the minds of most of the American public. Voluminous amounts of disinformation circulate; much of it is perpetrated deliberately by those who know better but have political or personal reasons for concealing the truth. This chapter will set the record straight and give a true accounting of the long controversy over religion in public schools.

Children *Can* Pray in School

One thing needs to be stated up front: Absolutely *nothing* in the Constitution, the laws of the United States or any state, city, or municipality anywhere prohibits children from praying in public schools. The Constitution, in fact, explicitly *protects* the rights of children to pray in schools. No student can lawfully be denied the right to say a prayer in school.

So why all the confusion? The problem stems from two widely misunderstood Supreme Court rulings of the 1960s, decisions in which the high court ordered school officials and other government bureaucrats to stop writing prayers for children or forcing them to participate in religious exercises in public schools. True, the court ruled 6-1 in 1962 and 8-1 in 1963 to get the government out of the prayer and Bible-reading business, but never once did the justices say that students can't pray on their own or read the Bible during free time if they choose. Today, many youngsters undoubtedly do so, but when it comes to an issue as emotional as school prayer, it seems no one ever thinks to ask the students what actually goes on in American public schools. Rather, too many people just take the old myth "Kids can't pray in school" and use it in efforts to raise money, win converts, or collect votes.

I will return to the school prayer decisions, but before that it is necessary to briefly review the rise of American public education and the role religion has played in it. Examining this history is important because it shows the hostility that has often developed over religion in public schools. Americans would do well to look at this past before adopting any proposal to reintroduce sectarian elements into our schools.

The Origins of Public Education

First, it is crucial to remember that the concept of free, universal public education as we know it today is a relatively recent idea. While public education existed in some parts of colonial America, many parents ignored laws requiring children to receive schooling. Early American society was heavily agrarian, and children often worked the fields alongside parents and other family members. Every available hand was needed to work the crops. If the children were educated at all, they either received schooling in church or perhaps at home.

The New England colonies made the strongest effort to establish public elementary schools, and several states in this region passed laws mandating schooling for children, usually just boys. Public education was scarcer in the middle colonies such as Pennsylvania and Maryland and virtually non-existent in the South outside of the cities. (Ironically, however, one of the first "public" schools was established in Charleston, South Carolina, in 1720. Under the school's bylaws, the headmaster was required to be a member of the Church of England, and the staff had to teach religion according to the church's precepts.)

The gap between the rich and the poor was extremely wide during these years. Most people were poor or led modest lives tied to the land. But at the top was a small corps of wealthier landowners, merchants, and leaders. Naturally, the wealthy of colonial society provided for their children's education, often through private tutors. When sons got old enough for college, they were often shipped off to Europe to study or sent to one of the few colleges that were operating in America by this time. But this aristocracy was a minority, and, since there was no middle class to speak of in early America, most people fell into the great collective of the working people. For these people, formal education was not considered necessary.

Although Massachusetts had created public schools as early as 1635, in most of the colonies education of the masses was not a priority. Following the Revolution, some enlightened leaders began proposing a system of free, universal education.

Thomas Jefferson, again thinking ahead of his time, proposed a bill in 1779 before the Virginia legislature that would have established a series of elementary schools to teach the basics—reading, writing, and arithmetics. Ever mindful of church-state separation, Jefferson even suggested that "no religious reading, instruction, or exercise shall be prescribed or practiced, inconsistent with the tenets of any religious sect or denomination."[1] Jefferson did not see public schools as the proper agent to change children's religious views.

Jefferson's bill did not pass, but he had set into motion a concept that would not die. Some years later, Virginia lawmakers took the main features of his idea and blended them into a public education plan.

As years passed, the idea of public education supported through taxation evolved in the United States and came to be accepted. The schools, however, were in no way religiously neutral. Schools tended to reflect the religious views of the predominant religious body in a given community. By design, they took on a generic Protestant flavor. Lessons in otherwise secular subjects were often tied to the Bible. For instance, children might learn to read by using Bible stories.

Obviously, such a system could not long survive. As the population of the post-Revolution United States expanded, sections of the country became less and less religiously homogenous. Soon members of what had been minority religious groups were clamoring for their rights of representation in the schools, too. Sectarianism's days in the public school system were numbered.

Enter Horace Mann

In his book *Church, State, and Freedom*, the late church-state scholar Leo Pfeffer recounts Horace Mann's struggle against sectarianism in public schools. Mann, a Massachusetts Unitarian who served in the state senate, helped engineer a new state law mandating that no textbooks could be used in public schools that "are calculated to favor any religious sect or creed."

As secretary of the first Massachusetts Board of Education, Mann enforced the law vigorously. Religious leaders and many educators opposed to Mann's reforms denounced him as an atheist, but Mann stuck to his plan. All efforts to have him removed from the post failed and Mann remained in the slot until 1848, when he resigned to enter Congress.

Mann was not opposed to general programs of religious instruction in public schools; he simply opposed sectarianism. He did not oppose using the Bible in schools, for example, and he argued that it could be viewed as a non-sectarian work. Ironically, Mann today is attacked by some Religious Right advocates even though he favored using the Bible in public schools!

Although Mann was not a separationist as we understand the term today, he blazed an important trail by at least suggesting that sectarianism in public schools was inappropriate. Clearly there remained problems with his approach. Many modern religious leaders, for example, would dispute Mann's claim that the Bible is a non-sectarian work or that it can be used in a non-sectarian manner. Still, in spite of his faults, Mann was a progressive thinker who helped lay the groundwork that led to the development of a modern system of public education that is religiously neutral and open to all students.

Protestant-Catholic Strife Over Schools

When Mann and other educators of the 19th century talked about the Bible or religion in public schools, they almost always meant the Protestant version of the Scriptures. Roman Catholics were still a rarity in the country at this time. Catholics did not start arriving on American shores in significant numbers until the late 1830s and 1840s and with the great waves of immigration in the post-Civil War era and in the early 20th century.

The small numbers of Catholics that did choose to live in America could find life difficult. Guaranteed the right to worship by the Constitution, they no longer had to worry about their priests being shackled and thrown into prison or their churches being raided by agents of the state. Many overt forms of prejudice still existed, especially in employment, but the one area where Catholics encountered the greatest frustration was in the public school system.

The de facto Protestant establishment was not kind to Roman Catholics. Bible reading and prayers were common in schools, but they were not Catholic prayers, and the version of the Bible read was the King James, not the Catholic Douay.

To understand why Roman Catholics were so upset over religion in the public schools of the 19th century it is necessary to know a little about the theological divide between Catholics and Protestants.

In 19th century public schools, the Bible was generally read by a teacher or administrator "without comment." This was seen as one way of getting around Mann's bar on sectarianism, but it overlooks the fact that reading Scriptures without comment is in itself a Protestant practice.

Generally speaking, many Protestants believe they are free to interpret the Bible as their individual consciences dictate. Catholics do not believe this to the same degree as Protestants do and recognize the authority of priests and other religious leaders in assisting church members in interpreting the Bible. Thus, reading the Bible "without comment" forced Catholic children in public schools to participate in a fundamentally Protestant practice.

Also keep in mind that the Lord's Prayer, seen as "non-sectarian" and agreeable to most Protestant groups of the time, is not the same as the similar Catholic prayer known as the "Our Father." Yet it was the former that was recited in public schools every day, and needless to say never uttered was a wholly Catholic prayer such as the "Hail Mary."

Catholic children were not simply required to sit through religious exercises alien to them; they were often forced to take an active role in them. Great insensitivity reigned as the Protestant majority laid down the rules for religious exercises in public schools.

In many parts of the country, teachers and administrators brooked no dissent when it came to daily religious exercises. In 1859, an eleven-year-old boy in Boston named Tom Wall was ordered by his teacher to read the Ten Commandments from the King James version of the Bible. Knowing that the Douay version lists the commandments in different order, the boy refused and was beaten until he relented. The teacher was taken to court, but a judge dismissed all charges.[2]

As the number of Catholics grew, slowly but steadily, priests and bishops came to believe that they could no longer keep silent about what they rightly perceived as a great violation of religious freedom. In 1840 a council of Roman Catholic bishops met in Baltimore and issued a statement urging Catholic parents to resist Protestant prayers and the practice of reading the Bible "without comment" in public schools.

Catholic Protests Escalate

Some Catholics living in the country's quickly growing urban areas decided to push for their rights. In New York City, where Catholic parents had been protesting mandatory religious practices for years, the superintendent of schools responded to Catholic concerns and ruled that prayer could not be required as part of the school day and that Catholic pupils had the right to opt out of school exercises when the Protestant King James Bible was used.

Things quickly got ugly. Even though the Catholic parents were not requesting that the religious practices be terminated—merely that their children not be required to sit through them—violence erupted. The local bishop posted armed guards in front of Catholic churches to ward off attacks by vandals and other troublemakers.

During a similar flap over religious exercises in Philadelphia's public schools in 1843, an even uglier riot broke out. It lasted three days. Violence erupted after the city's Board of Education voted to allow Catholic children to be excused from mandatory religious exercises or use their own version of the Bible. (Again, all the Catholics were asking for was that their beliefs be respected, not that the Protestant practices be stopped entirely.) Catholic churches and the homes of Catholic parents were burned; thirteen people were killed.[3]

In later years violence on a smaller scale broke out in other areas. In 1854 in Ellsworth, Maine, an outraged mob tarred and feathered a missionary priest, John Bapst, after he urged a parishioner to go to court and fight a school board regulation requiring children to read the King James Bible.[4]

Abuses such as these led to the creation of the Catholic school system in America. Fed up with the overt Protestant flavor of the public schools and desiring a system that would inculcate their own values, American Catholics simply built one.

Early conflicts over religion in public schools led to court battles in several states. In many cases, the actions were filed by disgruntled Catholic parents, sometimes backed by Jews, who desired a secular educational system. In light of this history, it is remarkable that today some conservative Catholics have joined the movement for a school prayer amendment. How easily some forget their own history!

Early Court Rulings

In Cincinnati, Ohio, Catholic parents in 1869 challenged the common practice of Bible reading in public schools and urged the Board of Education to pass a resolution ending the practice. After heated debate, the measure passed 22-15. The action was promptly challenged in court by a group supporting state-sponsored prayer.

A local court agreed with the prayer boosters and asserted that the board had no authority to exclude the religious practices from school, going as far as to call Christianity a requirement of good government.

On appeal, the Ohio Supreme Court overturned the ruling and said the school board had the right to exclude the Bible if it so chose. The court did not rule that prayers and Bible reading in public schools were unconstitutional—such rulings would come later—only that the public schools were not required to hold daily religious exercises.

In eloquent language the court observed, "United with government, religion never rises above the merest superstition; united with religion, government never rises above the merest despotism; and all history shows us that the more widely and completely they are separated, the better it is for both. . . ."[5]

Eventually state courts in some areas of the country began to rule that the practices of mandatory vocal prayer and Bible reading "without comment" were unconstitutional in public schools.

One of the earliest rulings was in Illinois, where in 1910 the state supreme court struck down a variety of religious exercises in public schools, including required prayer, Bible reading, and daily hymnals that students were required to take part in. The case had been brought by a group of Catholic parents.

In a major step forward, the Illinois high court found the practices unconstitutional even though objecting students could in theory be excused. The court, ruling that the purpose of public schools is secular education, not the inculcation of religious doctrine, wrote, "The exclusion of a pupil from this part of the school exercises in which the rest of the school joins, separates him from his fellows, puts him in a class by himself, deprives him of his equality with the other pupils, subjects him to a religious stigma and places him at a disadvantage in the school, which was never contemplated. All this is because of his religious belief."[6]

Supreme courts in other states struck down similar practices. Many were in the West and Midwest, where several state constitutions contain especially strong church-state separation provisions and require public schools to remain free from sectarian control. The Wisconsin Supreme Court ruled required public school devotional practices unconstitutional in 1890. Nebraska followed suit in 1903. But several state courts—notably Iowa, Massachusetts and Kentucky—examined the practices and found them constitutional. In the bulk of the states, however, the matter never came up in court.

Despite these early court actions, many Americans today continue to believe that state-sponsored prayer and Bible reading occurred all over the country until the Supreme Court rulings of 1962 and '63. History proves this simply was not the case.

How Common Was Religion in Schools?

In 1960, two years before the first prayer case reached the U.S. Supreme Court, Americans United for Separation of Church and State undertook a survey of Bible reading in public schools. The findings were illuminating. Only five states had laws on the books requiring daily Bible reading. Twenty-five states had laws allowing "optional" Bible reading. Courts in eleven states had declared the practice unconstitutional. The remaining states had no laws on the books one way or the other.[7] The practice, it seems, was not as common as is today believed, and one could argue that the trend was running in favor of a court-mandated, state-by-state phase-out.

Other evidence indicates that school-sponsored prayer and Bible reading simply weren't as common in public schools as the Religious Right today claims.

Boardman W. Kathan, a United Church of Christ minister, has

researched this area extensively. In 1989 he reported his findings in the journal *Religious Education*. Kathan found that as public schools evolved in the post-Revolutionary War period, there was a general attitude of indifference toward religion among the American public. While the Bible was often used in schools as a reader and speller, formal daily prayers and devotional readings were held sporadically, often only when a local clergyman visited the school.

Shortly before the Civil War, a great interest in educational reform arose in the United States. Alongside that came the Second Great Awakening, which created a renewed interest in religion among Americans. During the Awakening, which was a Protestant phenomenon, some people began to argue that public schools should inclucate Protestant values. As a result, formal rituals of prayer and Bible reading developed in some schools.

However, it was not until the 20th century that such practices began to find their way into state law. Kathan reports that prior to 1900, only Massachusetts had a law on the books dealing with prayer and Bible reading in public schools. Between 1910 and 1930, seventeen states and the District of Columbia passed similar laws.[8] The movement to get these ordinances on the books was spearheaded by a powerful lobby of conservative church groups, led by the National Reform Association.

The laws were quickly challenged in court. Many of the early school prayer cases took place in state courts because church-state cases were a rarity in the federal courts prior to the 1940s. The Supreme Court had not yet ruled that the Fourteenth Amendment applies the Bill of Rights to the states. Hence, in matters of religious freedom the U.S. Supreme Court was quick to defer to lower state courts.

The Supreme Court Gets Involved

By the 1960s that had changed, of course. A number of other factors in American society had also changed. For one thing, religious minorities were growing in numbers and becoming more confident of their rights in society. The burgeoning black civil rights movement undoubtedly inspired religious minorities, who came to believe that they too should enjoy the full fruits of American liberty—including religious freedom.

Jews, atheists, Catholics, minority Protestants and others who felt disenfranchised because of the religious flavor of the public schools began looking to the federal courts for relief. In doing so, they initiated a series of landmark court rulings that increased religious freedom for all Americans; however, they remain controversial and poorly understood until this day.

The first school prayer case was decided by the U.S. Supreme Court in 1962. However, the high court had heard disputes over religion in public schools before. In 1948 the court struck down voluntary religious instruction programs run by outside groups on site at public schools. Four years later, the court upheld such plans occurring off of school property during the school day.

But the famous 1962 case, *Engel v. Vitale*, was something different: a direct challenge in the nation's highest court to a school-sponsored program of prayer. The facts of the case were not in dispute. The prayer was clearly state supported. Indeed, the challenge revolved around a prayer written by school bureaucrats. The New York Board of Regents composed what they believed was a "non-sectarian" prayer and urged local school district officials to tell teachers to lead students in the prayer at the start of each day. The Regents believed the prayer would ward off the evils of juvenile delinquency and Communism.

About 10 percent of the school districts in New York elected to use the prayer, one of them being the Herricks School District of New Hyde Park on Long Island.

A group of New Hyde Park parents quickly challenged the prayer practice. Although the parents lost at the first court level, when the dispute reached the Supreme Court the decision wasn't even close. The justices struck down the prayers by a 6-1 vote. (One justice did not participate, and there was a vacancy on the court.)

The court majority ruled that the prayer program had the effect of unconstitutionally involving the government in religious matters. Observed the justices, "It is no part of the business of government to compose official prayers for any group of the American people to recite as a part of a religious program carried on by government."[9]

Reaction was swift. Some members of Congress, ever eager to exploit complex, emotion-laden issues for personal gain, denounced the decision. Sen. Robert C. Byrd, a West Virginia Democrat, remarked, "Can it be that we, too, are ready to embrace the foul concept of atheism? Somebody is tampering with America's soul. I leave it to you who that somebody is."[10]

Byrd's comment was the first of many attempting to link application of church-state separation by the courts to Soviet hostility toward religion. Since then, the argument has been repeated time and time again by those who oppose the separation principle. Some have gone as far as to suggest that the Soviets invented church-state separation. Such a statement unveils an abysmal ignorance of U.S. history. Jefferson coined the wall metaphor in 1802, a full *115* years before the Communist state arose in Russia in 1917.

Far from being an expression of Communism, the court's ruling in *Engel* increased religious freedom in America. For the first time parents had complete control over what prayers their children would say and what religious texts they would be exposed to. It is difficult to understand how anyone could oppose a court ruling that allows parents to decide what religious exercises their own children take part in.

In a press statement issued shortly after the ruling, Americans United for Separation of Church and State pointed out that the *Engel* decision increased religious freedom. "The Court's decision is a blow to the totalitarian concept of government," observed the group. "There are those among us who want government to take over everything. Now this thinking invades the most intimate and personal realm known to man—that of religious experience."

Continued the statement,

> Public school children in New York State have been, in effect, required by law to pray and have been regimented in their prayers. To establish such a religious exercise upon these citizens is an unconstitutional use of governmental authority. . . . The decisive point of difference between a free government and a Communist or Fascist government is this—that the free government does not try to run everything. Certain matters are deliberately left to the personal conscience and decision of the people themselves. Religion is eminently

one of these matters and the Supreme Court has now enabled us to keep it so.[11]

Religious Right propagandist David Barton claims in his books and videotapes that the Supreme Court failed to based the *Engel* decision on history or prior church-state precedents.[12] Barton has apparently not taken the time to actually read the decision he so roundly criticizes. In it, Justice Hugo Black reviews church-state relations in the colonial period in making the case against government involvement in religion. In his concurring opinion, Justice William Douglas cited several previous church-state cases.

Madalyn Murray O'Hair

At this point, the reader might be wondering, "What about Madalyn Murray O'Hair? Wasn't she involved in all of this?" O'Hair's role in the prayer cases constitutes one of the great myths of American church-state relations.

Briefly, the myth goes something like this: Until 1962, prayers occurred in every public school in America. Madalyn Murray O'Hair, an atheist, filed a lawsuit and had them all removed. Millions of people in fundamentalist churches all over America believe this story. There is only one problem with this scenario: It isn't true.

As history indicates, several states had already removed school-sponsored devotional exercises, some as early as 1890, long before O'Hair arrived on the scene. Secondly, O'Hair's case was only one of three cases heard by the Supreme Court in 1962 and '63 concerning school prayer.

O'Hair, who in the 1960s was a resident of Maryland, filed her case to block the mandatory recitation of the Lord's Prayer in Baltimore public schools at the start of the school day. At the same time, Pennsylvania resident Ed Schempp was pursuing litigation to stop mandatory devotional Bible reading in Philadelphia-area public schools on behalf of his son, Ellory, a student at Abington Senior High School.

The Schempps won the case at the federal appeals court level, and

Pennsylvania lawmakers responded by changing the law to allow students to opt out of the religious exercises with parental permission. The Schempps said the new scheme still unconstitutionally promoted Christianity at state expense and returned to court. The appeals court agreed, but the school district appealed. The Supreme Court agreed to settle the controversy.

The Supreme Court consolidated the Schempps' case with Murray O'Hair's case, *Murray v. Curlett*, under the name *Abington Township School District v. Schempp*. In an 8-1 ruling released on June 17, 1963, the court struck down both exercises.

Thus, while Madalyn Murray O'Hair has proclaimed herself the woman who "got prayer kicked out of schools" and has used her notoriety to establish a nationwide atheist network, her claims are wildly exaggerated. Make no mistake, O'Hair was vilified for bringing the case, and her unpopular stand required considerable personal courage on her part. But the legal effort removing government-sponsored prayers and other religious exercises in public schools involved lots of other people who should not be overlooked. No one person can take the credit.

Like the *Engel* ruling before it, nothing in the *Schempp* decision in any way infringes the right of students to voluntarily read the Bible or pray during free time. The justices also went out of their way to stress that the decision should not be construed as hostile to religion or to imply that secular programs of education involving the Bible are not legal.

Observed Justice Tom Clark, "It might well be said that one's education is not complete without a study of comparative religion or the history of religion and its relationship to the advancement of civilization. It may certainly be said that the Bible is worthy of study for its literary and historic qualities. Nothing we have said here indicates that such study of the Bible or of religion, when presented objectively as part of a secular program of education, may not be effected consistently with the First Amendment."[13]

Clark also asserted, "The place of religion in our society is an exalted one, achieved through a long tradition of reliance on the home, the church and the inviolable citadel of the individual heart and mind. We have come to recognize through bitter experience that it is not within the power of government to invade that citadel, whether its purpose or effect be to aid or oppose, to advance or retard. In the relationship between man and religion, the State is firmly committed to a position of neutrality."

Congress Speaks Up

Despite language like that, the decision, like *Engel* before it, was marked by a massive outpouring of outrage. Newspaper editorials denounced the ruling, and politicians across the country took up the cause of "restoring" prayer to public schools.

Nowhere was this battle more pitched than in Congress, where numerous measures were introduced to amend the Constitution to allow for state-mandated prayer programs.

About a month after the *Schempp* ruling was handed down, Rep. Frank Becker, a New York Republican, introduced a school prayer amendment. Although at least sixty other similar proposals had been introduced, Becker's was the first to see movement in the House. Hearings were held on the Becker amendment during the spring of 1964. They lasted seven weeks. Despite rabble-rousing from conservative religious leaders and a mail campaign aimed at members of Congress, Becker was unable to obtain the 210 votes he needed to get the amendment out of the House Judiciary Committee.

Members of the Senate also tried to pass a school prayer amendment. Unlike its companion in the House, the measure, sponsored by Sen. Everett Dirksen of Illinois, was able to get out of the Senate Judiciary Committee but failed to garner the two-thirds majority it needed to pass the full Senate. (The measure did receive a simple majority of 49-37.)

The battle over school prayer split the nation's two major political parties. The Republicans were quick to endorse the Becker amendment, and the Republican National Convention went on record supporting a school prayer amendment in the party platform, a position it retains to this day. The Republicans also tried unsuccessfully to use the issue against the Democrats during the 1964 presidential campaign. This issue still splits the two parties today and usually flares up at least once during presidential elections.

Although school prayer amendments continued to be introduced every year in Congress, the routine quickly became pro forma, and most were assigned to languish in congressional subcommittees, never to emerge.

Reagan's "Voluntary Prayers"

In the mid-1980s, however, the school prayer issue again achieved prominence in Congress and became a matter of public debate. Ronald Reagan, who was elected president in 1980, campaigned on a platform calling for "traditional values" and promised, if elected, to "return" prayer to schools.

Reagan talked incessantly about the need for "voluntary" prayer in schools, but since truly voluntary religious exercises have always been legal in public schools, observers on the church-state scene speculated that Reagan and his supporters must have wanted something more. Sure enough, when the Reagan school prayer amendment was introduced in 1982, a White House briefing paper submitted with it bluntly stated, "[S]tates and communities would be free to select prayers of their own choosing. They could choose prayers that have already been written, or they could compose their own prayers. *If groups of people are to be permitted prayer, someone must have the power to determine the content of such prayers.*"[14] (Emphasis mine.)

There were many parallels between the scene in 1982 and the unsuccessful effort nearly twenty years earlier to pass the Becker and Dirksen amendments. Celebrities holding conservative views but with no background in either education, religion, or child psychology were brought in to testify on behalf of the amendment. Politicians again attempted to use school prayer against opponents. But in the end, the outcome was the same. The Senate mustered a simply majority in favor of the amendment by a vote of 55-43, but the vote was eleven short of the required two-thirds majority.

Two years later Reagan and his backers took advantage of another widely misunderstood Supreme Court ruling to fan the flames of hysteria and again promote a school prayer amendment. The high court ruled 5-4 that year in the case *Wallace v. Jaffree* that an Alabama law mandating that public schools set aside a moment of silence for prayer was unconstitutional. The high court ruled that states have no business designating prayer time for anyone. Once again, a decision that actually increased religious freedom was poorly reported in the media and widely denounced by politicians and anti-separationist religious leaders.

Since the unsuccessful attempts of the mid-1980s, efforts to pass a school prayer amendment have continued, but none has reached the Senate or House floor and most quietly wither away in committee. Most recently, in January 1992 North Carolina Senator Jesse Helms, a Republican and frequent ally of the Religious Right, attempted to attach a "sense of the Senate" resolution favoring school prayer to an education bill. The Helms gambit was defeated by a 55-38 vote.

Related Issues

Outside of prayer, the Supreme Court has issued other rulings dealing with religion in public schools. In 1990, the court ruled 8-1 that the Equal Access Act, legislation designed to allow voluntary student prayer and Bible clubs to meet at public schools during non-instructional time under certain conditions, was constitutional.[15]

In 1987, the court struck down a Louisiana law that required public schools to teach "creation science" alongside evolution. The justices, in a 7-2 ruling, held that creationism is a religious doctrine, not a science.[16] The court had earlier ruled in 1968 that Arkansas lawmakers could not ban the teaching of evolution in public schools.

The Louisiana case produced some good language from the high court on how the application of separation of church and state to public education protects family rights. Observed Justice William Brennan, "Families entrust public schools with the education of their children, but condition their trust on the understanding that the classroom will not purposely be used to advance religious views that may conflict with the private beliefs of the student and his or her family."

Despite this clear defeat, the well organized and well funded creationist lobby has not given up. They have repackaged their idea and are again trying to sell it to public schools under the name of "intelligent design." Alongside this tactic, creationists are working feverishly to water down instruction about evolution in schools. Unfortunately, they have managed to frighten and confuse so many educators and administrators that some public schools now avoid the subject of evolution all together, seeking to dodge controversy. Creationists are responsible for the dumbing down of an entire generation of American students and have done great damage to science education in this country.

The Religious Right Gets Excited

By 1992, a series of changes had occurred on the Supreme Court. Several members of the court's staunchly separationist wing, including Justice Thurgood Marshall and Justice Brennan, perhaps the strongest defender of church-state separation on the high court since Hugo Black, had retired. They were replaced by more accommodationist justices appointed by Presidents Ronald Reagan and George Bush.

Religious Right groups began predicting that a revolution in church-state issues would occur. The new Reagan court, they said, would soon modify or overturn outright the court's school prayer rulings and other matters of church-state jurisprudence.

Early on it appeared that the anti-separationists were correct. One of the new conservatives, Justice Anthony M. Kennedy, was quick to criticize the high court's church-state cases. In a 1989 controversy dealing with the display of religious symbols on public property, Kennedy bluntly stated, "Substantial revision of our Establishment Clause doctrine may be in order."[17]

The high court did not have to wait long for the perfect test case to begin its "substantial revision." A controversy soon bubbled up from the federal courts testing the constitutionality of prayers before public school graduation ceremonies. The dispute was brought by the Weisman family of Providence, Rhode Island, whose case I described in the opening chapter. The Weismans protested the inclusion of prayers during the graduation of daughter Deborah from middle school in 1989.

Although pundits on both sides of the church-state controversy predicted at the very least a chipping away at Jefferson's wall, the resulting decision was quite a surprise. On June 24, 1992, the court issued a narrow 5-4 ruling striking down the state-backed prayers and upholding separation of church and state. In an ironic twist, the majority opinion was written by Justice Kennedy in language that harkened back to the strict separationism of the 1960s and 1970s!

"It is beyond dispute that, at a minimum, the Constitution guarantees that government may not coerce anyone to support or participate in religion or its exercise, or otherwise act in a way which 'establishes a [state] religious faith, or tends to do so,'" wrote Kennedy in the *Lee v. Weisman* ruling. "The State's involvement in the school prayers challenged today violates these central principles."

Continued Kennedy, "The First Amendment's Religion Clauses mean that religious beliefs and religious expressions are too precious to be either proscribed or prescribed by the State."[18]

Kennedy was joined by Reagan appointee Sandra Day O'Connor and David J. Souter, a Bush appointee. The three, joined by remaining separationists John Paul Stevens and Harry Blackmun, declared that the school prayer decisions of the 1960s are still good law and that government has no business coercing anyone into participating in religious exercises. The fact that three Reagan-Bush appointees joined the majority should lay to rest for good the notion that opposing school prayer is strictly a "liberal" position. Support for our nation's commitment to religious freedom cuts across ideological lines.

Separationists may have breathed a collective sigh of relief, but there was a feeling that they had merely dodged the bullet. The ruling, after all, was 5-4. The school prayer decisions of the 1960s saw only one dissenter. In the wake of the *Weisman* ruling, separationists were acutely aware of how precarious their position at the Supreme Court had become. One new appointee could change the balance.

What the Polls Really Say

Lee v. Weisman, like the other high court prayer rulings, was widely misunderstood by the American people and, in some cases, deliberately distorted by those with political agendas. Once again, untrue charges that God had been "expelled from the classroom" were levied. Critics glossed over Kennedy's eloquent language explaining how the ruling protects religious belief and unfairly accused the court majority of "hostility toward religion."

As we have seen, there are a number of misconceptions in the public mind about the scope and effect of the Supreme Court's school prayer rulings. This is reflected in public opinion polls, which commonly show numbers as high as 80 percent in favor of "school prayer." *Time* magazine, for example, published the results of a December 1991 poll in which 78 percent of the respondents said they favored "allowing children to say prayers in public schools."

Many of these polls, including the one quoted in *Time*, however, have been flawed in the manner in which they phrased the crucial question. Most people, when asked, will say they are in favor of "prayer in schools" because such a phrasing implies a voluntary system of prayer (and because many people still believe that even voluntary prayer in schools is illegal). Support drops, however, when respondents are asked if they favor required prayer or state-mandated devotional activities.

In 1989 *Parents* magazine performed a valuable public service by commissioning a public opinion poll that asked the proper question. Respondents were asked to choose from three possible prayer scenarios that could occur in public schools.

In the survey, 68 percent agreed with the statement, "Although no prayer should be said aloud, there should be a minute of silence each day so that students could pray silently, meditate, or do nothing if they prefer." Only *17 percent* agreed with the statement, "A prayer should be said aloud once a day in public schools, and students should be required to participate." Twelve percent favored the statement, "There should be no prayers or moments of silence in public schools."[19]

The vast majority of Americans—nearly 70 percent—simply want time to be available for students to say prayers in public schools. Ironically, more than half of the states already have such a moment of silence. If these moments are neutral—that is, not specifically designed to promote prayer—they are perfectly constitutional.

Thus, it seems, a countless amount of time and energy has been spent debating an issue that has already been solved in most states and could be solved tomorrow in the others through a simple, neutral moment of silence law.

The fact is, most Americans do not want to go back to 1962, when school bureaucrats wrote prayers for children to say. Most Americans want to choose for themselves what prayers their children are exposed to or are asked to say. For all their posturing, school prayer boosters have never once explained why it is desirable to have children participate in religious devotions composed by government officials. The prayer boosters' attempts to portray such policies as protective of freedom of religion stand logic and common sense on their heads.

Make no mistake, prior to 1963, a great deal of religious intolerance and forced participation in religion existed in many American public schools. In Pennsylvania, the Bible reading exercise was *mandatory*. The Religious Right often pines for the days when "voluntary prayer and Bible reading" were permitted in schools. Ironically, that's exactly the situation we have today in schools.

There was nothing "voluntary" about the state-mandated exercises in Pennsylvania and other states. In many cases, students could not be excused even if their parents objected. Seeking to avoid litigation, officials in Pennsylvania agreed to change the law to allow for "voluntary" participation in the religious exercises, but it was simply too little too late. Insensitivity and intolerance still reigned. In fact, Ellory Schempp, the brave sixteen-year-old who sparked the case, got things rolling one day by bringing a Koran to class and reading it silently during the morning devotionals. He was promptly sent to the principal's office. Today our public schools are free from such intolerance. We should be proud of this fact and resist vigorously any attempt to drag us back to the days of prayer mandated by the government.

Disinformation from the Religious Right

The issue of school prayer is really a non-issue. It is one of the greatest frauds ever perpetrated on the American people. Millions of Americans continue to believe that a schoolchild cannot, at any point in the day, bow his or her head in prayer. They are wrong.

Why does this massive fraud continue to circulate? The primary reason is the Religious Right. The various groups that make up this conglomeration have never been much concerned with accuracy. They have attempted to turn the American people against public education and church-state separation in general. Making people believe the public schools are hostile to any religious expression is one of their key strategies. Sadly, it has been a very successful one.

A good example of this is the often-repeated story about the tiny first-grader who is seized by the brutish public school principal for daring to say a prayer over her lunch. As the story goes, the child is hauled off to the office and berated with the law on school prayer and told to never do "that" again.

But when asked, Religious Right activists are unable to name where this event happened, when it occurred or who was involved. Not only that, the basic details often vary from telling to telling. The child's sex, age, and grade level vary wildly.

Televangelist Pat Robertson told a variant of this tall tale on his "700 Club" on December 4, 1992. This time the incident supposedly took place at a public elementary school in Kingsville, Texas, and involved a five-year-old named Shannon. Local reporters decided to look into the matter and called officials at the school.

The school officials' conclusion? "As far as we know, it did not occur," the school's public information director told the press.[20] The school official, Tony Morales, said administrators had "checked and checked and cannot find out anything. We called the principals at all three of our kindergarten campuses, and they are unaware of any incident resembling what was said by Pat Robertson. They do not even know of a girl named Shannon."

Scott Stanford, editor of the *Kingsville Record*, called Robertson's offices in Virginia Beach, Virginia, to see if he could track down the source of the story. He was told that Robertson had received the details from the American Center for Law and Justice (ACLJ), Robertson's own legal aid group. But when Stanford called the ACLJ, a staffer told him, "What was said on the air today was the first I had heard of it." Stanford published his findings, hoping that if the incident did occur those involved would come forward. No one ever did.

Concluded Morales, "We keep getting the runaround from the Robertson people. I called them. The school board president called them. But we still don't know any more than we did."

That's no surprise. By now it is clear that this story is an urban myth invented out of whole cloth by the Religious Right. It may circulate incessantly in Religious Right circles, but it is not true; it never happened. In spite of all of their allegations, the Religious Right has not been able to produce *one bona fide* instance of a violation of a student's right to pray in public schools. Not one!

The Religious Right, of course, would dispute that allegation. But the fact remains that when these stories are examined under the harsh light of scrutiny, it always turns out that certain key factors have been conveniently omitted.

In 1991, for example, a Virginia-based Religious Right legal aid group called the Rutherford Institute charged that an eleven-year-old fifth grader in Norman, Oklahoma, had been ordered by school officials to stop reading her Bible in the playground during recess and to stop holding informal Bible studies with other students.

The group trumpeted the case as a gross violation of religious liberty, and on the surface it appeared they were correct. But the entire story crumbled after a television reporter from ABC News went to Norman to investigate. Correspondent Walter C. Rodgers quickly learned that the child, Monette Rethford, had been disturbing other children with aggressive proselytism in the playground and that she had frightened her fellow schoolmates with vivid stories of hell.[21] The child had obviously been prodded to do these things by her parents; her father told Rodgers that, "Satanism, humanism and atheism" are being taught in public schools. Concerned parents had simply asked the school to keep the child from disrupting recess, and the school complied. Rutherford filed legal action, but the case was settled out of court.

Many of the cases the Religious Right points to as violations of religious liberty are in fact tensions wrought by hyper-aggressive students (usually spurred by adults outside the school) who quickly turn off their classmates with loud, continuous preaching. In tiny Blue River, Oregon, the local public high school was torn apart in 1991-92 by interfaith tensions when student members of a local Baptist church decided to "save" their fellow classmates. Shouting matches erupted between Baptist students and others who did not believe they needed to be saved. Soon the entire rural community was fighting over the incident, and two school board members were ousted during local elections for failing to take the problems seriously.[22]

Many parents send their children to public schools with the understanding that the children will not be pressured there to change their religion. When religious wars do break out, the confrontations can be ugly, and attempts by school officials to keep the peace are often interpreted as attacks on religion. One false step by a principal or superintendent can lead to disaster.

In Metropolis, Illinois, for example, a 1991 squabble over prayers around a public school's flagpole quickly got out of hand and resulted in yet another Religious Right attempt to claim a violation of religious freedom.

The incident started when a group of adults affiliated with a local church arrived on school grounds to pray with students around the pole. School officials had earlier told the adults that, as a matter of school policy, outsiders are not permitted on school grounds during the day. The principal, alarmed over the collection of outsiders on school grounds, followed the superintendent's orders and called the police. Officers came and promptly removed the adults from the school's grounds. Pat Robertson later aired reports about this incident on the "700 Club" but failed to point out that the adults were taken away for trespassing, not because they were praying. No students were arrested. Robertson's "reporters" later stuck a camera in the principal's face and demanded an apology. The principal, seeking to end the ugly incident and heal the community, complied.[23]

The list goes on. In numerous cases, incidents described as great violations of religious liberty in public schools by the Religious Right simply fall apart when someone takes the time to make a few phone calls. Unfortunately, those calls are usually not made, or if they are, they are not reported in the mass media. Thus, the claims of assorted far-right groups go unchallenged and enter the media or Religious Right rumor network as truth.

The tragedy of the school prayer issue is that it has unnecessarily divided the American people along theological lines. Denominations have been forced to take sides, and the debate has often been quite ugly. The Southern Baptist Convention, for example, switched positions on school prayer in the early 1980s, flip-flopping from opposition to a school prayer amendment to favoring one. The rift on that issue and numerous others has pitted Baptist against Baptist and wounded the denomination.

Likewise, religious minorities, understandably wary of state-supported religion in schools, have been attacked by unthinking clerics and others who characterize their opposition as some sort of anti-religious plot. Jews have taken many unfair hits in the arena of public opinion simply because many Jewish leaders have insisted on the right of Jewish children to attend public schools without being subjected to Christian religious exercises. Jewish objections arise not from any hostility toward Christianity but rather a perfectly understandable desire to maintain their own religious traditions. Surely Christians would demand the same rights were the situation reversed.

More Religious Right Distortions

A few final words must be said about religion in schools. The charge is often made that since "prayer was taken out of schools," the quality of American education and American life in general has declined. The school prayer rulings have been blamed for everything from juvenile delinquency to the American military disaster in Vietnam.

When it comes to simplistic thinking, this argument is the grand-daddy of them all. Still, despite its obvious flaws, it is sometimes taken seriously by Religious Right activists and others. Evangelical author David Barton has written an entire book full of charts and graphs purporting to show America's decline since the 1962 *Engel* ruling.[24] In

January 1992, Republican Sen. Jesse Helms of North Carolina used the charts on the floor of the Senate to argue for school prayer.

Because prayer has not been removed from school, the argument immediately fails. However, giving the argument the benefit of the doubt and going one or two steps farther really unmasks how ridiculous it is.

The argument that if two events occur in sequence then the former must have caused the latter is a common fallacy of logic known as *post hoc ergo propter hoc* (Latin for "after this, therefore on account of this"). As a moment's thought will demonstrate, the fact that two events occur at the same time does not mean they are related. Such an argument is analogous to stating, "Ever since men went to the moon, the world has been getting warmer." Maybe, but one must be able to do more than just note a coincidence; one must prove there is some type of connection between the two events.

In the case of the alleged decline of American society, no link has ever been shown relating to the prayer rulings. In fact, the alleged "slip" was caused by wholly unrelated factors. Barton and others, for example, are fond of claiming that SAT scores have declined since 1962. Under their reasoning, God is displeased with the prayer ruling and has retaliated by making students dumber. But a quick look at the facts unveils the real reason for SAT slippage: More students take the test today.

In the early 1960s, the SAT was taken almost exclusively by upper-class, well-educated youngsters who went on to study at prestigious universities. Today the SAT is taken by just about everyone who wants to go to college. Since many more young people from a much wider variety of socio-economic backgrounds take the test today, it's only natural that the scores would drop. Sadly, the type of slipshod "reasoning" typical of Barton is what passes as scholarship among Religious Right groups.

American society is plagued today by a variety of problems. The public school system has not remained unaffected. These problems are caused by complex socio-economic factors and shifts in the way Americans live and work, not to mention the changing dynamic of the American family. Some may search for a simple cause for these disturbing changes, but it just doesn't exist. To blame all of today's problems, from AIDS to the divorce rate, on a 1962 Supreme Court ruling is simplistic thinking.

Besides, not all indices of quality of life have declined since 1962. Many have escalated. Life expectancy is up, and impressive medical advances have occurred. Labor-reducing technologies are commonplace. Are these also a result of the 1962 ruling? Quite a powerful decision! One might also wonder why God has allowed the Japanese to prosper economically, have a top-line public school system and live in a society largely free from violence when their society is less than 1 percent Christian.

Opinion polls provide a final fatal blow to Barton's theory. Polls taken since 1962 have shown absolutely no reduction of interest in religion among American teenagers. If the school prayer rulings were as detrimental to religion as Barton and others in the Religious Right claim, it stands to reason that the religiosity of teenagers would have sharply dropped since those rulings were handed down.

In fact, just the opposite is true. Teenagers remain highly religious. A 1993 poll conducted for the Princeton Religion Research Center by George H. Gallup Jr. and Robert Bezilla found that 95 percent of all teens surveyed believe in God. An additional 93 percent believe that God loves them, and 91 percent believe in heaven. Finally, 86 percent said they believe in the divinity of Jesus Christ.[25] Results like these indicate what separationists have said all along: The school prayer rulings have helped religion, not harmed it.

The Secular Humanism Canard

Religious Right activists also constantly charge that public schools promote "secular humanism," which the Religious Right defines as a "religion" that fosters atheism. Again a quick look at the facts exposes this claim as nonsense.

There is no doubt that an organized humanist community does exist in the United States. However, it is so small that "humanist" does not even register as a category when pollsters ask Americans to describe their religious or philosophical beliefs. (In fact, more than 90 percent of all Americans say they are believers.) Given the decentralized nature of public education in America, there is no way that such a minuscule group of people could take over the public schools.

The fact is that polls have shown that the majority of people who teach and work in public schools and sit on school boards reflect the religious trends of America at large. That is, the overwhelming majority are Christians of one variety or another.

In 1986 the *American School Board Journal* published the results of a nationwide survey of school board members. The magazine had hoped to compile a profile of the "typical" school board member. Surveys were mailed to 4,441 school board members, and more than 1,400 responded, an excellent return rate that gave the survey a 95 percent accuracy rate.

What did the journal find? The typical school board member is a white married male between forty-one and fifty years of age. He has children in school, is a college graduate and works in a professional or managerial role and earns between $40,000 and $49,000 annually. Most significantly, he is a registered Republican who describes his views on education as "conservative."[26]

This is hardly the profile of the secular humanist that Religious Right groups would have us believe is running our public school system.

The humanism myth got started because the Religious Right defines "secular humanism" as anything they don't like that goes on in the public schools. The situation was much the same in the 1950s, when the great bogeyman threatening our schools was Communism.

Ironically, lately the Religious Right has realized that the secular humanism canard has failed to catch on and has shifted its claim, now alleging that public schools are teaching witchcraft and/or "new age" philosophies. This charge also quickly crumbles with a quick reality check. Polls have shown that the number of Americans following New Age teachings seriously is about 28,000—a miniscule number out of the 250 million people who live in the United States. An even smaller number are involved in Wicca, a witchcraft-based religion.

The secular humanism/witchcraft/new age charges are more than simply untrue. They are insulting to the hundreds of thousands of men and women who work in public education in the United States. Education is one of the most demanding careers a person can pursue. The hours are long, the pay is often low and the work is hard. Instead of being appreciated for their efforts, public school teachers are often ridiculed or abused. The Religious Right, instead of applauding our teachers for doing their best under exacting circumstances and urging teachers to improve public schools constructively, repeatedly asserts that teachers are dupes for whatever anti-religious idea comes along.

Despite the long history of conflict over religion in public schools in the United States and the especially ugly battles in the 19th century, many Religious Right activists continue to look to this period as a model for our schools to follow today. They are either ignorant of the history outlined here or are simply unwilling to extend a measure of toleration to those who do not believe exactly as they do.

"We want to have it like it was 100 years ago, when God, the Ten Commandments and prayer was the focus of the schools," Don Smith, who was elected to the La Mesa/Spring Valley, California, School Board told the *San Diego Tribune* in 1990.[27]

In Vista, California, school board member Deidre Holliday told *The Wall Street Journal* in 1992 that public school teachers should tell students about Christ and lead them in religious exercises.

Remarked Holliday, "It would be wonderful to see the scripture read in schools so that children learn the truth. This is our heritage. Anyone who comes into this country is welcome, but we shouldn't be diluted by others' beliefs."[28]

The Religious Right is correct about one thing: Many who work in public education are suspicious of their agenda as it relates to the schools. In light of the intolerance expressed by Smith and Holliday and those like them, is it any wonder?

Notes

1. Leo Pfeffer, *Church, State, and Freedom* (Boston: Beacon Press, 1953), 279.
2. Ibid., 376-377.
3. Ibid., 375.
4. Ibid., 376.
5. *Board of Education of Cincinnati v. Minor,* 23 Ohio St. 211 (1872).

6. *Ring v. Board of Education,* 245 Ill. 334 (1910).

7. "School Bible Reading Survey," *Church & State* 13(January 1960): 5.

8. Boardman W. Kathan, "Prayer and the Public Schools: The Issue in Historical Perspective and Implications for Religious Education Today," *Religious Education* 84(Spring 1989): 232-248.

9. *Engel v. Vitale,* 370 U.S. 421 (1962).

10. Leo Pfeffer, *Church, State, and Freedom* (Revised Edition) (Boston: Beacon Press, 1967), 466.

11. Protestants and Other Americans United for Separation of Church and State news release, undated.

12. David Barton, *The Myth of Separation* (Aledo, TX: WallBuilders Press, 1989), 163.

13. *Abington Township School District v. Schempp,* 374 U.S. 203 (1963).

14. Joseph L. Conn, "Reagan Backs Government Sponsored School Prayer," *Church & State* 35(June 1982): 3.

15. *Board of Education of the Westside Community Schools v. Mergens,* 88-1597, June 4, 1990.

16. *Edwards v. Aguillard,* 85-1513, June 19, 1987.

17. *County of Allegheny v. ACLU,* 87-2050, July 3, 1989.

18. *Lee v. Weisman,* 90-1014, June 24, 1992.

19. *Parents* magazine, January 15, 1989.

20. Roddy Stinson, "Now this, ladies and gentlemen, is just Robertsonesque." *San Antonio Express-News* (December 17, 1992): 2A.

21. "Press Reports On 'Playground Bible Bust' Weren't Accurate, Says ABC Reporter," *Church & State* 44 (June 1991): 18.

22. Rob Boston, "American Public Schools: Mission Field USA?" *Church & State* 45(January 1992): 8-12.

23. Ibid., 11.

24. David Barton, *America: To Pray Or Not To Pray?* (Aledo, TX: WallBuilders Press, 1988.)

25. George H. Gallup Jr. and Robert Bezilla, "Poll: U.S. Teens Believe That God Loves Them," Religious News Service, April 21, 1993.

26. "The Secular Humanist Witchhunt: Some Burning Evidence," *Church & State* 40(February 1987): 13.

27. Community Coalition Network press statement, San Diego, Calif., January 1992.

28. Sonia L. Nazario, "Crusader Vows To Put God Back Into Schools Using Local Elections," *The Wall Street Journal,* June 15, 1992.

6

Parochiaid

The Rev. Jerry Falwell was in a fix. Although eager to expand his Lynchburg, Virginia, fundamentalist Christian school—Liberty University—and consolidate its debt, the Lynchburg-based TV preacher was short on cash.

But Falwell was not entirely without resources. Virginia law allows municipalities to float bond issues on behalf of local business, in the hopes of spurring economic development. Accordingly, Falwell turned to the city of Lynchburg and requested a bond issue.

Lynchburg's city leaders were happy to oblige. After all, Falwell, though a controversial character, had brought jobs to the city with his school and other aspects of his religious empire. Once before city officials had consented to a tax break for Falwell in the face of his threats to pull up and relocate elsewhere. The bond issue seemed trivial by comparison.

But there was one catch: State law explicitly states that bonds cannot be issued on behalf of any religious ministry or pervasively sectarian institution. Although such a prohibition would seem to rule Liberty out from the start, Falwell insisted otherwise. Liberty University, Falwell asserted, is not pervasively sectarian and does not exist primarily to impart religious doctrines.

A number of cosmetic changes were soon made to the school's catalog. Weekly chapel attendance was changed to "convocation" sessions. Prospective students were no longer required to offer their "personal testimony for the Lord Jesus Christ" and to submit a letter from their pastor attesting to their salvation experience. Opening prayers at the beginning of classes were dropped.

Claiming that Liberty was just another quasi-religious institution of higher education akin to Georgetown University or Baylor University, Falwell requested $60 million in taxpayer-backed municipal bonds.

Falwell might have quietly collected the bonds and started construction had it not been for the efforts of three Lynchburg residents— Nathanael "Nick" Habel, Haynie Kabler, and Jeff Somers. When the three learned what was going on at Liberty, they took legal action. The three separationists insisted that Liberty is pervasively sectarian and thus could not qualify for any type of state support, including municipal bonds. Unable to convince the city council, they took the matter to court.

Although they lost at the first court level, the three, now backed by Americans United for Separation of Church and State, appealed to the Virginia Supreme Court, which ultimately ruled 7-0 that the bond issue would violate not only the state bond act but also the Virginia Constitution and the U.S. Constitution. It was a resounding victory for separation of church and state.

Long-Running Battle

The incident at Lynchburg was just one skirmish in a long-running battle centering on the question of state aid to sectarian educational institutions. The dispute was a bit unusual in that it involved a university. Today's fight over public aid to parochial schools, sometimes called "parochiaid," usually revolves around elementary and secondary schools.

The United States, unlike many Western European nations, has no tradition of granting public funds to parochial and other private schools. In fact, just the opposite is true. Throughout our history as a nation, explicit steps have been taken to forbid this type of funding. In this country, public education has been seen as the primary vehicle for educating the masses. As such, state funds have been reserved exclusively for it. Although the Supreme Court in 1925 upheld the right of private schools to exist and ruled that states cannot force children to attend public schools, private schools have been kept off the government dole.

This is due in large part to America's tradition of separation of church and state. Religious schools, as ministries of the religious groups that sponsor them, are seen as extensions of churches. To award them public money would be the equivalent of taxing all citizens to support religious activities. This idea has been anathema since the days of Jefferson and Madison.

Nevertheless, some religious bodies have persisted in pressuring local, state, and federal governments to give them tax assistance. Most persistent at this has been the Roman Catholic Church, which has clamored for state aid almost from the day the Catholic school system was founded.

During the Cincinnati "Bible war" of 1869 (see chapter 5), Archbishop John Purcell, declaring that Catholic parents should not allow their children to participate in Protestant religious exercises in public schools, suggested that one way to solve the problem would be for the Cincinnati School Board to give parents money to offset the cost of private education "as has been done in England, France, Canada, Prussia and other countries."[1]

But a spirit of anti-Catholicism, prevalent in 19th century America, ensured that no public funds flowed to Catholic schools. The fact that a bias against Catholics may have been a driving force behind withholding funds in no way diminishes the power of the constitutional argument against parochiaid. In fact, many of those opposed to aiding Catholic schools did argue their case from a purely constitutional context. Others insisted that a public school system was required to bring the various immigrant groups together, to teach their children a common language and common customs of the nation. Catholics could choose to remain outside this effort at homogeny, the argument went, but they should not be given public funds to make it easier for them to do so.

By the 1870s emotion was running so high over the "school question"—that is, whether or not public aid would be extended to private schools—that Congress was pressured to act. James G. Blaine, a noted politician of the day, proposed a constitutional amendment applying the federal religion clauses to the states as well as prohibiting any expenditure of public funds for sectarian schools.

Blaine's amendment failed to pass Congress, though the vote was close. Many states, however, adopted variations of the Blaine Amendment and incorporated them into their own constitutions. As a consequence, almost half of the states today have some type of language in their constitutions barring tax aid to sectarian schools.

Widespread public wariness over the Roman Catholic Church steadily diminished as the 20th century progressed. To be sure, there was still much bias around. In 1928, Al Smith, the first Catholic to run for president on a major party ticket, was defeated by Herbert Hoover, in large measure due to fantastic and virulent anti-Catholic propaganda that circulated throughout the nation.

Catholics, however, achieved footholds in several parts of the country. Southern Louisiana, for example, has a strong Catholic tradition dating back to its days as a French territory. Large numbers of Catholics also settled in northeastern states such as Massachusetts, Pennsylvania, and New York.

Early Parochiaid Cases

As Catholic schools increased in number and Catholics grew politically powerful in some states, it became inevitable that agitation for legislation offering various types of assistance to Catholic schools would escalate.

Louisiana was the site of the country's first parochiaid court battle, which occurred in 1930 after the state legislature passed a law allowing public money to be used for the purchase of secular textbooks for public and private school students.

The Supreme Court ruled in *Cochran v. Louisiana State Board of Education* that the law was constitutional because it was aimed at benefitting children, not the schools, a legal principle known as the "child benefit theory."[2]

Parochiaid proponents were quick to use the ruling to secure other types of aid. In a landmark 1947 ruling, they scored another limited victory when the court ruled in *Everson v. Board of Education* that states could provide public bus subsidies to parochial school children.

Although parochiaiders won bus subsidies in the *Everson* case, the ruling as a whole was a significant loss for them. The high court seemed to go out of its way to indicate that more expansive parochiaid programs would face tough sledding before the justices. This quickly turned out to be the case.

In ringing language that is some of the high court's most separationist to date, Justice Hugo Black said in *Everson*: "The First Amendment of the Constitution means at least this: Neither a state nor the federal government can set up a church. Neither can pass laws which aid one religion, aid all religions, or prefer one religion over another. . . . No tax in any amount, large or small, can be levied to support any religious activities or institutions, whatever they may be called, or whatever form they may adopt to teach or practice religion."[3]

The court's language was a type of prophecy that was soon borne out. Although advocates of parochiaid won another limited textbook aid program in 1968,[4] after that they faced a series of stinging defeats that dealt the entire movement a considerable setback.

1971's *Lemon v. Kurtzman* was the first of the high-profile losses. Here the Supreme Court struck down laws in Rhode Island and Pennsylvania that allowed the state to pay some portion of parochial school teachers' salaries in subjects deemed "secular."[5]

But in their *Lemon* decision the court did more than simply strike down parochiaid plans. The justices also devised a strict three-part test for determining church-state violations. Under what became known as the *Lemon* Test, a law is deemed to violate church-state separation if any one of three conditions are present: The law does not have a secular legislative purpose; the law has the primary effect of advancing or inhibiting religion; the law fosters excessive governmental entanglement with religion.

Since then, the *Lemon* Test has been cited in virtually every major church-state case before the high court, including several parochiaid cases. While not always consistently applied by the justices, the test affords a grand measure of protection to religious freedom by making sure that government adheres to the principle of separation of church and state. Religious Right activists have repeatedly attacked the *Lemon* standard and asked the court to discard it. Some justices have agreed and criticized the test—notably Antonin Scalia—but so far the court's finding in *Lemon* remains intact.

Two years after the *Lemon* case was decided, another black day for parochiaiders occurred. The high court in *PEARL v. Nyquist* struck down a series of New York laws offering a package of aid to parochial schools. One segment of the law was a voucher-type plan giving direct state grants to private schools that served low-income families. Another section allowed for state grants to repair and maintain parochial schools. A third section was a plan allowing for private school tuition reimbursement for parents.[6]

In 1975 the high court struck down yet another parochiaid plan from Pennsylvania, this one dealing with the loan of audio-visual materials, maps, periodicals, and other materials as well as various "auxiliary services" that the state provided to the schools—guidance counseling, psychological testing and remedial reading offered by state-paid personnel who came onto the grounds of the parochial schools.[7]

Into the Modern Era

But in 1983, the high court, by a narrow 5-4 majority, upheld a Minnesota plan that granted parochial and public school parents a tax deduction for expenses incurred by "tuition, textbooks and transportation."[8] Since public school parents do not pay for these services, just about all of the program's largess went to private school patrons.

Then, two years later, also by a narrow 5-4 margin, the high court struck down the federal government's plan for implementing "Chapter One" services for private school students needing remedial education. At parochial schools, Chapter One services had been provided by public schools teachers on site at the private schools. The Supreme Court said this arrangement entangles church and state.[9]

The court has, however, seen fit to extend tax assistance to handicapped students attending sectarian schools under some conditions. In a case from Washington state, the high court ruled that a blind man could use public funds to attend a seminary.[10] In 1993 the justices ruled 5-4 that it does not violate the First Amendment if a public school chooses to provide a publicly funded interpreter to a deaf student in a sectarian school.[11] Both of these rulings were narrow and did not open the door to broader forms of parochiaid.

Unlike religion in public schools, where the high court has maintained a more or less consistently separationist line, the decisions concerning parochiaid have been all over the spectrum. As a result, in some states parochiaid has persistently been a problem. Legislators have sought to push the pro-parochiaid decisions to the limits and award private sectarian schools as much public money as possible. However, states have stopped short of implementing full scale voucher programs, plans whereby a variety of private schools are funded alongside public schools.

In the late 1970s and early 1980s, however, the political picture surrounding parochiaid began to change. Ronald Reagan, elected president on a platform of "getting government off people's backs," advocated spending public funds on private schools. He was joined by a new school of economists and would-be education reformers who sought to privatize formerly public institutions—including education. Although Reagan's tuition tax credit proposal failed to pass Congress, the national debate over the issue gave the parochiaid question new visibility and boosted the movement's supporters.

For the first time, groups other than the Catholic bishops began advocating for voucher plans, tuition tax credits, and other forms of parochiaid. As a consequence, various plans advocating forms of parochiaid filtered down to the states. Since then, these plans have been a constant feature in state legislatures. Most never get out of the various committees to which they are assigned. Others die on the floor of the statehouse.

There have been a few exceptions. Iowa passed a tuition tax credit and deduction plan similar to Minnesota's in 1987. The plan was later upheld by a federal court. In 1990, lawmakers in Wisconsin approved a controversial private school "choice" plan that had been inserted into the state budget by an aggressive pro-voucher lawmaker. The plan is limited to the city of Milwaukee and does not include sectarian schools. (An "independent" Catholic school that tried to get into the program was turned down.) The scheme was later upheld by the Wisconsin Supreme Court.

But for the most part, parochiaid boosters have little to show for their efforts legislatively. However, by keeping the issue alive in statehouses, the pro-parochiaid forces believe they are meeting an important public relations goal by keeping the controversy in the public eye.

Referenda in the States

Unfortunately for advocates of parochiaid, the public seems to have little desire to see private school aid plans implemented. In recent years, parochiaid boosters have managed to place voucher questions on several state ballots as referendum questions. The results have not been encouraging for those who favor these types of plans.

Colorado voters, for example, trounced a proposed voucher system by a 2-1 margin in 1992. Identical results occurred in Oregon two years earlier when a voucher referendum was rejected by voters. In 1988 voters in Utah turned down tuition tax credits by an even bigger margin— 70 percent to 30 percent.

In fact, since 1967 voters in thirteen states and the District of Columbia have defeated parochiaid proposals at the ballot, often by wide margins. Only one plan managed to pass—a limited proposal in South Dakota that allows public schools to "lend" textbooks to private schools.

Who supports parochiaid these days? Other than the Catholic hierarchy, the idea's most ardent supports are economic conservatives who believe in a free market approach to just about everything. This includes activists with the Libertarian Party, a fringe political movement that wants to do away with most forms of government, and the so-called "neo-conservatives," who favor privatizing as many public services as possible.

Also jumping on the parochiaid bandwagon as of late have been various Religious Right leaders such as Pat Robertson and Robert Simonds of Citizens for Excellence in Education, a Religious Right pressure group that seeks to "take over" public schools by getting fundamentalists of their stripe elected to school boards. The involvement of Protestant fundamentalists marks a flip-flop in their thinking. Until recently, many hard-right Christians have been wary of accepting any state support for their schools, fearing, rightly so, that government controls will quickly follow. Many Religious Right leaders still oppose vouchers for this reason and argue that a fundamentalist academy must pay its own way to be truly independent.

Answering Pro-Parochiaid Arguments

No matter which group is promoting vouchers, the arguments they use tend to be the same. Most of them, in fact, are merely the same tired arguments put forth by the Catholic bishops during the first big push for parochiaid in the late 1940s. As weak as they are, these arguments have become prevalent in the states and are worth responding to in depth. Let's look at some here.

Parochiaid will promote school "choice." The parochiaiders' appropriation of the word "choice" to describe their misguided crusade is perhaps their most devious tactic. Choice conjures up all the right images to Americans, primarily freedom. What the parochiaid forces don't point out is that when it comes to private schools, the concept of educational "choice" is meaningless, since private institutions remain free to discriminate in admissions. The religious leaders who operate 85 percent of all private schools have the only real "choice" about who gets in and who doesn't. Sectarian schools have the right to expel students for *any* reason, including concerns over discipline or simply to free up space for other children.

In 1988, a Christian school in East Moline, Illinois, forced an eighteen-year-old student to withdraw because he had contracted AIDS from a blood transfusion. The boy's father enrolled him in the nearby public school.

That same year, a New York City woman complained that her ten-year-old niece was denied admission to three Catholic schools after the girl's family complained of unsafe conditions at one of the schools. Obviously, a stack of vouchers a mile high and talk of "choice" would not get these children, and others in similar situations, into private schools that do not want them. These schools should not be permitted to discriminate in this manner and still receive public funds.

Parochiaid will force public schools to improve by making them compete with private schools. Real competition can never exist between public and private schools as long as private schools retain the right to expel any student for whatever reason they please or maintain selective admissions policies. Obviously, the playing field is uneven. Public schools must by law accept all who apply; private schools do not. Public schools must meet a host of state and federal regulations that control every aspect of their operation. Private schools are free from most of these. There can be no competition between two such dissimilar systems.

Private school parents are forced to pay taxes twice—once for public schools and once for private. "Double taxation" does not exist. Private school tuition is *not* a tax; it is an additional expense that some parents have chosen to pay. People should not expect reimbursement for state services that they chose on their own to duplicate. After all, people who build their own swimming pools don't receive a tax kickback because they don't use municipal pools.

It is also important to keep in mind that all citizens are expected to support basic public services such as fire departments, police, and public schools, whether they use them or not. In addition, an educated populace benefits everyone, not just those with children. That's why childless couples and single people still must pay taxes to support public education.

Ironically, double taxation *would* result if a parochiaid plan is ever passed by Congress. All Americans will pay first to support public schools, which are free and open to all, and second to support private schools, which are totally unaccountable to the public, discriminate on who is admitted, and teach sectarian doctrines that some may find offensive.

The inner-city poor would benefit from a voucher plan and other forms of parochiaid. This claim is one of the cruelest frauds perpetrated by parochiaid advocates. Yearly tuition at a private school can easily top $3,000. Yet most voucher plans offer at most $500 to $1,000 in payment or a limited tax break. The poor would have no way of supplying the rest. Vouchers and other forms of parochiaid would benefit primarily the wealthy and upper middle class, people who can already afford private school fees.

Additionally, most private schools are located in suburbs or small cities. Most would flatly refuse to accept educationally disadvantaged children from inner cities or any child with a discipline problem or difficult learning disability. Even if a few were accepted, the costs of transportation would be prohibitive.

The Constitutional Problem

These arguments, however, fail to address the central church-state problem presented by parochiaid. Even if tomorrow all of these obstacles were somehow magically solved, public aid to sectarian schools would still be unconstitutional.

Parochiaiders frequently argue that vouchers and others forms of aid are constitutional because they are aid to parents, not students. The argument is a mere semantic ploy. An estimated 85 percent of all private schools are religious in nature. Since a voucher could be used only to purchase educational services, on average 85 percent of voucher money would be used to subsidize religious institutions.

Various courts have explicitly ruled that the government may not use parents as a conduit for unconstitutional practices. In 1967, a federal court struck down a voucher law that had been passed in Louisiana by the state legislature in response to efforts to integrate the state's public schools.

In the *Poindexter v. Louisiana* case, the court said flatly, "The United States Constitution does not permit the State to perform acts indirectly through private persons which it is forbidden to do directly."[12] The U.S. Supreme Court later upheld this ruling in a per curiam decision.

No public aid should be used to subsidize religion. Just as the government cannot fund churches by funneling the money through individual citizens, it cannot fund church schools through like means. Religious schools, as affiliates of the faith groups that sponsor them, are really just one more component of a church's mission. Government has no business paying for any aspect of a church's operation. That is the job of those who believe in what the church stands for.

Any honest religious leader will readily admit that church-related schools exist first and foremost for the benefit of the sponsoring denomination. Leaders of the Catholic Church have been very up front about this, especially in recent years. In fact, many have expressed a desire to increase the schools' Catholic nature and have talked about ways to use the schools as instruments of evangelism. This is their right, of course, but clearly such blatantly sectarian goals simply cannot be underwritten with state funds in a country that takes separation of church and state seriously.

During a November 1990 meeting of Catholic bishops in Washington, D.C., the church hierarchy lauded its schools as "proven instruments of evangelism." Responding to a suggestion that Catholic schools water down their sectarian flavor to attract non-Catholic parents, Cardinal Anthony J. Bevilacqua of Philadelphia remarked, "We must keep the Catholic identity while reaching out to non-Catholics through evangelism."[13]

But while affirming the religiosity of their schools, the bishops also overwhelmingly approved a policy statement calling for increased public assistance to their parochial schools. The bishops, it seems, want it all— a strong network of thoroughly Catholic schools that boost the faith, free from most state regulations and accountable only to church authorities, yet funded with taxpayer dollars drawn from Catholics and non-Catholics alike! The bishops are asking all Americans to pay for their evangelistic efforts. It is easy to see the injustice in this plan.

Given the Catholic Church's controversial stands on many public policy issues, stands that are taught as absolute truth in its schools, it's no wonder so many Americans remain wary of parochiaid. The church has tried repeatedly to cast this opposition as "anti-Catholicism." The charge is offensive to many separationists. Far from being rooted in anti-Catholicism, opposition to parochiaid more commonly springs from a desire to protect religious freedom and church integrity. For that reason, the view is shared by a majority of Catholics and non-Catholics alike.

Experiences Abroad

Nevertheless, many advocates of parochiaid insist they can thwart public opinion and prevail. Some of the more radical ones even assert that the days of the public school system are numbered. Jerry Falwell once remarked that he is looking forward to the day when all schooling in America is run by churches.

To win advocates over to their side, those who favor parochial school aid often point to experiences in other countries where this type of aid is common. Great Britain and Canada are two of their favorite examples.

There are two problems with these types of international comparisons, however. First, neither England nor Canada has a history of civil liberties and church-state separation similar to that found in the United States. Indeed, Great Britain to this day has an established church. Canada, while it does not have an established church, was a British colony for many years and adopted many aspects of the British system.

Second and more importantly, parochial school aid in these nations has not been implemented as smoothly as voucher advocates would have the American people believe. When the Canadian province of Ontario extended public funding to the Roman Catholic "separate" school system in 1984, Catholic officials demanded that a number of public school buildings be turned over to them to meet space needs. Many communities were torn apart by the ensuing conflict, with citizens divided along religious lines. This conflict continues today.

Furthermore, the extension of public funds to Canadian Catholic schools set in place a competition for funds between the two systems. With tax revenue scarce, many public school parents complain that public schools are being seriously underfunded.

In addition, religious leaders in other denominations are now arguing that the province's policy of funding only Catholic schools violates Canada's anti-discrimination laws and have gone into court to seek public funding for their own schools. In the end, Ontario may wind up with a system of education fragmented along sectarian lines and a budget busted by an influx of new sectarian schools seeking handouts. After all, why not go ahead and build schools if the government is willing to foot the bill?

England has suffered similar problems. There the country's Muslim minority is demanding that public assistance be extended to its schools alongside those of the Anglican and Catholic churches. Parliament and the courts have refused, increasing interfaith tensions. In addition, English religious leaders have lost a measure of control over their schools thanks to parochiaid. Under the country's laws, a majority of a given school's parents can vote to "opt out" of the local education system and become "independent" (though still receiving government funding). This action can effectively sever a private school's denominational ties.

Despite the problems that other nations have encountered with parochiaid, U.S. voucher boosters continue to point to them as models for America to follow. Parochiaiders are waiting for one state to break the logjam. If they can push a voucher plan through somewhere and have it declared constitutional by the Supreme Court, they figure, other states will quickly follow. They came close in Pennsylvania in 1991 when the state Senate approved a full-scale voucher plan. It was later derailed in the House by a vote of 114-89, largely due to concerns over the measure's $300 million price tag at a time when Pennsylvania faced a severe budget shortfall.

The parochiaid boosters' approach overlooks one key fact: Many state constitutions explicitly bar any diversion of public funds to sectarian schools. And, even if a plan is passed somewhere, disgruntled parents whose children are denied admission to the private school of their "choice" are sure to file lawsuits. These legal efforts may in turn open the door to state control of parochial and other private schools, leading to the day when parochial schools become mere adjuncts to the existing public school system. Robbed of their independence, the schools would be no better than those church leaders originally sought to escape from.

The Church College Example

The issue of state control is put into stark perspective by looking at the history of church-related universities. In the 1970s the Supreme Court upheld government assistance to church-related colleges and universities, provided they are not "pervasively sectarian." That is, institutions founded for religious purposes can get public money as long as they are not too religious or refrain from being serious about it.

Most church colleges today are completely secularized and maintain only loose affiliations with the churches that founded them. In some cases, church leaders have lost the ability to have a say in the religious lives of students and have had to permit student groups to operate on campus that espouse doctrines at odds with church teachings. Only church colleges that eschew all public funding have been able to remain truly independent.

In light of the experience of church-related colleges, parochiaid boosters would do well to be careful of what they ask for. They just might get it.

Notes

1. Leo Pfeffer, *Church, State, and Freedom* (Boston: Beacon Press, 1953), 379.

2. *Cochran v. Louisiana State Board of Education,* 281 U.S. 370 (1930).

3. *Everson v. Board of Education,* 330 U.S. 1 (1947).

4. *Board of Education v. Allen,* 392 U.S. 236 (1968).

5. *Lemon v. Kurtzman,* 403 U.S. 602 (1971).

6. *Committee for Public Education and Religious Liberty v. Nyquist,* 413 U.S. 756 (1973).

7. *Meek v. Pittenger,* 421 U.S. 349 (1975).

8. *Mueller v. Allen,* 463 U.S. 388 (1983).

9. *Aguilar v. Felton,* 105 S.C. 3237 (1985).

10. *Witters v. Washington Dept. of Services for Blind,* 474 U.S. 481, 1986.

11. *Zobrest v. Catalina Foothills School District,* 92-94, June 18, 1993.

12. *Poindexter v. Louisiana Financial Assistance Commission,* 275 F. Supp. 833, 835 (E.D. La. 1967).

13. Rob Boston, "Parochial Concerns," *Church & State* 44(January 1991): 4.

7

Free Exercise

The First Amendment consists of just forty-five words. Of those, only the first sixteen concern religious freedom and separation of church and state. About half of those sixteen deal with the free exercise of religion.

Those few words have had a powerful impact on American society. The right to practice religion freely—or to refrain from participating in religion at all—is one of the most cherished rights of the American people. When asked to describe what makes America unique, many people are quick to respond "freedom of religion."

But over the years, Americans have squabbled incessantly over what religious freedom means and how far the principle should be extended. The United States, lacking an established religion, quickly became a haven for those seeking the right to religious free exercise. In the fertile soil of freedom new religious movements took root. They continue to do so today. Unfortunately, these new movements sometimes came into conflict with state policy. The scope of those sixteen words has been the center of the resulting debate.

Testing the Boundaries

The boundaries of religious freedom are not tested by a country's mainstream faiths. Instead, it is the new, unorthodox religions that usually push things to the limits. This was certainly the case in the United States. Religious minorities were the first to test the limits of the First Amendment. Many of the early free exercise cases were brought by members of three religious minorities—Mormons, Seventh-day Adventists, and Jehovah's Witnesses.

Because of their efforts, by the 1970s religious freedom in America was expanded and the First Amendment was interpreted by the federal courts to offer its widest extent of protection in U.S. history. Although many critics say recent Supreme Court rulings have reversed the trend and curtailed religious freedom, there is no denying that during a relatively short period of time the country took several giant steps forward in the area of religious free exercise.

With the exception of the Church of Jesus Christ of Latter-day Saints, (the Mormons) most American religious groups have not experienced direct, government-sponsored efforts to eradicate their beliefs. Surely a certain degree of inter-religious tension has always existed in America, and it has flared in ugly ways at different points in our history. But generally speaking, after 1800 even small religious groups were safe to meet for worship without worrying about their doors being kicked in by the local constable.

The main free exercise problems, then, did not stem from government's outright attempts to stamp out certain religious beliefs but rather from conflicts stemming from the specific practices of certain religions. From the beginning of history to the present day, some believers have felt compelled by faith to engage in certain activities the state has declared illegal. The opposite also occurred, of course. Some believers felt compelled by faith to refrain from engaging in certain activities that are mandated by government.

A good example of the former that also provides a capsulized overview of the free exercise debate is the unusual practice of snake handling. Although most mainstream Christians view this activity as quite bizarre, it is still practiced by small pockets of dedicated believers, mostly in the rural South. Snake handlers insist they have a sound biblical basis for the activity and point to a passage in the New Testament book of Mark that refers to the practice (see Mark 16:15-18).

Obviously handling poisonous snakes (and drinking strychnine, as some snakes handlers also do) can be extremely dangerous. Accordingly, several southern states have laws on the books making it a crime to handle poisonous snakes during religious services.

On its face, this would seem to be a classic church-state free exercise controversy, and some may see it as an open-and-shut case. Since the First Amendment means that government has no authority to tell religious groups what they can and can't do in church, the snake handlers must prevail, right?

Wrong. In this case there is an additional factor that makes all the difference: People have died from handling rattlesnakes and copperheads in church (and from drinking poison). The government, it is argued, has an obligation to safeguard human life that in this case overrides religious freedom. Courts therefore have ruled consistently that states and communities have the right to ban snake handling and the consumption of poison in church. Today, only West Virginia allows the practice of snake handling for religious purposes.

As the example about snake handling shows, no sixteen words, no matter how eloquent or well crafted, can answer every conflict over religious freedom that will arise in a modern, growing, religiously diverse society that seeks to maximize religious liberty. This means that the courts have been forced to hammer out guidelines for determining what types of religiously motivated activities can be suppressed by the government. And therein lies the difficulty.

Mormons and Polygamy

For a long time after the Constitution was ratified the federal courts were loath to enter this territory. Church-state cases dealing with the free exercise of religion were a rarity before the federal courts in the 19th century. The first few cases to bubble up to the Supreme Court centered on the Mormons.

Many people today see Mormons as just another member of America's mainstream religious community, known for their theologically conservative views and large families. But in the 19th century many Americans held a much different view of the Mormons. The group, then just getting off the ground, was a despised religious minority viewed by many as threatening to the American way of life. The chief reason for this vituperation was polygamy.

Some Mormons practiced plural marriage. Although few rank-and-file Mormons engaged in the practice, church leaders, including founder Joseph Smith and Brigham Young, one of his top lieutenants, had several wives apiece. (Smith had forty-nine wives; Young ultimately married twenty-seven women.) Plural marriage was alien to America, and its adoption by Mormons led to conflict and tension that forced the members of the new religion to flee westward, from state to state, seeking safe haven.

It should be pointed out that Smith is not entirely innocent in this drama. There are indications that he may have been involved in fraudulent banking scams early on in his career as a religious leader. Whatever the case, a mob killed him in Nauvoo, Illinois, in 1844, and Young led most of Smith's followers farther west into what is today Utah, where they settled. Young, who became governor of the territory, officially named polygamy as a church tenet in 1852. Ten years later, Congress passed legislation designed to stamp out polygamy in the western territories.

Federal agents began arresting Mormons living in polygamous households. One of those arrested was George Reynolds, a secretary to Young. During a trial in a territorial court, Reynolds argued that the law could not be applied to Mormons because they were religiously compelled to practice polygamy.

Reynolds lost the case but appealed to the U.S. Supreme Court. On Jan. 4, 1879, the high court issued a unanimous opinion upholding the territorial court. Never before asked to rule on such a matter, the high court formulated what is known as the "belief-action" standard, holding that while the First Amendment makes freedom to believe absolute, it does not similarly protect actions based on those beliefs.

Declaring that, "Polygamy has always been odious among the Northern and Western Nations of Europe," the Supreme Court deemed the anti-polygamy statute constitutional and opened the door for further prosecutions of Mormons engaging in plural marriage.[1]

Believing they had the blessings of the Supreme Court, federal authorities continued to vigorously prosecute Mormons for the next twelve years. In 1890 another Mormon case reached the Supreme Court. In *Davis v. Beason* the court, again unanimously, ruled that an Idaho Mormon who practiced polygamy could be prosecuted for falsely swearing that he did not believe in plural marriage.[2] The oath was part of the Idaho territory's voting regulations.

Later that year, the high court upheld a federal law designed to reduce the power of the Mormon church in Utah by turning church lands over to the government.[3] Realizing that they were outgunned by the federal government, church officials in 1890 issued an executive order banning polygamy. Six years later, Utah was admitted to the union under a constitution that specifically bans plural marriage.

Jehovah's Witnesses

Following the Mormon cases, the free exercise front was quiet at the Supreme Court for nearly fifty years. But beginning in the late 1930s and early 1940s, a series of cases went before the Supreme Court concerning yet another unpopular religious group, Jehovah's Witnesses.

The Witnesses, founded in Pennsylvania in 1872, are known to most Americans for their aggressive proselytism and often overt anti-Catholicism. Though disliked by many, this small group (U.S. membership is less than one million) has not been reluctant to stand up for its rights in federal court. As a result, Jehovah's Witnesses are responsible for a series of high court rulings that expanded religious freedom for all Americans.

For instance, in a string of early Witnesses cases the Supreme Court invalidated a succession of state and local laws designed to place unreasonable curbs on groups seeking to distribute literature door to door. Short-sighted politicians had ignored the dangers such statutes could pose to civil liberties at large. If the state were to gain the power to stamp out one religion's message merely because it was deemed unpopular, a dangerous precedent would be set. Many religious and civic groups at the time may not have been supportive of the Witnesses, but they are today thankful for their efforts on this front.

The literature distribution cases were important victories for religious liberty, but perhaps the most important case the Witnesses were involved in was 1940's *Cantwell v. Connecticut*. This landmark legal dispute got under way after police in New Haven, Connecticut, arrested a Witness and his son, who were broadcasting a virulently anti-Catholic record on public streets. The two were charged with failure to obtain a "certificate of approval" from state authorities, a document that allowed "bona fide" charitable and religious groups to solicit for funds.[4]

Ruling unanimously, the Supreme Court threw out the conviction as well as the Connecticut law requiring a "certificate of approval" to present religious messages. More importantly, the high court for the first time made it clear that the religion clauses of the First Amendment— indeed the entire Bill of Rights—are applicable to the states because of the Fourteenth Amendment, a doctrine known as incorporation. Incorporation gave Americans greater access to the federal courts in seeking redress of church-state grievances and increased the number of religious liberty disputes before the high court.

In another important case involving Jehovah's Witnesses, the Supreme Court ruled in 1944 that free exercise of religion cannot override child labor laws. The case arose in Massachusetts after a group of Witnesses, who often used children to distribute literature for long hours at night, challenged state statutes regulating the hours children may work.

Observed the high court in *Prince v. Massachusetts*, "The right to practice religion freely does not include liberty to expose the community or the child to communicable diseases or the latter to ill health or death."[5]

Medical Treatment Controversies

In recent years, this decision has been cited as precedent in some cases involving forced medical treatment for minors. Some religious groups, primarily Christian Scientists and assorted Pentecostal Christian groups, do not believe in seeking medical care for any reason, holding that religious faith alone can cure disease. (Strictly speaking, this is true more of Pentecostals; Christian Science theology holds that disease is an illusion that can be taken away by prayer and other spiritual means.)

While adults have a right to refuse medical treatment for any reason, courts have tended to rule that this right does not extend to children, who are considered too young to make an informed decision about their own health care. As a result, children belonging to these groups in some states have been inoculated or been given medical treatment against parents' wishes.

In other cases, parents whose children died because they received no medical treatment for serious illnesses have been charged with manslaughter or endangering the welfare of a child. State court rulings in this area have produced a mixed bag of opinions. Some parents have been found guilty (generally receiving probation, not prison sentences), while others have been acquitted. It should also be noted that forty-five states have laws on the books shielding parents who use spiritual healing from criminal prosecution. Recently, some medical authorities have begun calling for the repeal of these laws. The issue of the legality of spiritual healing for children is emotional and complex, involving a host of parental rights concerns beyond those of a church-state character.

Proselytism and Flag Salutes

Jehovah's Witnesses refuse blood transfusions and have also been involved in some of the spiritual healing cases, but most of the court rulings they sparked deal with activities related to religious proselytism in public places. In 1943, for example, the Supreme Court handed down an important decision dealing with the right of religious groups to distribute literature. In a narrow 5-4 vote, the high court struck down a Pennsylvania statute requiring that groups wishing to distribute literature pay a special tax.[6]

These rulings were grudgingly accepted by the American people, but public sympathy for Jehovah's Witnesses did not run high. Witnesses had a habit of making nuisances of themselves, and undoubtedly many Americans saw the efforts to curb the group's evangelical fervor through government action a good thing. But given the benefit of forty-five years of hindsight, it is easy to see how dangerous the anti-Witnesses statutes were and how destructive to religious and political freedom they could have become if they had been permitted to stand. Being forced once in a while to shut the door in the face of an aggressive religious proselytizer is a small price to pay for complete religious freedom for all.

In the midst of these rulings another issue concerning Jehovah's Witnesses ended up in the federal courts. This issue, more emotional than any previous case involving Witnesses, focused on the Pledge of Allegiance.

Jehovah's Witnesses do not believe in earthly allegiances. Their only duty, they say, is to God. They do not participate in secular government. They will not hold office or vote in elections. They also steadfastly refuse to recite oaths of any kind—including the Pledge of Allegiance— or to salute the flag. Saluting flags, they say, is a form of idolatry.

In 1940 the United States was on the brink of entering World War II, and an exaggerated sense of patriotism ran through the population. Many states had laws mandating the recitation of the Pledge of Allegiance and a flag salute every day in public schools. Children of Jehovah's Witnesses, who refused to participate in the exercises, were frequently expelled from school or otherwise punished.

Although their timing could not have been worse, the Witnesses took the pledge matter into federal court in the late 1930s. In 1940 the Supreme Court issued one of its worst church-state opinions ever and held by an 8-1 vote that a Pennsylvania law requiring recitation of the Pledge of Allegiance in public schools was constitutional, de-claring that schools had no obligation to exempt Jehovah's Witnesses or other objectors.[7]

The high court's ruling in *Minersville School District v. Gobitis* was followed by an outbreak of violence against Jehovah's Witnesses across the country. Although the Witnesses lost the case, just the fact that they had dared to bring it outraged millions of Americans. What followed is one of the darkest and most disgraceful periods in American church-state history.

In Richwood, Virginia, the chief of police rounded up a group of Jehovah's Witnesses, forced them to drink castor oil and paraded them through the streets before running them out of town. In Jackson,

Mississippi, members of a local veterans' organization attacked a trailer park where many Witnesses were known to live and drove several from their homes.

The list gets worse: A Witness in Nebraska was lured away from his house and castrated by a mob. In Rockville, Maryland, local police assisted a marauding crowd that attacked a Witness church (called a Kingdom Hall) to break up a religious meeting. In Kennebunk, Maine, an unruly mob charged the local Kingdom Hall and set it on fire, burning it to the ground.[8]

In the eight days following the flag salute ruling, the U.S. Justice Department received hundreds of reports of attacks on Jehovah's Witnesses. When schools went back in session that fall, some zealous teachers and principals stepped up their efforts to expel Witness children and even threatened to imprison the children in juvenile homes unless they recited the pledge.

By 1943 the Supreme Court had realized its mistake. Changes had occurred on the court by then. Some justices had retired, and others had changed their minds about the Minersville case. The high court accepted a new case dealing with mandatory flag salutes in public schools—this one from West Virginia—and issued a decision strongly upholding religious freedom.

Speaking for the 6-3 majority in *West Virginia State Board of Education v. Barnette*, Justice Robert Jackson eloquently wrote, "If there is any fixed star in our constitutional constellation, it is that no official, high or petty, can prescribe what shall be orthodox in politics, nationalism, religion, or other matters of opinion, or force citizens to confess by word or act their faith therein."[9]

Continued Jackson, "The very purpose of the Bill of Rights was to withdraw certain subjects from the vicissitudes of political controversy, to place them beyond the reach of majorities and officials and to establish them as legal principles to be applied by the courts. One's right to life, liberty, and property, to free speech, a free press, freedom of worship and assembly, and other fundamental rights may not be submitted to vote; they depend on the outcome of no elections."

Sadly, many Americans apparently do not agree with that reasoning. During the 1988 presidential race, George Bush attacked Democratic nominee Michael Dukakis because Dukakis, as governor of Massachusetts, had in 1977 vetoed a bill requiring recitation of the pledge in the state's public schools. Dukakis, pointing to the *Barnette* ruling, noted that the measure was clearly unconstitutional. Bush accused Dukakis of being opposed to the pledge, and one opinion poll showed a majority of Americans favoring mandatory recitation of the Pledge of Allegiance in public schools, even if some religious groups or individuals object.

The Zenith of Free Exercise

Jehovah's Witnesses and another religious minority, Seventh-day Adventists, have also been involved in free exercises cases concerning workers' rights. Seventh-day Adventists, who hold Saturday as the sabbath, have a special interest in this area of free exercise law. Because devout Adventists refuse to work on Saturday, they have had frequent problems with employment laws and have been forced to go to court several times to assert their rights. In doing so they expanded religious freedom for all Americans—at least until recently, when the high court overturned some previous rulings and stepped away from awarding free exercise special protection.

A series of four cases from 1963 until 1989 set down a basic principle that workers cannot be penalized for refusing to work on their sabbath. The earliest case, 1963's *Sherbert v. Verner*, dealt with a Seventh-day Adventist who was fired for refusing to accept Saturday employment at a textile mill.[10] When the woman, Adell Sherbert, applied for unemployment benefits, she was rejected. In reversing that finding, the Supreme Court ruled 7-2 that Sherbert could not be compelled by the state to choose between her religious beliefs and her livelihood. In a 1989 case, *Frazee v. Department of Employment Security*, the high court unanimously extended the principle to cover Sabbath keepers unaffiliated with any specific church.[11]

Sherbert and the cases that followed it established a broad principle of free exercise law known as the "compelling state interest" test. Under this standard, government may not restrict a person's free exercise of religion unless it can first prove a compelling interest on the part of the state and show that no less restrictive means are available to achieve the state's goals.

The Supreme Court used the standard again in a 1972 case dealing with the Old Order Amish. Members of this community protested Wisconsin's compulsory education law and refused to send their children to school beyond the eighth grade. The Amish argued that sending children to school beyond this level would expose them to corrupting and "worldly" ideas that would conflict with the simple, religious lifestyle of the Amish.

In a 7-0 decision (two justices did not participate), the high court ruled unanimously in favor of the Amish, declaring that Wisconsin's interest in educating youngsters was compelling, but that an exception should be made for the Amish so they would not be forced to violate their sincerely held beliefs. The court's ruling in *Wisconsin v. Yoder* was the high-water mark of free exercise rights at the Supreme Court.[12]

Later Free Exercise Rulings

Things quickly went downhill from that point. With the exception of a few minor cases related to employee rights, in the years following *Yoder* the Supreme Court seemed to give only passing acknowledgement to the "compelling state interest" standard, and religious groups began losing free exercise cases. In a surprising 1990 ruling, the high court scrapped the "compelling state interest" test altogether in a case from Oregon known as *Employment Division v. Smith*.[13]

The *Smith* opinion, written by an arch-foe of separation, Justice Antonin Scalia, threw free exercise jurisprudence into a state of flux from which it has yet to recover. Fallout from the case is still being felt. Basically, the high court, by a narrow 5-4 majority, declared that the government no longer must meet a "compelling state interest" in regulating religion. All that matters, said the court, is that laws that might infringe on religious belief be "neutral and generally applicable."

In other words, any law that is neutral on matters of religion will be considered constitutional, even if its practical effect is to eviscerate a given religious belief. Under this reasoning, religious groups have begun losing a steady stream of free exercise cases in the federal and state courts. Autopsies can now be performed on those who die in accidents, even if family members object for religious reasons. Church leaders can literally lose control of their buildings if the facilities are deemed historic by municipal governments. Policies of church confidentiality have been placed in jeopardy. Things have gotten so bad that some state court judges, frustrated by the Supreme Court's new doctrine, have begun extending protection to religious freedom via state constitutions.

What shocked so many religious groups about the *Smith* ruling was the extent of its reach. The high court had not been asked to reformulate its free exercise case law and gave no indication that it would do so. The facts of the case, though somewhat exotic, did not lend themselves to such a sweeping decision: Two American Indians in Eugene, Oregon, had been fired from their jobs as substance abuse counselors because they ingested small amounts of peyote, a mild hallucinogenic, during rites of the Native American Church. When the two applied for unemployment benefits, they were turned down by state officials.

The high court not only rejected the two men's claim, but used the occasion to refashion free exercise law and scrap the old "compelling state interest" standard. Critics of the *Smith* ruling—and they came from both liberal and conservative camps—said the high court could have denied the Indians' claim without throwing out the "compelling state interest" test. (Justice Sandra Day O'Connor made much the same argument in her opinion, although she agreed with the majority's ultimate conclusion denying the men the benefits.)

Perhaps the most shocking feature of the *Smith* ruling, however, was that Scalia brazenly based portions of the decision on the loathsome *Gobitis* decision, the first flag-salute case from 1940. Civil libertarians were shocked that a Supreme Court justice had based a key church-state ruling on a case that had been expressly overturned and discredited by the court in 1943. The *Smith* decision clearly leaves the rights of minority religions in the hands of state and local lawmakers and fosters majoritarianism. The court had hit another low mark in church-state jurisprudence.

Smith was such an unpopular ruling that it sparked a move in

Congress to mute its effects through legislation. The proposed bill, known as the Religious Freedom Restoration Act, gained support from both liberal and conservative civil liberties and religious groups but for two years was unable to pass Congress when it became bogged down in an unfortunate dispute over abortion. In early 1993 a tentative compromise was announced that may lead to the bill's passage.

Two years after the *Smith* ruling, the Supreme Court agreed to hear another free exercise case, this one from Florida. The facts in the dispute are even more unusual than those in *Smith*, centering on whether communities may pass laws banning the practice of animal sacrifice.

The issue arose in south Florida in a suburb of Miami named Hialeah. Here an estimated 50,000 followers of an Afro-Cuban religion known as Santeria reside. Members of the faith, which blends animism and Roman Catholicism, practice animal sacrifice during certain feast days. The animals sacrificed, most often chickens and goats, are usually consumed afterwards.

Shocked at the activities, officials in Hialeah passed four ordinances designed to outlaw animal sacrifice for religious purposes. Opponents of the laws argued they were unconstitutional even under the new *Smith* standard since they are aimed specifically at a religious practice and thus are not "generally applicable." Hialeah officials respond that they have the right to ban religious practices that pose a threat to the community.

In June 1993 the high court ruled unanimously that the Hialeah ordinances had gone too far and struck down all four. The opinion, written by Justice Anthony M. Kennedy, declared that the intent and effect of the laws was to suppress the Santeria religion. Observed Kennedy, "Our review confirms that the laws in question were enacted by officials who did not understand, failed to perceive, or chose to ignore the fact that their official actions violated the Nation's essential commitment to religious freedom."

Elsewhere Kennedy wrote in the *Church of the Lukumi Babalu Aye v. City of Hialeah* decision, "The Free Exercise Clause commits government itself to religious tolerance, and upon even slight suspicion that proposals for state intervention stem from animosity to religion or distrust of its practices, all officials must pause to remember their own high duty to the Constitution and to the rights it secures. Those in office must be resolute in resisting importunate demands and must ensure that the sole reasons for imposing the burdens of law and regulation are secular. Legislators may not devise mechanisms, overt or disguised, designed to persecute or oppress a religion or its practices."[14]

The *Church of the Lukumi* decision, while a solid victory for religious liberty, left the findings of *Smith* intact, although three justices criticized *Smith* in concurring opinions. This left religious freedom advocates with at least a hope that in time, with new appointments, a court majority could arise opposed to the new rule announced in *Smith*.

Free Exercise in Transition

What is to be made of all this? First of all, that free exercise law at the Supreme Court is in transition. Ironically, this came about because of the new, conservative appointments to the high court in the 1980s and early 1990s. Many Religious Right leaders eagerly supported these appointees, hoping they would reinterpret the Establishment Clause and pave the way for the return of state-sponsored religious exercises in public schools. Not only has that not happened, but the new, right-leaning majority has turned the full force of its judicial attack on the Free Exercise Clause and severely restricted its protections.

A few years after *Smith*, Justice Scalia, speaking at a church-state conference at Baylor University, asserted that the high court should look to society's historical traditions when dealing with church-state controversies. In the case of the free exercise of religion, he said, societal majorities will decide which religiously motivated activities should receive special protection from government's reach.

Such an approach should send a chill down the spine of all church-state separationists and advocates of religious freedom. "Societal tradition" is most assuredly *not* an appropriate guideline for determining constitutional rights. For a long time in the United States, the "tradition" was majority rule in religious matters. If the majority decided to force its religious exercises on all students in the public school, that practice became "tradition" and minority rights were trampled.

Scalia's views underscore one of the greatest dangers facing religious liberty advocates today: the majoritarian and statist bent at the Supreme Court. Contrary to Scalia's assertions, the First Amendment is not a blueprint for the majority to run roughshod over the minority or for the government to always have its way in church-state conflicts over free exercise. Yet under his reasoning, that is exactly the result to be expected.

Sixteen words cannot possibly be expected to answer every question about religious liberty that will arise in a modern society marked by expanding religious pluralism. Until recently, the Free Exercise Clause was seen as a command that government give religion every benefit of the doubt and as much leeway as possible in seeking to resolve these disputes. As the federal courts move away from this ideal, religious freedom is placed in jeopardy. The first to feel the hit, as usual, are religious minorities.

Phony Free Exercise Claims

Before leaving the discussion of free exercise, one more important point should be covered: Religious Right activists like to play up the supposed tension that exists between the Free Exercise Clause and the Establishment Clause. Actually, no such tension exists. Interpreted properly, the two clauses complement one another and do not clash. The problem occurs in the way the Religious Right interprets "free exercise."

All Americans have the right to worship as they see fit within the bounds of the law. But no American has the right to expect the state to endorse or promote his or her religious beliefs or to demand the power of the government for help in spreading sectarian messages. The understandable refusal of the government to support religion is often what the Religious Right means when they talk about "free exercise problems."

For example, Religious Right groups often complain that teachers cannot pray with students in public schools and labels this a free exercise problem. As usual, they have skewed the facts. Teachers have the right to pray on their own, but they do not have the right to abuse the authority of the public school, a government-owned institution, to promote their personal religious beliefs or encourage students to adopt new or different beliefs. The government is not inhibiting any teacher's free exercise rights by demanding that the public school system remain neutral on religious matters.

Religious Right activists expect the government to provide them with religious freedom *and* a public forum that enables them to spread their message to win new converts. This makes perfect sense to many on the Religious Right, since they believe their message is the "true" one. But obviously the government is under no obligation to provide that forum and is, in fact, constitutionally forbidden to do so.

Consider the following analogy: Every American has the right to express his or her ideas, but that does not mean the government has to buy each of us a newspaper to more efficiently spread those views. It is ludicrous to assert that the government is "discriminating" against anyone for refusing to provide him or her with a ready-made forum for the expression of their views, be those views religious, political, or whatever.

Advocates of parochiaid sometimes make a similarly contorted argument when the contend that they cannot practice their religion fully unless the government pays for parochial school tuition. Again the logic fails. The government has no obligation to assist anyone in practicing religion. Indeed, the government is absolutely forbidden from taking on this role. This argument is analogous to asserting that one is not free to practice religion unless the government provides Bibles, choir robes, candles, prayer books, and other religious items free of charge. The state can only make sure that religious freedom is not infringed upon by bureaucrats or burdened with undue regulation. From that point you're on your own.

Phony arguments aside, free exercise is facing some real threats today. It is no exaggeration to say that the situation is critical as the Supreme Court continues to turn a deaf ear to legitimate claims of church-state abuses, and Congress is unwilling or unable to help.

There is one bright spot: Religious freedom remains a cherished right of the American people. If government tampers with it too much, a backlash is inevitable. That backlash may be building now. Unfortunately, the country may have to travel through some difficult periods—periods especially troubling for minority religions—until its full impact is felt.

Notes

1. *Reynolds v. United States*, 98 U.S. 145 (1878).

2. *Davis v. Beason*, 133 U.S. 333 (1890).

3. *Church of Jesus Christ of Latter-Day Saints v. United States*, 136 U.S. 1 (1890).

4. *Cantwell v. Connecticut*, 310 U.S. 296 (1940).

5. *Prince v. Massachusetts*, 321 U.S. 158 (1944).

6. *Murdock v. Pennsylvania*, 319 U.S. 105 (1943).

7. *Minersville School District v. Gobitis*, 310 U.S. 586 (1940).

8. Leo Pfeffer, *Church, State, and Freedom* (Boston: Beacon Press, 1953), 523.

9. *West Virginia Board of Education v. Barnette*, 319 U.S. 624 (1943).

10. *Sherbert v. Verner*, 374 U.S. 398 (1963).

11. *Frazee v. Department of Employment Security*, 87-1945, March 29, 1989.

12. *Wisconsin v. Yoder*, 406 U.S. 205 (1972.)

13. *Employment Division, Department of Human Resources v. Smith*, 88-1213, April 17, 1990.

14. *Church of the Lukumi Babalu Aye v. City of Hialeah*, 91-948, June 11, 1993.

8

Symbols and Sunday Laws:
Other Church-State Problems

As previous chapters have indicated, disputes over parochiaid, religion in public schools, and the free exercise of religion account for the bulk of America's church-state difficulties. However, there are other issues in the church-state field that should not be overlooked. Many of these issues have been litigated in state and federal courts, adding much to the body of church-state law. This chapter will review some of those controversies.

Religious Symbols on Public Property

Every year around Christmastime people in communities across the nation squabble over religious symbols on public property. Some years see outbreaks of these types of disputes in cities big and small in every corner of the country. These fights mar the holiday season every year for someone.

The script goes something like this: Town officials stick up a nativity scene or menorah in front of the courthouse or city hall building. Someone complains. City officials say they aren't taking it down. The matter goes to court, where the display is struck down or upheld, depending on the circumstances of its display and, seemingly, the mood of the judge.

The Supreme Court has wrestled with this issue, and, in a line of decisions, some general guidelines have emerged. If followed, these rulings could give city officials a good idea of what is constitutional and what is not regarding holiday displays. Unfortunately, few members of municipal government, it seems, are willing to wade through the rulings. Or, more likely, they simply choose to ignore them and put the symbols up, hoping no one will complain. These same folks then turn around and label as "grinches" those who speak out against the symbols.

Through all the high court rulings on religious symbols, one fact is clear: Government may not sponsor displays of religious symbols standing alone at government sites. Creches put up by the city council on the steps of the city hall are not constitutional.

The government may, however, include nativity scenes, menorahs, and other religious symbols as part of larger holiday displays that also contain secular holiday symbols such as Christmas trees, figures of Santa Claus or reindeer.

Also, private groups—the Jaycees, religious organizations, etc.— may display sectarian symbols on public property provided that the property has been open to other free-speech activities in the past. A public park, for example, that has been the site of demonstrations or political rallies can be used by private groups to display religious symbols. But even then, the symbols cannot be erected permanently.

Confused? It's really not that complex. Generally speaking, the government should stay out of the business of erecting, maintaining, or encouraging the display of sectarian symbols on public property. If government officials insist on doing so, they should add a generous mix of secular symbols to abide by the so-called "plastic reindeer" rule.

In a nutshell, that is the policy the Supreme Court has articulated. Whether or not it makes sense is open to debate. Many separationists believe the "plastic reindeer" rule is dodge at best and argue that the presence of secular symbols does not mute the inherent religiosity of creches and menorahs. There is much to be said for this argument.

Conversely, a lot of religious people argue that mixing the secular and the sacred is offensive to the devout and ought to be avoided. Again, this is a valid argument.

The tragedy of the religious symbols cases is that every year someone's holiday is ruined by often mean-spirited fights that simply aren't necessary.

It doesn't have to be that way. There is an obvious solution to this annual seasonal tussle: Let the churches and other faith groups in a given community sponsor religious displays. Keep the government out of it entirely.

Even most small towns have at least one large church or synagogue occupying space on a prominent thoroughfare. There is no reason why the creches and menorahs could not be erected on the front lawns of these facilities. Better yet, each house of worship could erect its own display, thus increasing the number and variety of religious symbols for citizens to see.

Such an approach has worked in Pittsburgh, site of a major battle over religious symbols at the courthouse and city-county building in the late 1980s that reached the Supreme Court. Weary of the annual fight, Mayor Sophie Masloff in 1990 asked that religious symbols be displayed across the street from the government buildings on private property.

Court intervention or not, disputes over religious symbols tied to Christmas or Hanukkah eventually blow over when the holiday season passes. But recently in some parts of the country battles have broken out over permanently erected crosses on public property.

The problem seems especially bad in California. In the San Diego area, church-state separation activists sued to have two large crosses removed from public property. A federal judge ruled in 1991 that the crosses violate the California Constitution's "no preference" religion clause, a decision that was later upheld by the U.S. Ninth Circuit Court of Appeals. Meanwhile, a group of state lawmakers has launched a drive to amend the state constitution in the event the decision survives further appeals. Municipal officials are now scrambling to deed the land the structures sit on to private groups, a solution that is unlikely to satisfy those who brought the legal action. More litigation seems inevitable.

Richard John Neuhaus, a Catholic priest and frequent critic of church-state separation, argues that efforts like this to remove religious symbols from public property result in a "naked public square" and encourage government hostility toward religion.[1]

Neuhaus and those who make this and similar arguments overlook several salient points. First of all, the "public square" is more than just a physical place. It is also a forum where various ideas are advocated, defended, and exchanged. Under this definition, church leaders in the United States have most certainly not been excluded from the public square. Religious groups enjoy absolute freedom to enter the public square and contend for various issues that are important to them. Some people may not like it when churches undertake such a role, but it is perfectly legal and appropriate under the Constitution.

A multitude of religious groups maintain lobbying offices in Washington, D.C., and the state capitals. Collectively they enjoy significant influence over the political system—influence many secular PACs would like to have. Religious leaders, in fact, continually make pronouncements on the burning issues of the day. In Neuhaus's own tradition, one need look no further than the pastoral letters often issued by the United States Catholic Conference of bishops. Such a grand measure of freedom hardly sounds like a system that seeks to silence the voice of religion.

Second, when looking at the public square as a physical place, it must be pointed out that the government allows certain public forums to be used by religious groups on an equal basis with non-religious organizations. True, religious groups do not enjoy monopoly power over the public square, but clearly they have no right to expect such exaggerated influence.

Third, the government must represent people of divergent backgrounds and faiths. No American should be made to feel like an outsider because of his or her religious beliefs. In light of that obvious fact, it is clearly inappropriate for the "public square" to be taken over by the government and filled with sectarian messages that only divide our people.

If the "public square" is really a "government-sponsored square," then it should be a forum for messages that unify us, not tear us apart and suggest that some citizens are more favored by the government than others. Alternately, it should be a place where all citizens and groups have the right to make their say, including religious groups, but not a place where religion receives special favors. Special treatment is what Neuhaus and his crowd really mean when they talk about "hostility toward religion" and access to the "public square."

Addressing the symbols issue during a church-state conference in Philadelphia in 1991, Marvin E. Frankel, a retired federal judge, made some wise observations. The effort to flood the public square with sectarian symbols is offensive to many, he pointed out. "The demand is no less and no more than an attempt by some people to show who's boss," Frankel remarked. "It says, 'This is a Christian country. If you don't like it, you know what you can do.' "[2] Frankel is exactly right.

The problem of religious symbols on public property may seem trivial to some, but to those involved in litigation such as that described above, it is a very important issue. Obviously the display of a 103-foot Latin cross on government-owned property, maintained with public funds, sends a signal that Christianity occupies a special place in the eyes of the government. These symbols, which are overt and often impossible to avoid, are the best example of the "in your face" school of church-state thought. To religious minorities they send a clear message of who the majority is and suggest that this majority enjoys special status in government, a status religious minorities clearly do not share. Obviously, this is an inappropriate message for the government to send.

But it is not only religious minorities who are offended by such displays. Often Christians oppose them, too. Many Christians believe that the cross, as the sacred symbol of Christianity, ought not to be appropriated by the state for any reason. They are offended to see a religious symbol to which they attach deep significance wedded to the naked power of the government—or, for that matter, junked up by being paired with tacky plastic elves and holiday garlands.

Symbols do have meaning, and the intermixing of sectarian and government symbols reeks of a two-bit theocracy. These displays cheapen both the church and the state. For all involved, it is best that they be removed at once. If that is absolutely not practical, then the land the symbols stand on should be sold to private groups, with all maintenance costs shouldered by voluntary contributions.

Civil Religion

In American society, religious leaders are generally looked upon more favorably than government officials. Civic leaders, perhaps hoping to capitalize on some of religion's good public image, often seek the prestige of religion. Many government officials see cloaking themselves in religion as one sure way to boost their poor public persona.

But there is a catch: Religion that is promoted in the public arena by politicians must be sufficiently "non-sectarian" so as not to offend any constituent. For this reason, chaplains who appear before legislative bodies usually end their prayers "in God's name," not "in Jesus' name." Prayers are usually addressed to "Our Lord," "God" or something vague like "the one who watches over us."

Civil religion—religious practices performed for the benefit of government agencies or the type of generalized religion pushed by politicians—is therefore a bland exercise that sometimes offends the devout with its watered-down flavor. Nevertheless, civil religion is definitely on the upswing in the United States. From city halls and school boards to the White House and Congress, government officials are clamoring for religious leaders to open their sessions with invocations and prayers.

A 1983 Supreme Court decision upheld the concept of legislative chaplains and may have sparked the new drive for every school board, city council, and sewer authority in the country to find a preacher for its monthly gathering. In *Marsh v. Chambers*, the high court ruled 6-3 that states may hire chaplains and even pay them out of public funds to open governmental sessions with prayers.[3]

The justices were clearly afraid to make the ruling that the First Amendment demands—mainly that state-paid religious ministers do not square with separation of church and state. Under the court's own precedents the state-paid chaplains should have been struck down, but the justices, perhaps believing such a ruling would be too unpopular, decided to dodge precedent. They ruled that government chaplains have a long history in the United States and are thus "traditional." The majority pointed out that the first Continental Congress had appointed state-funded chaplains, and thus no constitutional violation was found. The justices were also probably reluctant to axe legislative prayers knowing that action would spell an end to their own opening prayer, "God save this honorable court!"

Justice William Brennan, pointing out that founding father James Madison opposed state-funded legislative chaplains, concluded that the practice had been unconstitutional all along and was not saved by its long history. He argued that the first Congress had acted more out of political concerns than respect for the Constitution some of them had helped draft.

But the damage was done. The decision has since been cited by municipal bodies of every sort to justify their pre-meeting prayers. Few other courtroom challenges on this issue have seen the light of day, except for a 1992 ruling by a state judge in Utah. The judge ruled that prayers before the City Council of Salt Lake City were unconstitutional because public funds were used to line up the chaplains. Third District Court Judge J. Dennis Frederick ruled that the plan violates sections of the state constitution.[4] The case was appealed to Utah's Supreme Court. In the wake of the ruling, Utah's lawmakers tried unsuccessfully to alter the state constitution to permit the prayers and move church and state officially into closer union.

This is not to suggest, however, that municipal prayers have always gone off without a hitch. Just the opposite is true. In many cases, citizens have criticized the prayers or their content. In 1990 an atheist in San Diego was arrested for protesting during prayers at a meeting of the San Diego Board of Supervisors. The following year, two school board members in the San Diego area challenged the board president's practice of opening the meetings with overtly Christian prayers. One board member said he would prefer a moment of silence because "that does not offend anybody."[5]

Less commonly, members of government themselves are offended by the content of legislative prayers. In 1989 a guest minister offering a prayer before the Florida House of Representatives used the occasion to launch an anti-abortion tirade, angering pro-choice members of the delegation. The state representative who had invited the minister later apologized for the incident.

Although prayers have been upheld before legislative bodies such as state senates, it does not follow that state-sponsored prayers can intrude on other branches of government. A county judge in North Carolina, for instance, was sued by the ACLU in 1990 after he refused to stop opening sessions with vocal prayers. The federal Fourth Circuit Court of Appeals ruled against the judge, and the U.S. Supreme Court later refused to hear the case. The lower court said the prayers violated the religious neutrality of the courtroom, an essential feature of the secular legal system.[6]

Aside from prayers, the biggest church-state problem in the civil religion field today centers on ceremonial proclamations. Every year lawmakers in Congress, state legislatures, and city councils pass thousands of these resolutions. Most are inoffensive, marking, for example, occasions like National Dairy Goat Week or National Cauliflower Appreciation Day.

But sometimes resolutions that deal with religious themes create controversy. Specifically, proposals put forth in many communities to designate 1990 the International Year of Bible Reading led to church-state problems.

In the California town of Benicia, Mayor Marilyn C. O'Rourke refused to sign a Year of the Bible resolution that had been passed by the town council on a 3-2 vote because it described the Bible as "the Word of God." Mayor O'Rourke argued that it was no business of the government to tell people when to pray or what religious texts to consult. Benicia's city council, O'Rourke insisted, should not take it upon itself to decide which religious texts qualify as "the word of God."

To buttress her argument, O'Rourke asked a local Catholic priest, David K. O'Rourke (no relation), to examine the resolution and offer an opinion. Rev. O'Rourke offered some keen insights that are worth repeating here.

"If this proclamation is inconsequential—another National Asparagus Week or Year of the Grandfather—none of us, I suspect, is going to care one way or the other," observed the Rev. O'Rourke. "If it is intended as a serious action, and I gather it is, then I don't think it is the sort of thing that the council should be involved in. It is neither a good idea, nor a constitutional practice, for the government to tell people how to pray, the form of prayer to use, who to pray to, when to pray or even that they should pray. Our parishioners may call us to task on any of these areas, but for constitutional reasons the city council should not."

Continued the priest, "Every religious group in the United States is a minority group. Some may be unhappy with this status and wish they had official standing. I am not unhappy with it. The Catholic Church, the largest of these minorities, has prospered greatly in this country where we separate church and state."[7]

Rev. O'Rourke is correct. In matters of civil religion, government officials would do well to remember the voluntary principle. A moment of silence before a meeting would afford everyone an opportunity to pray, meditate, or simply clear the mind in preparation for the business at hand. Moments of silence avoid the divisiveness and acrimony that often occur during debates over civil religion. And best of all, they exclude no one. In a free country, no one should be made to feel that they have better standing before the government because they belong to the "favored" religion. Conversely, no one should be made to feel like an outsider on account of religious belief or lack thereof.

Before leaving this topic, it is important to look at two related issues that are continually cited by Religious Right activists who dislike separation of church and state. These are the motto "In God We Trust," which appears on U.S. currency, and the idea that the United States has a "Judeo-Christian heritage."

The argument that America is a Christian nation because "In God We Trust" appears on its money is very weak. To begin with, this practice is not long rooted in our nation's history. The phrase first began appearing on coins sporadically around the time of the Civil War. "In God We Trust" was not designated the country's official motto until the 1950s, in reaction to hysterical fears of creeping Communism that swept the United States during the heyday of Wisconsin Sen. Joseph McCarthy, a notorious Red-baiting demagogue.

Arguments that the United States has a "Judeo-Christian heritage" are even less persuasive. "Judeo" was added only recently, in a feeble attempt at ecumenism. There is no consensus on what this term means among American religions. Consider the commandment, "Thou shall not kill," which is said to be part of this heritage. Some U.S. Christians and Jews interpret this as a mandate for pacifism, that is, a statement that all killing is wrong. Others do not extend it that far and say the commandment only forbids certain types of killings, carving out exemptions for self-defense, war, and the death penalty for crimes. Compounding the situation is that certain great ethical principles—such as the Golden Rule to love thy neighbor as thyself—appear in some guise or another in all the world's religious and philosophical systems, thus negating any Judeo-Christian claim of a monopoly on them.

Christianity and Judaism are, to be sure, religions found in abundance in America. But when a Religious Right activist says something like, "The country must return to our great Judeo-Christian heritage," it is important to remember that his or her interpretation of that heritage is likely to colored by sectarian and/or political bias. It certainly is not something all American religions agree on.

In sum, references to a U.S. "Judeo-Christian heritage" are meaningless. More often than not, they are simply semantic devices used by fundamentalists who really mean, "The country should adopt my far-right Christian views."

Mandatory Sunday-Closing Laws

The Supreme Court is often accused of "legislating from the bench," that is, forcing policies on the American people that they do not want. This accusation is levied especially often in controversial church-state issues. But the issue of mandatory Sunday-closing laws proves that some church-state controversies can be resolved in a manner favorable to the separation principle without court mandates.

As indicated in chapter 4, mandatory Sunday-closing laws were typical in many states until well into the 20th century. Despite their clear religious basis, Sunday-closing laws were often not considered a church-state problem. The statutes, also known as "blue laws" in many communities, simply *were*. Shops did not open on Sunday because it had always been that way.

Jews were early protesters of mandatory Sunday-closing laws. In some cities, Jewish shop owners argued that forcing them to close on Sundays created economic hardships. Observant Jews, who hold Saturday as their sabbath, were forced to close two days out of the week.

Some Christians who also keep a Saturday sabbath joined Jews in this protest, notably Seventh-day Adventists and Seventh-day Baptists. With this type of spirited opposition, it was inevitable that the issue would go to court. Ironically, the first case challenging blue laws to reach the Supreme Court was brought by neither a Jew nor a Seventh-day Adventist. It did, however, revolve around issues of commerce.

By 1961, the year the Supreme Court decided its first contemporary blue law case, some states had begun to relax their Sunday-closing laws a bit. At one time, the laws outlawed absolutely all business transactions on Sunday, but gradually certain exemptions were permitted. Medicine and other health-related goods, for example, could be sold on Sunday. Some states allowed food to be sold. Other states permitted small stores, the "mom and pop" type groceries, to open but ordered that large department stores remain closed. The result was a crazy patchwork of laws in some states governing which items could be sold and which could not. The lists seemed to have little relationship to logic. Some states, for example, allowed frozen food to be sold but not canned food.

This type of confusion only increased cries for reform. In states where legislators did not take action, the courts were invited to step in. The first major legal battle started after employees at a discount store in Anne Arundel County, Maryland, were charged with selling the following items, all illegal to purchase on Sunday: a loose-leaf binder, a can of floor wax, a stapler and a toy submarine. (The mind boggles at the planning that must have gone into this undercover police sting!) The employees' attorneys argued that Maryland's blue law, which limited Sunday sales to foodstuffs, medicine, gasoline, and newspapers, violated the Establishment Clause of the First Amendment.

The Supreme Court consolidated the case with a similar dispute involving a department store in Allentown, Pennsylvania, and ruled 8-1 that mandatory Sunday-closing laws do not violate the Constitution. In one of the high court's lowest church-state moments, the justices put the First Amendment aside in the *McGowan v. Maryland* ruling and lamely asserted that blue laws, though they indeed originally had a religious purpose, had become secularized over the years. Their only purpose now, the court declared, was to provide a "day of rest" for weary retail workers.[8]

But even the court's poor logic could not save blue laws. Their days were clearly numbered. Even as the Maryland case awaited decision before the Supreme Court, lawmakers in that state were taking steps to make the state's blue law less restrictive. Other states were taking similar actions.

Eventually, strict blue laws began to fade away. The public wanted to shop on Sundays (as evidenced by the fact that many shoppers would cross state borders to do so), and retailers, eager to increase their profits and keep dollars in state, urged state and local lawmakers to change or scrap the laws. Politicians, always attentive to the needs of business and cognizant of the economic boost brought by Sunday shopping, did not require much persuading.

Of course, there was some opposition to this liberalization, mostly from religious leaders who argued that Sunday shopping violates the "sacredness" of the day. But the public will could not be thwarted, and most people apparently found the arguments of religious leaders unpersuasive. Store owners opened their doors on Sunday, and people came to shop.

The Religious Right has always found it difficult to accept that blue laws died a natural death and were not blasted out of existence by the Supreme Court. In his 1991 book *The New World Order*, television evangelist Pat Robertson falsely accuses the high court of having struck down mandatory Sunday-closing laws in the *McGowan* case. Another Religious Right leader, Tim LaHaye, made the same mistake in one of his books. To the Religious Right, it is inconceivable that a majority of people might not want a state-imposed "day of rest."

For the most part, blue laws are a dead issue today, but occasionally a dispute flares up somewhere in the country. In 1991 the North Dakota legislature repealed what was probably the nation's strictest blue law after efforts by shopkeepers to have it declared unconstitutional at the state Supreme Court failed. The vote in the state House of Representatives was not even close at 72-33, and Gov. George Sinner immediately signed the measure into law.

Town council members in Prospect Park, New Jersey, were forced to scrap an extremely strict blue law in 1991 after the American Civil Liberties Union threatened a lawsuit. The law was so severe it forbade even *leisure* activities outdoors on Sundays, and police occasionally told children riding bicycles outside to go home. A resident of a nearby town threatened to sue over the law after he was cited by police for fixing a broken radiator hose on his van while visiting his daughter one Sunday. In response, the town council modified the law to bar loud noises on Sunday.[9]

But these types of stories are exceptions. Most states and communities ditched blue laws years ago, and today department stores and other shops across the United States are open on Sundays, albeit usually with curtailed hours.

Religious leaders still occasionally pine for the old days. In recent years, Pope John Paul II has spoken out against Sunday commerce several times. Addressing French bishops in 1992, the Pope bemoaned the fact that more people now work on Sundays, charging that today, "The traditional function of Sunday, day of the Lord, tends to be truncated."

The Pope has even gone so far as to recommend that governments reinstate blue laws. In an encyclical issued in 1991, John Paul called for governments to recognize Sunday as a day of rest, calling the position "a human right, which is based on a commandment."[10] John Paul has also urged the leaders of the European Economic Community to impose blue laws, a move that has met with some success.

Some American bishops have picked up on the Pope's crusade. In 1991 and 1993 Cardinal Bernard Law of Boston wrote to Massachusetts Gov. William Weld in opposition to Weld's proposal to allow stores to open at 9 o'clock on Sunday mornings instead of noon.

"In the Christian tradition we are reminded that man was not made for the Sabbath, the Sabbath was made for man," wrote Law. "As a society, as families, as individuals, we need the quiet, the change of pace, the worship that a communal day of rest affords. Rather than a further erosion of what is a common good, we encourage the governor and the legislators to help our society restore a sense of the Sabbath."[11]

Pat Robertson agrees with this crusade and bemoans the loss of blue laws in *The New World Order*, but as full mall parking lots indicate, the public does not necessarily believe it needs quiet or peace of mind on Sunday. Most don't share the view of Robertson, the Pope, or Cardinal Law and favor Sunday shopping. As Americans work longer and longer hours during the week, they seem to need an extra day to run their errands. For the time being at least, this is one church-state issue that appears to be settled.

Churches and Taxation; Churches and Politics

Because the issues of churches and taxes and church involvement in politics are closely related, I will consider the two together in this section.

Religious groups, like other not-for-profit organizations, enjoy tax-free status. That is, they do not have to pay taxes on the donations they receive and are usually exempt from state income tax on the goods they purchase and the land they own. (Individual clergy members, however, must pay federal and state income taxes.)

Occasionally, however, the suggestion is made that churches ought to be taxed. Religious groups, some say, have amassed great wealth and if we tax them we can balance the budget.

Theoretically, no legal barrier to taxing churches and other religious groups or non-profit organizations exists. In a landmark 1971 ruling in *Walz v. Tax Commission of the City of New York*, the U.S. Supreme Court declared that it is not unconstitutional for states to give churches tax exemption. The high court did not say, and has never said, that the federal government or states are *obligated* to give churches tax exemption. They said merely that it does not violate the Establishment Clause for government to choose to do so. [12]

But no state, of course, has seriously entertained the notion of directly taxing churches. Many states do tax churches if they are involved in for-profit ventures unrelated to their religious mission, but otherwise the general tax exemption afforded to churches is fairly safe.

One reason churches stay free from taxation is that most offer a wide array of social services. Government believes these services provide a valuable safety net for society and reduce some of the burden on the state. In other words, if a church runs a homeless shelter, that's one less such shelter the government need open. The government does not want to discourage the social mission of churches by slapping them with burdensome taxes.

There is also a fear that taxing churches would require the government to get intimately involved in churches' affairs and private matters, fostering entanglement of church and state.

But the issue of taxing churches is not without controversy. In order to remain tax free, churches must refrain from getting too heavily involved in politics. For instance, groups considered non-profit by the Internal Revenue Service may not endorse candidates for public office. Likewise, they may not attack someone running for public office to the extent that they effectively endorse his or her opponent. Therein lies a gray area. Some churches are known for their political activism, and many have been accused of going too far in their political activities.

In 1980 an abortion-rights group based in New York sued the IRS in an effort to force the tax agency to revoke the tax-exempt status of the Catholic Church over the bishops' anti-abortion activities. To bolster their case, the New York group pointed to several Catholic parishes where candidates for state and federal office had been openly endorsed in church bulletins.

It took nine years, but the Supreme Court ultimately decided that the abortion-rights group lacked the authority to sue the IRS in this manner. The case was dismissed due to lack of "standing"—a legal term meaning the right to sue—and the central issues it raised were never dealt with by a court.[13]

But the case might have had some positive fallout. Just before the 1988 presidential election, the U.S. Catholic Conference issued a twelve-page memo to churches warning clergy not to endorse candidates, form political action committees, or distribute campaign literature. Many religious groups issued similar bulletins during the 1992 campaign.

Most people think of the Internal Revenue Service as a fierce bureaucracy, determined to get every dime of tax revenue owed the government. This image may be accurate for private citizens, but when it comes to churches the IRS has tended to play the game a little more softly. There are signs, however, that the tax agency is toughening up even here.

In 1991 the IRS conducted a lengthy investigation of television preacher Jimmy Swaggart and found him guilty of violating IRS rules by twice endorsing Pat Robertson for president during the 1988 campaign. Swaggart received no monetary fine but was ordered to sign a statement promising to refrain from intervening in future political campaigns.

The IRS's action, to be sure, was a slap on the wrist. However, it was a sign of things to come. By going after Swaggart, who by then was down on his luck due to sex scandals, the IRS might have been sending a not-so-subtle warning to religious groups about the dangers of mixing religion and politics: Next time it could be you.

Sure enough, in 1993 the IRS struck again and fined televangelist Jerry Falwell $50,000 after determining that his non-profit Old Time Gospel Hour had illegally channeled money into a political action committee that gave money to conservative congressional candidates. The IRS also revoked the Old Time Gospel Hour's tax-exempt status retroactively for the years 1986 and 1987.

At about the same time, the IRS announced that it was investigating a Binghampton, New York, fundamentalist church that ran an anti-Bill Clinton advertisement in *USA Today* just before the November 1992 election. The tax agency also looked into a Korean Christian church in Los Angeles that had contributed money to a congressional candidate.

Aside from incurring the wrath of the IRS, religious leaders who chose to get involved in politics run other risks. Members of the denomination, for instance, may object to the involvement. Many religious people still think politics is a dirty business that the church should be above. Some groups, like Jehovah's Witnesses and some fundamentalist-oriented denominations, take this position to an extreme and refrain entirely from getting involved in politics; their members don't even vote.

The Roman Catholic bishops run an almost constant risk of sparking a backlash from American Catholics over the issue of abortion. In recent years, some conservative bishops have suggested that Catholic lawmakers who refuse to toe the church's severe anti-abortion line be excommunicated. But support for this position among Catholics in general is very low. Indeed, a majority of American Catholics, polls consistently indicate, are pro-choice. In light of that, the hierarchy wrestles with how far they can take this issue.

New York Gov. Mario Cuomo is in frequent conflict with arch-conservative church leaders such as Cardinal John J. O'Connor of New York. Cuomo says he is personally opposed to abortion but does not believe he has the right to impose that view on others through government action. Although right-wing Catholics frequently call for O'Connor to excommunicate Cuomo, so far the cardinal has taken no action.

Political activity by church leaders can polarize denominations. In the early 1980s, conservative forces in the Southern Baptist Convention orchestrated an effort to seize control of the denomination's leadership. They were successful and immediately reversed the denomination's historic stands in favor of separation of church and state. The group's leadership is now solidly anti-separationist.

In the process of switching positions, the SBC fell into line with the Republican Party. Top Republican officials regularly address SBC gatherings. In the early 1990s, both President George Bush and Vice President Dan Quayle appeared before Southern Baptist meetings.

The close ties between the SBC and the GOP have split the denomination. A dissatisfied splinter group of members who still favor church-state separation, known as "moderates," have slowly been building their own institutions and working to keep their ideas and the denomination's traditional views on church and state alive. Some observers believe the moderate wing will eventually branch off and form a separate denomination or align with more moderate Baptist bodies already in existence.

As the SBC experience shows, religion and politics make for a volatile mixture. Across the country, extremely conservative, anti-separationist forces are launching carefully planned campaigns to win local offices. Much of this activity is coordinated by Pat Robertson and his minions in Virginia Beach. They have been successful in some parts of the country because of low voter turnout.

Robertson's forces have focused their efforts almost exclusively on the Republican Party. In 1992 they managed to take control of state Republican parties in California, Iowa, Virginia, Colorado and Texas. Alarmed moderate Republicans organized to fight back, but their efforts were too little too late. The shock of what happened, however, will undoubtedly spur efforts to recapture the party in years to come. In 1992, for example, Religious Right activists suffered reduced success in state and local elections.

Conservative Christians have every right to participate in politics, of course. They can run for office and register voters just as all other Americans can. Religious Right activists often claim that their rights to do these things are somehow suppressed when efforts are made to expose their narrow agendas. Nothing could be further from the truth.

Anyone who runs for public office should be prepared to accept thorough and ongoing scrutiny of his or her views. In California, Religious

Right activists ran a variety of "stealth candidates" in 1990. These people ran low-key campaigns based in several large fundamentalist churches in a given area, making few if any public appearances at voter forums. Many won local races due to low voter turnout.

The Religious Right can only get away with that once, and the activists who did win office should not expect a low-key campaign the next time around. Exposing candidates who have narrow, sectarian agendas that run counter to democracy is not bigoted. It is not "anti-Christian." Providing information to voters about candidates is the American way. The Religious Right fears it because so often when this information is released, their people are soundly rejected. Why else would they run "stealth campaigns"?

One other point needs to be made before leaving this issue: When a church or religious leader speaks out an a controversial issue of the day, the cry is occasionally heard, "He can't do that! What about separation of church and state?"

Such complaints are misguided. The church leader *can* speak out, of course; separation of church and state does not affect free speech. Churches have an absolute right to speak on moral issues of the day. However, they do not have the right to expect that their pet theological notions be written into law. They must persuade people that their religious views are correct, not attempt to compel obedience through the power of the government.

Finally, it is not illegal for members of the clergy to run for and hold public office. Years ago the state of Tennessee had a law barring "Ministers of the Gospel, or priests of any denomination whatever" from holding public office. In the 1978 case *McDaniel v. Paty* the Supreme Court struck the law down by a unanimous vote.[14] The high court's action was appropriate. In a free society, everyone should have the right to run for public office. If the voters are upset at the thought of clergy running for office, they can make their feelings known at the ballot box.

Abortion

Is abortion a church-state issue? Separationists differ on the answer to that question. But one thing is for certain: At the very least, abortion is an issue with strong church-state overtones.

Many of the anti-abortion laws that are now pending in some states in anticipation of the demise of *Roe v. Wade,* the landmark 1973 Supreme Court ruling that legalized abortion, were drafted by church leaders or lobbyists. For example, a Missouri law designed to chip away at *Roe* that was passed by the state legislature in 1986 and later upheld by the Supreme Court was written by two lobbyists for the Catholic Church. The bill included a legislative finding that life begins at conception, a doctrine of the Catholic Church.

The legislative preamble was singled out for special mention in a friend-of-the-court brief filed by Americans United for Separation of Church and State before the Supreme Court in the Missouri case. Unfortunately, only Justice John Paul Stevens was swayed by the argument that the preamble violated the Establishment Clause.

Stevens noted that in the 13th century St. Thomas Aquinas taught that male fetuses received souls forty days after conception, and female fetuses at eighty days. Wrote the justice, "If the views of St. Thomas were held as widely today as they were in the Middle Ages, and if a state legislature were to enact a statute prefaced with a 'finding' that female life begins eighty days after conception and male life begins forty days after conception, I have no doubt that this Court would promptly conclude that such an endorsement of a particular religious tenet is violative of the Establishment Clause."

Continued Stevens, "In my opinion the difference between that hypothetical statute and Missouri's preamble reflects nothing more than a difference in theological doctrine."[15]

Commenting on the ruling in *Webster v. Reproductive Health Services,* William F. Schulz, former president of the Unitarian-Universalist Association, remarked, "To allow state legislatures to adopt one definition over another and to force all of us to conform to one theological standard is nothing short of religious totalitarianism."[16]

Other religious groups have attempted to make a free exercise argument in favor of abortion rights, asserting that a woman should have the right to follow her conscience, as dictated by her religious beliefs, when making a decision on abortion. Courts have not been sympathetic to this argument.

Paul D. Simmons, formerly professor of Christian ethics at Southern Baptist Theological Seminary in Louisville, Kentucky, has expertly outlined the case for abortion as a religious liberty issue. Observes Simmons, "One of the great values of the *Roe v. Wade* decision is that no woman is coerced to act in ways contrary to her religious scruples and moral value system."

Continues Simmons,

> For those who believe strongly that zygotes are persons, there is no coercion to terminate a pregnancy, even under the most problematic circumstances. On the other hand, those women whose religious and moral belief systems permit abortion under certain circumstances are respected and protected. It belongs to the woman to decide based upon her religious beliefs. Religious groups are also free to teach their followers whatever doctrinal formulations of personhood they believe consistent with their commitments to tradition and theology. Without ever saying so, *Roe v. Wade* was an exercise in protecting religious liberty.[17]

Although pro-choice and anti-abortion forces share little common ground, there is one thing they agree on: This issue is likely to be settled in the states in the years to come. State legislatures have already gained increased power to regulate the availability of abortion. As the trend escalates, religiously based lobbying has also shot up in state capitals across the country.

Pro-choice advocates often complain that in some states it is obvious that lawmakers are taking their marching orders from sectarian forces. The problem is that such activities, while inappropriate, are not illegal. Religious groups have the right to attempt to influence legislation, and denominations from very liberal to very conservative maintain lobbying offices in Washington and in state capitals.

Americans sometimes expect their court system to solve too many problems. In the case of religiously motivated lobbying, the hands of the courts are tied as long as all Internal Revenue Service regulations are being followed. If lawmakers appear to be unduly influenced by church officials, voters can express their displeasure at the ballot box.

One final thought on this issue should be expressed: Debate rages among religious denominations over whether abortion is a legitimate constitutional right. The Supreme Court may be leaning away from the *Roe* finding that it is. Some pro-choice religious groups argue that if abortion is a constitutionally protected right, then it is irresponsible for anti-abortion forces to try to persuade legislators to restrict it through state laws. Constitutional rights, after all, are not subject to up-and-down votes and may be modified only through constitutional amendments.

While this argument has a certain appeal, it is naive. Over the years many religious groups have shown a callous disregard for the commands of the Constitution. The Catholic Church has lobbied incessantly for parochiaid even though it would violate the freedom of conscience of millions of Americans. Fundamentalists constantly pressure lawmakers to pass school prayer laws, even though the courts nearly always strike them down because they run roughshod over the First Amendment. Many religious denominations, it seems, are all too willing to put aside the protections of the Constitution—the very protections that make it possible for them to prosper in the first place—in favor of acquiring some perceived short-term goal.

Such may be the case with abortion. Once we have allowed states to base laws on narrow theological precepts, we have established a dangerous standard that may one day lash out against the prevailing conservative religious forces of today.

Polls show consistently that young people are overwhelmingly pro-choice. The next generation to rule this country may follow the precedent being laid down today and write its laws in accordance with the views of more liberal religious groups. When that happens, will anti-abortion forces be able to argue plausibly that church-state separation is being violated? In that sense, today's religiously inspired abortion foes may win a temporary battle but definitely lose the war.

U.S.-Vatican Diplomatic Ties

Near the end of Ronald Reagan's first term, the president surprised the religious community with the announcement that he would establish full diplomatic ties with the Vatican. An ambassador-elect, William Wilson, was named, and the U.S. Senate was asked to confirm the nominee.

Reagan's action created an uproar in some segments of the American religious and civil liberties communities. In a rare display of ecumenism, mainline Protestants, represented by the National Council of Churches, joined more conservative elements on the spectrum of American theological thought in opposing the move.

The idea of a formal diplomatic relationship between the U.S. government and the Holy See was nothing new. In fact, an ambassadorial exchange had been proposed in 1951 by President Harry S. Truman. Truman was prepared to name Gen. Mark Clark Vatican ambassador, but the plan was derailed by widespread public outcry. Letters deluged the White House and Capitol Hill, and religious leaders denounced the move from pulpits across the nation.

The 1984 protest lacked much of that vigor. While many religious denominations went on record in opposition to the move, they seemed to lack the spirit for a aggressive fight to block the exchange of ambassadors. The Senate Foreign Relations Committee held hearings on the matter, but in the end the Senate voted overwhelmingly to approve Wilson's appointment, 81-13.

A coalition of religious and civil liberties groups, led by Americans United for Separation of Church and State, filed suit in federal court to block the move as a violation of church-state separation. The court, however, dismissed the suit on grounds of "lack of standing," holding that Americans United and the other groups did not have the authority to challenge Reagan's action. The central issue of the lawsuit—whether or not the establishment of diplomatic relations with the Vatican transgresses separation of church and state—was not addressed by the court.[18]

Since then, four men, all Roman Catholics, have held the ambassadorship. The last ambassador under George Bush, Thomas P. Melady, a former university administrator, is a member of the Knights of Malta, an international Catholic chivalric order with about 2,000 members in the United States. Melady's two predecessors, Wilson and Frank Shakespeare, were also members of the group.

Although the issue is rarely discussed today, it is clear from a constitutional perspective that U.S.-Vatican ties violate the First Amendment. The Vatican may claim to function as an independent foreign state, but clearly it is a "nation" in name only. The Vatican, which is only 108 acres in size, exists solely to serve as the world headquarters of the Roman Catholic Church. The United States government, as a secular entity bound by law to treat all religions equally, should not have a special relationship with one church. Such an action gives Catholicism a favored status with the United States government that other religions can never hope to achieve.

Wilson himself acknowledged the religious nature of U.S.-Vatican ties in a 1985 speech, calling the relationship "a quest for morality" on the part of the U.S. government. To say the least, this is a highly questionable motive for establishing diplomatic ties.

Vatican ambassadors have tried in vain to draw some distinction between the Vatican as a religious entity and the Vatican as a state. Shakespeare once remarked, "We don't have an ambassador to the church. We have an ambassador to the Holy See, which is a legal, juridical state. That's important. We have an ambassador for the same reason that 117 other countries do. It's in our national interest."[19]

But since the Vatican itself makes no such distinction between the sectarian and secular, Shakespeare's assertion is meaningless. The Pope is first and foremost the spiritual leader of the world's estimated one billion Roman Catholics. Any action the Vatican takes in world affairs or U.S. policy is filtered through the lens of sectarian bias.

Indeed, the creation of formal ties between the two entities, critics say, has given the church yet another avenue to lobby the U.S. government for political goals favored by the Catholic Church, most relating to social issues such as birth control, abortion, and aid to parochial schools.

In 1992 former Vatican ambassador Wilson told *Time* magazine that U.S. officials teamed up with the Vatican in the early 1980s to destabilize Poland's Communist government. As part of the deal, Reagan agreed to help implement the Catholic Church's narrow policy on birth control worldwide by sharply curtailing U.S. involvement in promoting family planning overseas. As a result, U.S. aid was cut off to international family planning agencies that fund birth control and abortions. [20]

The special relationship has also given Vatican officials immunity under U.S. law. In 1990, Bishop A. James Quinn told a conference of priests schooled in Roman Catholic Church law that the Holy See's diplomatic status could come in handy under certain conditions, such as when church officials are dealing with charges of clergy misconduct and accusations of child molestation by priests.

Noting that international law prevents police in host countries from searching embassies, Quinn pointed out that subpoenaed files may not be tampered with or destroyed, but added, "If there's something there you really don't want people to see, you might send it off to the Apostolic Delegate [another name for the Vatican Ambassador] because they have immunity. . . . Something you consider dangerous, you might send it there." [21]

It should be noted that Quinn's recommendation was not endorsed by the hierarchy of the church. In fact, a Roman Catholic lawyer-priest warned against such an action in a 1985 report to church officials, pointing out that sending sensitive material to the Vatican embassy could "insure that the immunity of the nunciature would be damaged or destroyed by the civil courts." [22] Still, the suggestion that church officials could exploit U.S.-Vatican diplomatic ties to cover up wrongdoing is chilling.

Critics have also argued that the diplomatic relationship gave the Catholic Church, which has become increasingly conservative under current Pope John Paul II, opportunities to team up with rightist elements in the Reagan and Bush administrations to meddle in world politics. The Knights of Malta, for example, have been active in funding various covert operations in Latin America ostensibly designed to subvert Communism. The Knights' close ties to the three Vatican ambassadors have undoubtedly facilitated these actions.

When Democrat Bill Clinton was elected president in 1992, separationists urged him to leave the Vatican ambassador slot vacant. But Clinton ignored the advice and appointed Boston mayor Raymond Flynn to the post. Flynn is the fourth Roman Catholic to hold the position.

In summary, then, although the establishment of diplomatic ties between the United States and the Vatican raised serious church-state questions that remain unanswered to this day, the action did not create sufficient concern among the American people to warrant close examination of the issue by the Senate. This is unfortunate. Now that the relationship is entrenched, it is unlikely to be undone.

Unfortunately, official U.S.-Vatican ties are probably here to stay, much to the detriment of both church and state in this country.

Notes

1. Richard John Neuhaus, *The Naked Public Square* (Grand Rapids, MI: William B. Eerdmans Publishing, 1984).

2. Rob Boston, "Religious Liberty At The Crossroads," *Church & State* 44(July-August 1991): 4-7.

3. *Marsh v. Chambers,* 463 U.S. 783 (1983).

4. *Society of Separationists v. Whitehead,* Civil No. 910906136, March 2, 1992.

5. "School Boards Struggle With Sex Ed. Classes, Distribution of Condoms," *Church & State* 44(April 1991): 17.

6. *North Carolina Civil Liberties Union v. Constangy,* 90-1880, 90-1881, 1991 U.S. App. 4th Cir.

7. David K. O'Rourke, "Bible Reading, Prayer And City Hall: Don't Make Anybody An Outsider!" *Church & State* 43(July-August 1990): 21.

8. *McGowan v. Maryland,* 366 U.S. 420 (1961).

9. "New Jersey Town Changes Sunday Law To Avoid Lawsuit," *Church & State* 44(October 1991): 3.

10. "New Papal Encyclical Endorses Religious Liberty, Sunday Laws," *Church & State* 44(July-August 1991): 21.

11. "Cardinal Law Attacks Sunday-Closing Reform In Massachusetts," *Church & State* 44(June 1991): 19-20.

12. *Walz v. Tax Commission of the City of New York,* 397 U.S. 644 (1970).

13. *United States Catholic Conference v. Abortion Rights Mobilization,* 87-416, June 20, 1988.

14. *McDaniel v. Paty* 435 U.S. 618, April 19, 1978.

15. *Webster v. Reproductive Health Services,* 88-605, July 3, 1989.

16. Rob Boston, "Different Doctrine," *Church & State* 42(September 1989): 7-8.

17. Paul D. Simmons, "Dogma And Discord: Religious Liberty And The Abortion Debate," *Church & State* 43(January 1990): 17-21.

18. *Americans United for Separation of Church and State v. Reagan,* 85-1309 (3rd Cir.), March 21, 1986.

19. "Vatican, U.S. 'Groping' For Relationship, Ambassador Says," *Church & State*, 41(September 1988): 16-17.

20. Carl Bernstein, "The Holy Alliance," *Time*, Feb. 24, 1992, 28-35.

21. Jason Berry, "Loose Canon," *Church & State*, 43(October 1990): 4-5.

22. Ibid., 5.

9

Thy Kingdom Come:
Christian Reconstructionism

The Religious Right is not a monolithic movement. Like the mythical Hydra, the Religious Right is multi-headed. While the various groups that make up the Religious Right may agree on many key issues, they fall out over others, especially issues of theology and its relationship to the political order.

Some groups, like the Christian Legal Society and the National Association of Evangelicals, while theologically conservative and generally accommodationist on church-state issues, are not unequivocally opposed to the concept of separation of church and state. Some of their supporters may agree that church-state separation is a good idea but argue that the concept has been taken too far in the modern age.

Other Religious Right organizations, such as Pat Robertson's Christian Coalition, Concerned Women for America, and Jerry Falwell's now defunct Moral Majority, are more vociferous in their attacks on Jefferson's wall of separation, brazenly proclaiming that they see no need for separation of church and state. They often attempt to portray separation as a myth or tie it to Communism or some other distasteful philosophy.

Extreme Anti-Separationism

At its most extreme, the Religious Right encompasses a loose conglomeration of organizations that forthrightly call for scrapping the First
Amendment and reordering government along the lines of the Bible's
Old Testament. This movement is known variously as Christian Reconstructionism, theonomy, or dominion theology.

Christian Reconstructionism is premised on the idea that people must
submit totally to God in all areas of their lives, including the governments
they form. At first thought, this may not sound so threatening to many
believers. Many religious people in America believe in submitting to God's
will. The problem with Reconstructionists is that they believe only *they*
have the correct and proper interpretation of "God's will." And their
interpretation is quite extreme. In a country where an estimated 2,000
separate religious denominations strive to live together in peace, the
problem inherent in the Reconstructionist approach is obvious.

Adding to the difficulty, Reconstructionists believe that the Old Testament contains a blueprint for a model society. Accordingly, they would
have the government enforce Old Testament dictates through law. They
have no use for democracy as we understand the concept today. They
are quick to label those who do not agree with them "apostates,"
"blasphemers," or even "tools of Satan." The society they burn to create
would severely restrict the religious freedom of most Americans.

The Reconstructionists' insistence on doctrinal purity has fractured
the movement more than once. Despite the infighting, elements of the
movement continue to surface in many American churches of various
denominations, especially those with a rigid fundamentalist or Pentecostal bent.

Because Reconstructionist ideas are so unusual, there is little threat
that the philosophy's adherents will ever have their way in the United
States. The primary threat of their ideas stems from the steady and
increasing influence they have on conservative Christianity. Some church
leaders, while not buying into the entire Reconstructionist package, have
adopted portions of the ideology, particularly the movement's opposition to separation of church and state. As a result, more and more
conservative church leaders are turning away from the idea that separation

protects religious liberty and toward adopting some variation of the notion that the state should enforce religious dictates by law. This is a tragic development. Separation of church and state will not survive unless it is supported by the religious community.

Even with the newfound support, Reconstructionists have a long way to go before achieving any of their public policy goals. Still, the movement has come a long way in just under thirty-five years and should be watched.

R. J. Rushdoony

The best known proponent of Reconstructionism in the United States is Rousas John Rushdoony, a writer and theologian who heads a California-based Reconstructionist think tank called the Chalcedon Foundation. In 1959 Rushdoony published the first Reconstructionist tome, titled *By What Standard?: An Analysis of the Philosophy of Cornelius Van Til.* Van Til, a Dutch theologian, is considered the movement's godfather.

Going back even further, Reconstructionists trace their ideas to John Calvin (see chapter 2), the French theologian who called for governments to purge "idolatrous practices" from the lands and advocated church-state union. As noted earlier, Calvin's Geneva was a harsh theocracy that suppressed religious liberty. Nevertheless, Geneva under Calvin remains the Reconstructionists' model society.

The Reconstructionist Agenda

What do Reconstructionists believe? A complete analysis of the movement is not possible in a few pages. Entire books have been written analyzing the philosophy. A survey of the movement's views, however, shows that a reconstructed society would bear little resemblance to the religiously neutral, pluralistic American society of today.

The first thing to understand about Reconstructionists is that they consider "pluralism" a dirty word. By their thinking, anyone espousing theological error—that is, anyone who fails to agree with them totally on religious matters—has no claim to religious freedom and may have his or her actions curtailed by the government. Religious toleration, a system whereby various faiths contend for members and public voice in an open dialogue, is anathema to the Reconstructionists because it affords people an opportunity to be exposed to theological error.

As Rushdoony put it, "In the name of toleration, the believer is asked to associate on a common level of total acceptance with the atheist, the pervert, the criminal, and adherents of other religions as though no differences existed."[1]

Virginia-based Reconstructionist Byron Snapp was even harsher in his analysis of the dangers of religious toleration and pluralism. Writing in a 1987 issue of *The Counsel of Chalcedon*, a Reconstructionist journal, Snapp observed, "The Christian must realize that pluralism is a myth. God and His law must rule all nations. . . . At no point in Scripture do we read that God teaches, supports or condones pluralism. To support pluralism is to recognize all religions as equal. Such a recognition denies God glory that belongs uniquely to Him. Clearly our founding fathers had no intention of supporting pluralism for they saw that the Bible tolerates no such view."[2]

From this starting point, Reconstructionists go on to formulate a reordered society that would strip away most forms of government, leaving citizens accountable to local church authorities. Taxes would be replaced with mandatory tithing, and social services would be provided by church groups. Security and police services would be provided by local militias.

Reconstructionists advocate the death penalty for a variety of offenses, and some observers have noted that the scope of punishable offenses is so great that if a reconstructed society is ever implemented in the United States, few will be left to live in it!

Reconstructionists go beyond advocating the death penalty for criminal acts such as murder and rape and would apply it to a variety of "offensive" acts, some of which are religious in nature. A partial list of offenses meriting the death penalty under Reconstructionism include: striking or cursing a parent, adultery, incest, bestiality, homosexuality, "unchastity," witchcraft, incorrigible delinquency, blasphemy, propagation of "false doctrines," and sacrificing to "false gods."

Commenting on this list, Rushdoony observed, "To the humanistic mind these penalties seem severe and unnecessary. In actuality, the penalties, together with the Biblical faith which motivated them, worked to reduce crime. Thus, when New England passed laws requiring the death penalty for incorrigible delinquents and for children who struck their parents, no executions were necessary: the law kept the children in line."[3]

Gary North

Rushdoony's unusual views won him an early disciple in Gary North, an economist. North later married Rushdoony's daughter, but the two men had a falling out over an obscure theological point some years ago and are reportedly estranged today. Rushdoony, if asked, does not acknowledge North and other theonomists outside his sphere of influence as real Reconstructionists.

North is a prolific writer whose bespectacled appearance hides an aggressive theocratic personality. In his books and newsletters he blasts popular culture and lambastes those who do not espouse his version of Christianity.

Based in Tyler, Texas, where he runs something called the Institute for Christian Economics, North also has little use for democracy and once wrote, "The modern world has been threatened by the rise of mass democracy, the politics of one man, one vote."[4]

When it comes to implementing the death penalty for various religious "crimes," North's preferred method is stoning. To North, stoning has a nice biblical ring to it. North has researched the issue extensively and once listed five reasons why stoning is the method of choice for executing today's idolater: stones are plentiful and available at no cost; no single blow can be traced to one person, thus reducing feelings of guilt; stoning displays the collective responsibility for crime prevention; executions should be public events; and stoning is symbolic of God's crushing the head of Satan as prophesied in Genesis 3:5.[5]

Reconstructionist Connections

Scholars H. Wayne House and Thomas D. Ice examined Reconstructionism in an interesting book published in 1989 called *Dominion Theology: Blessing or Curse?* (Not surprisingly, the two side with "curse.") House, a theology professor at Dallas Theological Seminary and Ice, a Baptist minister who once followed Reconstructionist teachings, make a good case that the movement is gaining influence in ultra-conservative fundamentalist Christian churches.

House and Ice say Reconstructionists are becoming more and more willing to put aside doctrinal differences and work with other conservative religious groups. They hope to draw into their network ultra-Calvinist strains of Presbyterianism, Baptists, and assorted charismatic Christians.

Some of these groups, hearing only part of the Reconstructionist message, are falling for it. Oddly enough, the new alliance includes some charismatics, Christians who believe in a "spirit-filled" theology often marked by speaking in tongues, faith healing, and loud, spontaneous worship services. Naturally, Reconstructionists don't tell the charismatics that under their system such forms of worship would be considered unlawful and might warrant the death penalty.

Rushdoony himself blasted charismatics in a 1982 book titled *Law and Society*. Wrote Rushdoony, "The mindless, meaningless babble of such worship is common to paganism, ancient and modern, where it is often associated with spiritistic possession. It is in any form alien to the Biblical faith. It is a form of the 'abominations' condemned by Biblical law. It is not found with any faithful and consistent affirmation of the sovereignty of God and a full trust in the atoning blood of Christ."[6]

Strong words. But when Rushdoony was asked by *Church & State* magazine in 1988 to explain how he expects to build bridges to charismatics after writing so harsh a denunciation, his response was rather lame: "I am not [charismatics'] judge. The Lord Jesus Christ is. Too many Christians feel they have been called to sit in judgment of everyone."[7] This from a man who advocates the death penalty for those propagating "false doctrines"!

The real answer is that the Reconstructionists don't intend to tell charismatics what they think of their worship. They are only interested in whatever support they can cull and hope charismatic leaders won't bother to do the research necessary to uncover statements like Rushdoony's.

The Coalition on Revival

More alarming than Rushdoony's musings or North's weird economic theories based on free market capitalism are the antics of the Coalition on Revival (COR), one of the more active Reconstructionist-based organizations.

COR is headed by Dr. Jay Grimstead, who founded the group in 1982. Though the California-based organization denies it is Reconstructionist, some of its views fall more or less into lock step with adherents of that philosophy.

At one time, COR's steering committee list read like a virtual Who's Who in Religious Right circles. The Rev. Donald Wildmon, head of the pro-censorship American Family Association, was a member. Other Religious Right luminaries who claimed membership included televangelist D. James Kennedy, Robert Dugan of the National Association of Evangelicals, the Rev. Tim LaHaye of the Traditional Values Coalition, former U.S. Rep. Mark Siljander, a Michigan Republican whose congressional comeback effort in Virginia failed in 1992, and Ed McAteer of the Religious Roundtable. Gary North is also a steering committee member.

Unhappily for COR and its sympathizers, the group's militant agenda, which calls for abolishing public education, forming county-wide "militias" and dismantling the Federal Reserve banking system, began to leak out in the late 1980s and early 1990s.[8] In the wake of the disclosures, the more prominent Religious Right leaders began scurrying away from the group; several hastily resigned from the steering committee. Wildmon went so far as to sue an official with the National Endowment for the Arts who attributed some of COR's ideas on capital punishment to him.

COR has issued a series of "Worldview" documents and a list of twenty-five theological tenets. Investigative reporter Frederick Clarkson, who often writes about fringe elements of the Religious Right, reports that one tenet reads in part, "We deny that anyone, Jew or Gentile, believer or unbeliever, private person or public official, is exempt from the moral and juridical obligation before God to submit to Christ's Lordship over every aspect of his life in thought, word, and deed."[9] Once again the Reconstructionist-type intolerance comes rapidly to the surface. Just who is to determine how to interpret "Christ's Lordship"? Could it be Jay Grimstead?

Grimstead himself seems to think so. In December 1991 Grimstead became infuriated when Bill Allen, a conservative California Republican, decided to run in a primary election for a U.S. Senate seat. Grimstead was angry because he wanted all California far-right forces to throw their support behind former U.S. Rep. William E. Dannemeyer, an ultra-conservative ally of the Religious Right. Allen's candidacy, he feared, would split the Religious Right vote.

COR activists drafted a harshly worded letter to Allen warning him of the consequences if he did not drop out of the race. Although the letter was never mailed, a copy somehow got to Allen. He was appalled by the strident tone it took.

Grimstead said three things would occur if Allen did not drop out. First, activists would work to "expose to our Christian network the foolishness and destructiveness of your efforts and encourage them to see your campaign for what it truly is—a political abortion which can only aid, indirectly, the forces of darkness." Second, the letter said, Allen's future political plans would be jeopardized. Last and most ominously, Grimstead warned, "We suspect that God Himself will take efforts to discipline you and judge this action of yours however He sees fit. Any of us who have been disciplined by our Heavenly Father can tell you He can deal very forcibly with us."[10]

Although the actual letter sent to Allen was softer in tone and deleted the reference to divine reprisal, the candidate took the original threat seriously and asked state officials to investigate. The California attorney general's office declined to do so. In the end, both Allen and Dannemeyer were trounced in the primary.

While Grimstead and company enjoy meddling in California politics, COR and other Reconstructionist groups by no means limit the scope of their activities to the political sphere. A COR document issued in 1990 contains a twenty-four point action plan that covers virtually all aspects of life, including the arts and popular culture. To counteract what they see as the negative effect of the television, COR calls for producing a Reconstructionist version of "Saturday Night Live."[11]

Other COR goals relating to film and television are not so amusing. Dr. Theodore Baehr, a COR steering committee member who heads the Christian Film and Television Commission, has called for implementation of a restrictive film code that would ban, among other things, "lustful kissing" and "dances that suggest or represent sexual actions" in movies. The code also declares that, "No movie shall be produced that will lower the moral standards of those that see it," a guideline so loose it would give COR censors what they really want: veto power over all films.[12]

Baehr's code was originally endorsed by Cardinal Roger Mahony of Los Angeles, an arch-conservative Roman Catholic who in 1992 called on the motion picture industry to voluntarily adopt the Baehr standards. If the industry refuses, Mahony said, the government should intervene. When reporters exposed Baehr's ties to Reconstructionism, Mahony quickly broke contact with him and backed away from the code.

Pat Robertson and Reconstructionism

At this point, readers might be wondering how Pat Robertson fits into all of this. After all, where there are wild-eyed anti-separationists to be found, Pat Robertson is usually not far behind. But when it comes to Reconstructionists, Robertson at least tries to keep a distance.

Robertson disagrees with a key component of Reconstructionist theology concerning the end of the world. Reconstructionists believe Christians of their stripe will rule over the world *before* the second coming of Christ and perhaps pave the way for His return. This view, common among evangelicals in the 19th century but largely out of favor today, is called *postmillennialism*.

Robertson, by contrast, is a *premillennialist*. He believes that "born-again" Christians will not rule over the planet until a period of chaos and conflict following Christ's return.

Robertson has said of Reconstructionism, "I admire many of these teachings because they are in line with the scripture. But others I cannot accept because they do not correspond with the biblical view of the sinful nature of mankind or the necessity of the second coming of Christ."[13]

In June 1992 Robertson told *Christianity Today*, "I don't agree with Reconstructionism, although I do believe that Jesus is Lord of all the world. I believe that he is Lord of the government, and the church, and business and education, and, hopefully, one day, Lord of the press. I see him involved in everything. And that's why I don't want to stay just in the church, as such. I want the church to move into the world."[14]

The comments sparked an interesting response from Gary DeMar, a Georgia-based Reconstructionist. In the letters to the editor section of the magazine, DeMar wrote, "I was a bit confused when Pat Robertson claimed that he doesn't 'agree with Reconstructionism' but does believe that 'Jesus is Lord of all the world . . . of the government, and the church, and business and, hopefully, one day, Lord of the press.' This is the heart and soul of Reconstructionism."

Concluded DeMar, "At the very least, Pat Robertson, as I've always suspected, is an operational Reconstructionist."[15]

Although Robertson shuns the title "Reconstructionist" and says he disagrees with the movement over "endtime" theology, that hasn't stopped him from using books by Rushdoony and North at his Regent University. Also, Herbert Titus, former dean of the university's School of Law, once attended a small, Reconstructionist-affiliated Orthodox Presbyterian church in Oregon and has allowed his essays to appear in Reconstructionist publications. Titus, however, says he is not a Reconstructionist.

More Reconstructionist Connections

Reconstructionist ideas also influenced John Whitehead, founder of the Rutherford Institute, one of the most active of the Religious Right legal aid groups. Whitehead says he is not a Reconstructionist but readily admits to liking some Reconstructionist ideas. Rushdoony wrote the introduction to Whitehead's first book, *The Separation Illusion*, an attack on separation of church and state, and the two appeared at a Washington, D.C., Religious Right conference in 1985.

Also apparently influenced by Rushdoony is John Lofton, a far-right columnist who was fired by the ultra-conservative *Washington Times* newspaper (controlled by the Rev. Sun Myung Moon and his controversial Unification Church). Lofton, who now puts out an anti-separationist newsletter, occasionally writes columns for Rushdoony's Chalcedon Foundation.

What do these spider web-like connections mean? How concerned should we be about Christian Reconstructionists?

To begin with, *any* group that advocates policies as radical as the Reconstructionist agenda should be watched. Like the U.S. neo-Nazi groups, the Reconstructionists are a potentially dangerous force that cannot be ignored just because they are currently scarier on paper than in real life.

At the same time, Americans must be cognizant of where the real danger lies. There is very little threat that Reconstructionists will seize power next week and institute their odd ideas. Rather, as has been pointed out, the real danger lies in the influence they have had on some churches.

With that thought in mind, the best strategy for fighting Reconstructionism is simply a strong defense of separation of church and state. The Reconstructionist agenda will not appeal to any church leader who sees the value in maintaining a healthy distance between church and state. It needs to be said time and time again, therefore, that separation protects churches and helps them grow. If American church leaders lose sight of this, they are open to being tempted to embrace portions of the Reconstructionist agenda. They won't become theonomists overnight, but they might sign up with a Pat Robertson crusade or agree to show an anti-separationist video at church. Those types of small victories are what the Reconstructionists want—for now.

Fighting the Reconstructionists

The fight against Reconstructionism must be two-pronged. Many mainstream Christian bodies find theonomistic teachings abhorrent and completely anti-biblical. These organizations must take the lead in working to persuade their brethren in other theological camps not to fall under the sway of Rushdoony and company.

At the same time, secular opponents of Reconstructionism must come to the forefront. While religious communities wage war against Reconstructionism from a theological perspective, secular groups can attack it from a public policy angle. The majority of Americans do not favor executing children for any reason. Nor do most Americans, even those who believe that the sexual revolution has gone too far, want to see adulterers or fornicators dragged into the streets and stoned.

Americans, by and large, do not believe that prosecuting people for blasphemy is a good idea. They also do not want to see the government making judgments about which religious beliefs are "true" and warrant state support and which are "false" and warrant state persecution.

Some Reconstructionists are now making feeble attempts to portray themselves as "moderates" on the religious scene, but few are fooled by this stance. Reconstructionists are radicals who would impose a religious state on America. They want to line those who disagree with them up against a wall and stone them to death. They favor mandatory tithing to churches and executions for blasphemy. No matter how one tries to recast it, this is what Reconstructionism is about. These are not moderate positions, and they are not positions that Americans, even conservative Americans, want to see implemented.

Exposing these facts should be enough to cut Reconstructionism off at the knees. If the past is any guide, it will do exactly that. In 1990 *Mother Jones* magazine, a journal of liberal opinion, exposed the theonomistic leanings of the Coalition on Revival. Almost immediately members of the mainstream Religious Right who had been flirting with the group began deserting it. When the dust settled, Religious Right luminaries Beverly LaHaye, Robert Dugan, Donald Wildmon, and others had jumped ship.

Unlike the Reconstructionists, COR does not advocate stoning or the death penalty for a variety of "religious crimes." Their agenda is much more vague, but portions of it are extremist enough to weaken its support once it is examined under the harsh light of media scrutiny. If COR's stated goals are radical enough to cause desertions like this, the even more extreme agenda of the Reconstructionists should be more than enough to scare away any religious leaders tempted to flirt with the philosophy and still be taken seriously in the American religious community.

Most Reconstructionists can't be argued with or persuaded to return to the more sane folds of American theology. Separationists shouldn't waste too much time on efforts like that. Rather, the emphasis should be on containing the spread of Reconstructionism and isolating it to where it belongs—the lunatic fringe of extreme right-wing Christianity. If successful, this strategy will eventually relegate Reconstructionism to the long list of forgotten ideas in American religious history.

As recently as thirty years ago some misguided religious leaders in America still preached that segregation of the races was "God's plan." It took a while, but eventually religious leaders came to realize that no worthwhile church would deny membership to anyone based on race or ethnic heritage. Today there are still faith groups that preach racism, but they are few in number and almost universally scorned in the United States. Separationists must work diligently to make sure that the same fate awaits the Reconstructionists.

American theology is diverse. Some Americans are deeply devout, others are completely irreligious. Such diversity keeps our country vigorous in spirit. It also guarantees, unfortunately, that certain strains of religious fanaticism will always be with us. Religious extremists will never hesitate to equate their twisted political and social notions with the word of God. This is their right in a free society.

But while these groups may have the right to exist, they have no right to demand to be taken seriously by the American people. They are, in fact, fair game for exposure and condemnation. In the end, these two powerful weapons may be all we need to spare America the tyranny of the Reconstructionists.

Notes

1. Rob Boston, "Thy Kingdom Come," *Church & State* 41(September 1988): 6-12.

2. Ibid., 7-8.

3. Rousas John Rushdoony, *The Institutes of Biblical Law* (Vallecito, CA: Ross House, 1973), 236.

4. Boston, 7.

5. H. Wayne House and Thomas D. Ice, *Dominion Theology: Blessing or Curse?* (Portland, OR: Multnomah Press), 73-74.

6. Rousas John Rushdoony, *Law and Society* (Vallecito, CA: Ross House, 1986), 160.

7. Boston, 10.

8. Fred Clarkson, "HardCOR," *Church & State* 44 (January 1991): 9-12.

9. Clarkson, 11.

10. Frederick Clarkson, "Divine Discipline," *Church & State* 45(March 1992): 13-14.

11. Clarkson, "HardCOR," 11.

12. "Cardinal Teams Up With Fundamentalist Radical To Censor Movies, TV," *Church & State* 45(March 1992): 19.

13. Boston, 9.

14. "Robertson Bullish On Family Channel, UPI," *Christianity Today* (June 22, 1992): 51-52.

15. Gary DeMar, "Letters," *Christianity Today* (August 17, 1992): 10.

10

Suggestions for the
Separationist Citizen Activist

In 1990 a series of short books with titles like *50 Things You Can Do To Save The Earth* and *50 Things You Can Do To Protect Animals* became popular among some cause-oriented Americans. The idea was to give average citizens suggestions for making a difference in the cause of their choice. *Save The Earth*, for example, contained suggestions for home recycling among other things.

While I don't have 50 things you can do to save separation of church and state, I do have a few ideas on how readers can best safeguard that vital principle. If separation is to survive, it will take a concerted effort on the part of ordinary Americans. In this chapter, I will try to share some suggestions for spearheading that type of involvement.

Keeping Informed

The first thing to remember is that information is vital. You have to know what's going on in your community, the nation, and the world. Americans are busier today than they have ever been according to some commentators who watch work trends, but everybody should try to find time to read a daily newspaper. You certainly don't have to read every story all the way through, but by at least skimming the headlines and spot reading some pieces you can keep up with what's happening. Follow up with the local and network evening news if you can.

Newspapers and TV news will give you general information, but when it comes to church-state issues you'll need something more specific. One way to keep up on the current church-state issues is through *Church & State* magazine, the monthly publication of Americans United for Separation of Church and State. This magazine is the only journal of its type published in the country—a specialty publication that provides news and analysis of the full range of church-state issues. Through guest columns and editorials, the journal provides activists with cogent arguments that make the case for separation.

There are other organizations that work on church-state issues that can serve as outlets for information. The American Civil Liberties Union, for example, is well known for its church-state legal work, although the group works on a whole range of additional civil liberties concerns. Aside from the ACLU, a variety of groups affiliated with religious denominations keep an eye on the church-state scene. Many Baptists belong to the Baptist Joint Committee on Public Affairs, based in Washington, and read the BJC's publication *Report from the Capital*. (See appendix 4 for information on how to obtain these publications.)

The American Jewish Committee and the American Jewish Congress also do excellent church-state work and occasionally issue bulletins on church-state topics. The Anti-Defamation League of B'nai B'rith is another good source. The Seventh-day Adventist Church maintains a religious liberty office and publishes *Liberty* magazine, which centers on religious freedom issues.

With all of these resources around, there is really no excuse for not keeping informed.

Grassroots Activism

However, watching the national scene is not enough. Separationists must bring their battle down to the local level. The Religious Right has done this with great success, and separationists must learn to parrot their model. Across the country, thousands of Religious Right extremists are pressuring school officials to ban books, asking city councils to introduce sectarian proclamations, and running for local office, among other things. Separationists need to counter each and every one of these actions.

Local elections are extremely important, and church-state separation activists should keep an eye on all of them, no matter how insignificant the office may seem. Because voter turnout in local races is often low, Religious Right activists have enjoyed great success in some parts of the country getting people elected to school boards as well as to city and county councils. Once seated, these people create untold mischief.

The only way to combat these types of tactics is to fight back by exposing Religious Right candidates. Attend voter forums and ask candidates some pointed questions. Be wary of any candidate who refuses to attend voters' forums. A favorite tactic of the Religious Right is running "stealth candidates" who make few public appearances. They win by exploiting public apathy.

Encourage the local press to do full reports on all candidates for local office and list where they stand on a variety of issues. Every candidate for school board, for example, should be required to explain his or her position on two education-related church-state issues—vouchers and state-sponsored religious exercises in public schools.

In small and medium-sized towns, editors and reporters at local papers or radio stations are often quite approachable and open to ideas from readers or listeners. Suggestions for regular "candidate profiles" can bear great fruit. Encourage the local press to investigate candidates who have Religious Right ties. The public has a right to know if a candidate for the school board is in the pocket of Pat Robertson.

Remember, the Religious Right can win only as long as it is able to keep its agenda in the dark. Experience has shown time and time again that when Religious Right candidates are exposed for the extremists that they are, they usually lose. Religious Right candidates often depend on the votes of a few large fundamentalist churches as their support base. An informed electorate from the general population can often beat them, but only if people know what is going on and care enough to vote.

Public Outreach

Separationists must also step up their public outreach efforts. Friends of separation of church and state who have a flair for writing might want to consider letters to the editor. Again, this strategy takes a page from the Religious Right's own play book: Their activists have flooded daily and weekly papers across the country with anti-separationist propaganda. Many of the letters are similar, even though they come from disparate geographical areas. Obviously, they are coming from a central source, most likely a slick magazine published by some Religious Right outfit.

Don't hesitate to respond to such letters. If you are unsure of your writing skills, ask a friend or family member who enjoys writing to help you get your ideas in order. Don't get overly concerned about your writing abilities. You don't have to be a best-selling novelist to write a letter to the editor; you simply need a statement that is as concise and as easy to read as possible.

Remember, letters to the editor are some of the most-read items in a newspaper. A pro-separation message in this forum can reach tens of thousands of readers.

For letter writers, here is some specific advice:

• Most newspapers and magazines have a letters policy that is usually printed on the editorial or letters page. Read it and learn the paper's rules before you write. Some newspapers, for instance, limit the length of letters or the number that a reader can submit in a month. Few papers print anonymous letters, so always be willing to provide your name, address, and telephone number for verification purposes.

• In general, shorter letters are better. They stand a better chance of being published and read. Use short, direct sentences in the active voice. If you are unsure of your writing skills, go to a book store and pick up a self-help book on better writing to get some tips.

• Strive to be polite. When responding to an anti-separationist letter or editorial, resist the temptation to engage in name calling or vituperation. Such letters are rarely printed, and if they are they can damage your credibility.

• Brush up on your grammar, and no matter how good your spelling is, try to find someone to proofread your letter before you mail it.

Despite your best efforts, little mistakes can get by you. (Of course, it won't be a disaster if you do make a grammatical error. Chances are it will be corrected by the newspaper's editors.)

• Mail responses promptly, the same day or the next if possible. You might want to ask if the paper accepts letter by fax machine. The longer you wait, the less timely the issue becomes and the smaller your chances of seeing the letter in print.

• Check your letter for accuracy. If you are in doubt about any fact, look it up for confirmation in a reliable source. Be prepared to back up anything you say in your letter; you may be challenged by another letter writer. If you make a factual error, you will be vulnerable to attack by other letter writers. If in doubt, leave it out.

Speaking of accuracy, it is important to remember that Religious Right activists are often quite loose with the "facts" when they write about church and state. Mistakes and distortions are common because much misinformation about separation of church and state circulates in the Religious Right. Many fundamentalists simply accept these distortions as gospel and don't bother to check them for accuracy. The high rate of errors gives church-state separationists an excellent opportunity to respond to set the record straight.

For example, Religious Right activists are fond of claiming that Communists in the Soviet Union invented separation of church and state.[1] This claim is patently untrue, and its frequent appearance in print provides separationists with an almost guaranteed letter placement to correct the misstatement. Keep a church-state resource handy to attack the Religious Right's historical errors and distortions. (See appendix 1 for a list of the Religious Right's most common myths about church-state separation and the responses to them. Feel free to use this material—indeed anything in this book—when responding to the Religious Right.)

Local Watchdog Groups

Work through the media need not be done alone. Letters to the editor can be handled by a special committee of a local separationist organization. It is vital that citizens form such groups across the country to counter existing anti-separationist Religious Right groups that have local chapters in large and small communities all over the nation. As the church-state controversy escalates, separationists must be willing to go head to head with the Religious Right in every town.

Many people are concerned about the inroads the Religious Right has made in society in the past fifteen years, and increasingly in various parts of the country activists are coming together to counter extremist forces. Where are these people found? In churches, fraternal organizations, social groups, and the like. Mainline religious leaders may be interested in such an effort. Enlist local teachers and school administrators in the effort to protect the religious neutrality of public education and combat religiously based censorship. Talk to your friends, neighbors and family members. Post notices in community bulletin boards and public places. Look into running free announcements on local cable television access channels.

Exploit everything local Religious Right activists do and turn their activities around to your own advantage. If the local chapter of Pat Robertson's Christian Coalition attacks a book used in the local public school, study the book and consider forming a committee to defend it. Use that incident as a starting point to form a separationist group that, as part of its activities, keeps an eye on the local Christian Coalition unit.

If Citizens for Excellence in Education fronts a candidate for the school board, expose her and use the opportunity to inform the public about CEE's radical agenda. Then form a group to keep an eye on future CEE activities and promote church-state separation.

Handling Church-State Problems

Despite your best efforts to keep an eye on church-state developments in your community, conflict may still erupt in your local public school or city hall. What should you do if a situation arises in your community? How do you handle it? Can one person or a small group of citizens make a difference?

The key to dealing with church-state controversy at a local level is assessing frankly what you are up against and determining what avenues of solution are open to you. You must choose your battles carefully and be patient and polite—but tenacious. If you keep at it, in many cases you can win.

Church-state problems come in varying degrees of intensity. Your first task is to determine exactly what you have on your hands. Assume, for example, that your local city council decides to pass a resolution recognizing the International Year of the Bible and calls on all citizens to read the Bible. While protesting this action is certainly appropriate—after all, it is no business of the city to tell citizens what religious texts to consult—you will probably have to accept the fact that, once your protest is on record, you may not be able to do much else about this. Courts have looked at resolutions like the one described above in the past and ruled that since they are symbolic and don't have the force of law, they pass constitutional muster. In my assessment that opinion is wrong, but this battle may be lost and it's often not worth your time and money to go into court over such a matter.

If you have any doubts about the constitutionality of the matter before you, seek a professional opinion. Write to Americans United for Separation of Church and State, the state branch of the ACLU or another separationist organization. Officials at these groups can give you a legal opinion and may be able to cite case law from similar situations that have occurred before. Find out if you are standing on firm constitutional ground before you complain.

Of course, there are other types of arguments you can make aside from a constitutional one. In the case of the resolution, you could point out that the wording excludes non-Christians and makes members of religious minorities feel like outsiders. It is insensitive and inappropriate. An argument like this, made directly to the city council, may win you enough support to sink the resolution. Members of city council, after all, usually take great pains to avoid alienating any member of their constituency.

But what if the issue is not ambiguous and looks to be a clear violation of separation of church and state? What should you do then? As an example, assume that instead of a city council issuing a sectarian proclamation, the problem centers around a public school teacher who is preaching to seventh grade students during math class and reading to them from the Bible in an effort to encourage them to convert to his religion. (Cases like this have actually happened.) Is this situation worth contesting in court if necessary?

Definitely. Such actions are absolutely unconstitutional and have in fact been struck down by the courts. In fact, courts have held that public school officials are within their rights to fire teachers who refuse to stop preaching to students. What's more, if school officials knowingly persist in breaking the law concerning school prayer, they can be held personally responsible for court costs and any damages assessed by the courts.

Chain of Command

Naturally you don't want to run into court right off the bat. Once you have determined the scope of what you're up against, you should first try other ways to solve the problem.

It may be helpful to imagine the school and government officials who will be involved in this case as a pyramid or chain of command. At the bottom of the pyramid or the beginning of the chain rests the teacher involved. At the very top is the court system. You must start your way at the bottom and work your way up until the problem is resolved at some level.

In the case of our hypothetical example, you should begin with the teacher. Explain that his activities are inappropriate. Tell him that you, as the parent, are solely responsible for your child's religious upbringing. Say you do not want your child exposed to religious beliefs at school that conflict with whatever religious or philosophical system the child is trained under at home. Make it clear to the teacher that you are willing to discuss this matter with the principal if his activities do not cease at once.

If that doesn't work, follow up on what you told the teacher and go to the principal. Do not assume a conspiracy exists if there is no evidence of one. School officials may not be aware that the teacher is proselytizing. A polite letter and complaint listing specific instances to the principal and outlining your discussion with the teacher (with a copy forwarded to the superintendent) may clear up the problem. If you live in a small community and can approach the principal directly for a face-to-face discussion, all the better. But still send a letter just to get your case in writing. Keep a copy of every letter you send. Date everything. Make it clear in your letter that you expect a response.

If it appears that school officials are aware of the situation but will not do anything about it or have in fact encouraged the teacher's actions, go over their heads. Try the superintendent first, but if that goes nowhere write to the president of the school board and send copies to all the members. If there is still no action, request an opportunity to address the board about the issue. Let the school board know that illegal activities are going on.

Before you contact the school board it may be helpful to have a preliminary consultation with a watchdog group such as Americans United for Separation of Church and State or the ACLU. Tell them that at this stage you want to try to handle the matter on your own and request copies of any information they can send you about similar situations that may have been litigated in the past. Tell them you are looking to buttress your argument. If officials at the group can cite a court case for you, mention it in your letter to the school board. That way, they know you've done your homework and are serious about the complaint.

When you contact the cause organization let them know you might be calling back later for more help. Get the name of a contact to deal with and keep a careful record of when you called and what was discussed for your growing file.

If your protest to the school board fails, write to the education officials in the capital of your state. Explain the situation fully and send copies of all of the correspondence that has been generated so far. You might want to call first and get the name of the staffer who handles legal affairs. It might be helpful to follow up with a telephone call in a few weeks if you haven't heard anything. State education departments have staff attorneys who will examine claims and look for constitutional violations. In many cases, they will contact the school officials and order them to cease and desist. In extreme cases, state officials will threaten to withhold funding until a situation is corrected.

By this time you might have found some allies in your struggle. If other parents are upset about the activity, have them join your cause with letters of their own. Keep up the pressure. Remember, an individual is easy to ignore, but a group is not. There is strength in numbers.

If all of this fails, if you've contacted everyone from the principal to the director of the state department of education and still have had no satisfaction, it is time to call on the professionals again. Contact Americans United, the local affiliate of the ACLU, or another separationist group, and explain the situation, again sending copies of all of the relevant documentation.

Sometimes a letter from an activist group can result in positive change. But if all else fails litigation may be necessary. If the watchdog group is willing to bring suit on your behalf, be sure to let school personnel know. At the prospect of going to court, many public school officials will back down and stop unconstitutional activities. They don't want to waste scarce resources fighting court battles they know they cannot win.

If you decide to enter a church-state fight, you must be prepared for criticism. Lots of people in your community will disagree with what you are doing, and some will want to let you know about that. You can look forward to being attacked in the letters to the editor columns of the local paper as well as receiving hate mail and unpleasant, maybe even obscene, phone calls. Consider changing to an unlisted number or using an answering machine to screen your calls. Remember, making harassing telephone calls is a crime, and if the problem gets especially bad, contact the phone company and the police. Likewise with mail. If the letters threaten your life, contact postal authorities.

The situation may not get this out of hand. While many people who have pursued church-state litigation have been harassed, others have been ignored. Simply be prepared for some ugliness that may come your way. Church-state disputes seem to bring out the worst in some people.

Accept the fact that your protest will probably find its way to the local media. News like this travels fast, especially in small towns. Consider going to the media first. If your cause is publicized and you are open and sincere about your complaint, it may help you find supporters or bring the newspaper's editorial staff over to your side. Be accessible to reporters and state your case as articulately as possible. Also, dealing with reporters directly greatly enhances the chances of your side being told accurately. Don't let the media piece together your story from secondary sources.

If you are publicity shy, explore the possibility of filing an anonymous lawsuit. Quite frankly, however, this ploy will probably not work. Although some church-state complaints are filed anonymously, people have a way of finding out who is behind them in many cases. Your name will be on many documents, such as the letters you sent to school officials. Don't expect to remain anonymous, especially in a small town.

While this model has used a church-state problem in a public school as its example, I hope you can see how it would translate into other areas of government. For instance, if the city council is considering an action that you believe is a violation of church-state separation, start your protest with the council member who made the recommendation and move up from there. Strive to be as open and courteous as possible, and don't threaten a lawsuit right at the beginning. You may be surprised what an open, friendly dialogue can do for you.

Taking a Proactive Stance

With the Religious Right becoming more and more active, local separationist groups must be prepared to not only initiate lawsuits if necessary but fend off those brought by anti-separationists. The number of Religious Right groups that litigate has skyrocketed in recent years. In some cases, these groups believe they can harass and bully local officials into doing things their way with threats of costly lawsuits. Separationist forces need to be on the lookout at all times for this deplorable tactic and must be ready to defend governmental officials if necessary.

For example, in 1990 a group of parents in Sioux Falls, South Dakota, read shrill and distorted reports from the Religious Right group Focus on the Family about a public school reading series called "Impressions" and promptly demanded the removal of the books from the local school system.

The parents, backed by Focus on the Family and other outside Religious Right groups, asserted that the books taught witchcraft because some of the stories in the series are fairy tales about magical characters— the types of stories that pervade children's literature.

Thanks to distortions by the Religious Right, the parents were able to collect 8,000 signatures on a petition calling for the removal of the books. Alarmed, a local group arose to oppose the Religious Right and swung into action.

In short order, a counter-Religious Right group was functioning that told the real story about Impressions. Led by concerned parents Kathy English and Kristi Devick-Beek, the separationist group went so far as to convinced a local advertising firm to make a pro-Impressions video. They lined up psychologists and educators to speak in favor of the books and organized a speakers' bureau to reach an understandably confused public. When a school board textbook review committee met to take public testimony on the matter, fifty pro-Impressions witnesses were waiting to speak. The books stayed.

Had the separationist forces remained apathetic, Focus on the Family might have triumphed in Sioux Falls. To avert controversy or avoid a costly legal battle, the school board might have quietly removed the books and substituted readers that children don't find as interesting. As it turned out, the Religious Right left town defeated.

Separationists must be constantly on the lookout for Religious Right activity. To do this most effectively, first find out if there are local chapters of the major Religious Right organizations operating in your town. Simply write to the organizations (see appendix 3 for names and addresses) and ask them. Tell them you are a concerned parent and would like to know. There is nothing sneaky or dishonest about this. It's the truth, after all!

If there are chapters of national Religious Right groups operating in your community, find out what they are up to by attending their public meetings. Don't try to disrupt their activities or argue with them. Simply gather what useful information you can. Keep a low profile. If they have a mailing list, get on it. To fight these people effectively, you must first know what they are doing.

Mailings from national Religious Right groups can also be helpful. Many of these groups will put you on their list for free, at least for a few months. A nominal donation may be required to keep you on the list and receiving materials. If the thought of contributing even one dime to a Religious Right group turns your stomach, have another separationist join up once your materials stop coming. In turn, a third confederate can sign up after that. By rotating requests, a small circle of people can keep the stuff coming indefinitely.

Don't hesitate to request all the free material you can from Religious Right groups. Most of them have large budgets and can easily afford the cost of mailing materials. By contrast, most separationist groups operate on tight budgets. If you request material from them, a small donation to offset mailing and handling costs helps a lot.

The Religious Right is fond of portraying the current struggle over church and state as a war. In their books and materials, they use battlefield imagery to stir up their supporters in an effort to make them believe they are part of some grand design—most often a war to crush "humanism" or "Satan."

In some respects they are correct about the war metaphor. In this case, your "enemy" is the Religious Right. This "enemy" is cunning and well organized. Do not underestimate its strength. And remember, this "enemy" is not above using "guerilla warfare," that is, sneaky and underhanded tactics done in the dark of night, away from the glare of public view, to achieve its aims. If you are going to take on the Religious Right, you have to be prepared for just about anything. Personal attacks are common. You will be vilified as a "secular humanist," "atheist," "pagan" or called "anti-God." You can take solace in remembering that hysterical broadsides like this only expose the Religious Right for the mean-spirited movement that it so often is.

Monitoring the Religious Right and keeping an eye on the local school board are important, but some activists might want to take things a step farther. Some people might want to consider running for local office themselves. True, a seat on the local school board or city council can take up a lot of a person's free time, but obviously someone must be willing to make the sacrifices necessary to ensure good government free from sectarian control.

In some small towns, seats on local governance boards go unfilled because no one wants to run. This is the type of power vacuum the Religious Right looks for. If voters are apathetic and decent candidates don't run, that only makes the Religious Right's job all the easier. Even if you don't run yourself, you must get involved in politics at the local level, including helping locate good candidates who will reject the oppressive agenda of the Religious Right. Voters need a good alternative if they are to reject extremism.

Support from Religious Groups

Before closing this chapter, there is one factor about citizen action that must be discussed—participation of churches and other religious groups in the fight against the Religious Right.

Only a small segment of the American religious community opposes church-state separation. Most church leaders are sophisticated enough to realize that separation has been a great boon to religion, a principle that enables various religious bodies to grow and prosper and freely take their messages to the people.

Encourage these people to join your side. Contact leaders of the mainstream religious groups in your community. Let them know what you are doing and ask for help. Don't let sectarian differences be a barrier to cooperation. Remember, the battle to preserve separation of church and state benefits everyone—from the deeply devout to the committed atheist. Don't leave anyone who is willing to help out of your coalition. Diversity is a great strength. It shows that your movement is not narrowly focused by sectarian concerns, as Religious Right pressure groups often are. Religious diversity adds to your credibility and can increase your numbers by showing people that yours is a truly open, diverse and democratic movement committed to the principles that exemplify American freedoms.

Most Americans don't agree with the Religious Right. In fact, polls have continually shown that Americans express a great deal of apprehension over the agenda of Religious Right organizations. The only way they can win is if public apathy remains high. Overcoming that apathy and rousing people to action is undoubtedly the greatest challenge separationists face today.

Note

1. David Barton, *The Myth of Separation* (Aledo, TX: WallBuilders Press, 1989), 45.

11

Whither Separation?

In 1988 the Williamsburg Charter Foundation released the results of a public opinion poll it had commissioned to determine Americans' views on a variety of church-state issues.

The results uncovered a curious ambivalence over the meaning of separation of church and state in the minds of the public. A majority said they favored retaining the wall of separation between church and state, but that didn't stop large numbers from also backing various schemes of state-supported religion that would undermine that wall.[1]

Asked whether they favored "a high wall of separation between church and state" or "special steps" by the government to "protect the Judeo-Christian heritage," 51 percent opted for the wall, and 32 percent favored the special steps. The rest were unsure.

But elsewhere in the survey, 52 percent said they favored government supporting all religions on an equal basis, a concept that does not square with church-state separation. Forty-four percent said government should not aid religion at all.

Things quickly ran downhill from there as the survey examined specific church-state issues. Large majorities saw no problem with prayers before public school events or meetings of governmental bodies. Eighty percent said the government should be allowed to erect creches and menorahs on public property.

There was bad news for religious free exercise, too. Sixty-five percent agreed that it should be against the law for "unusual religious cults to try to convert teenagers." Another 57 percent said the FBI should "keep a close watch on new religious cults." Forty percent backed laws making it illegal for preachers to ask for money on television.

Perhaps most discouragingly, the survey unveiled widespread ignorance about the Constitution and the First Amendment. Only 33 percent of all Americans knew that religious liberty is guaranteed by the First Amendment. Thirty percent were not even aware that religious freedom is mentioned in the Constitution at all!

Over the years, other public opinion polls have reported similar findings. In some surveys, support for "the wall" shoots up as high as 75 percent. That's a nice high number, but it still means that 25 percent, a full quarter of our people, don't agree with the concept of separation of church and state. What system, it is fair to ask, are these people prepared to substitute instead? A merger of church and state? Which church? By what mechanism? Unfortunately, public opinion polls are not the proper venue to pose questions like this. Therefore, except for the rantings of extremists like Christian Reconstructionists, who suggest a state based on Old Testament law, the questions remain unanswered and we don't know what this 25 percent would do.

Perhaps more disturbing than the 25 percent who reject separation outright are the large numbers who say they endorse the practice of church-state separation in theory but reject it in reality. When asked, most people will say they support church-state separation. Yet many polls also show majorities backing things like school-sponsored religious exercises and government promotion of religion.[2]

The results are all the more troubling when compared with surveys that seek to determine the depth of Americans' knowledge on issues pertaining to the Bill of Rights. As we have seen, the outcome is all too often discouraging. Some years ago, a survey was taken asking respondents to explain what the Bill of Rights is. Many did not know that it is simply the first ten amendments to the Constitution.

Manifestations of this ignorance that frequently pop up in the mass media are fully exploited by the Religious Right. For instance, the Religious Right plays on the low level of knowledge among Americans when it argues that the United States was founded as a "Christian nation."

As past chapters indicated, Religious Right groups point to documents like the Northwest Ordinance or even more obscure proclamations that contain religious references. "See!" they say. "This proves America was meant to be Christian!"

What the Religious Right doesn't tell people, and what, tragically, many Americans apparently don't know, is that when it comes to determining what the laws of the United States mean, the only document that matters is the Constitution. The Constitution, a completely secular document, contains no references to God, Jesus or Christianity. The Religious Right's constant appeals to documents like the Declaration of Independence, which contains a deistic reference to "the Creator," cloud the issue and makes some people believe their rights spring from these other documents. They don't. As important as those other documents are to history, the rights of all Americans are ultimately traced to the Constitution and its amendments, specifically the Bill of Rights. When we talk about religious freedom and separation of church and state, therefore, only one document matters—the Constitution.

In light of this situation—growing hostility to Jefferson's wall and widespread ignorance about the development and meaning of the concept of separation of church and state—it's fair to ask if the idea can survive in the United States.

The short answer is that it is highly likely that the United States will always at least claim to operate under a system of separation of church and state. The First Amendment's religion clauses will not be altered outright or done away with. No official church will be established. No one will ever be forced to participate in religious services against his or her will.

The much harder question is determining whether or not the United States will ever adopt a system whereby separation of church and state exists more or less in name only. Under such a system, religion would receive government support for its projects and government would promote religious belief at various turns. Separation of church and state would be merely a slogan held over from days gone by.

How likely is this to happen? The disturbing answer is that we may be well on the way to it. And, if certain Supreme Court justices had their way, we would already have such a system.

A few examples may be helpful to understand what type of system may be evolving in the United States. Remember, overt forms of church-state union are never likely to prosper in the United States. In Germany, the government deducts money from each worker's wages and turns it over to the religious group of the worker's choosing. Anyone seeking to opt out of the system must appear before a government official and sign a form stating that, for example, he or she is an atheist. A system like this will probably never develop in America. But what's more likely is no better and may in fact be worse. Consider this: Under the various parochiaid plans currently being put forth around the country, tax money collected from all citizens is turned over to a select few religious groups. There is no opt-out mechanism, and the individual taxpayer can do nothing to keep his or her hard-earned dollars from flowing into church coffers. Under such a system, all Americans would pay church taxes.

In Germany, the government is at least up front about what it is doing and offers an out—albeit an inconvenient one—for those who absolutely refuse to participate. In our possible United States of the future, no such out will exist to save conscientious objectors from religious taxes. Everyone will have to participate.

In some Latin American nations, the doctrines of the Roman Catholic Church are written into secular law. For example, divorce and abortion may be outlawed. In some cases, provisions in the law explicitly state that the regulations stem from the country's close ties to Catholicism. Some nations still have special agreements, *concordats*, with the Vatican that give the church the right to make public policy.

In the United States, we will not likely see the day when religious leaders stand beside the president and members of Congress signing concordats or special agreements that provide for church-state union. But again, what we might get won't be much better. Rather than seek special favors through treaties, sectarian special interests will simply lobby lawmakers to have their views on social issues written into law, as many are doing now. Courts will later uphold the laws as valid, arguing that they serve some manufactured secular interest of the government.

How a given church's views on social policy get written into law is irrelevant to the church in question. Be it by concordat or lobbying, the result is the same: Citizens are living under laws drafted by religious groups that reflect the beliefs and practices of those groups. The church is telling the state what to do. In America nothing as explicit as a concordat will probably ever exist, but the practical equivalent of this type of agreement very well might.

The tragedy is that even as these types of events unfold, Americans will continue to insist that they have all the protections listed in their Constitution, long after they have in fact been eviscerated. In recent years, civil liberties attorneys have argued that the Fourth Amendment, which guards against "unreasonable searches and seizures" has been so narrowly construed by the courts that it is rapidly losing any meaning. The same thing could happen to separation of church and state. The concept will remain enshrined in our Constitution and praised by our politicians, but it will have been stripped of all meaning by the courts.

Is this bleak scenario inevitable? Not at all. But it can only be blocked if the Religious Right is stopped. And the Religious Right can be stopped only if more Americans understand that the movement is a serious threat to our freedoms.

The only reason anti-separationists have gotten as far as they have is because of apathy. The views held by the Religious Right are minority views. The movement has power only because the Religious Right has successfully filled a vacuum left open by other Americans who have forfeited their voice in public discourse. If enough Americans get back into the game, the tide can easily turn.

Even though public opinion polls might show Americans waffling on specific issues such as crosses on government property, the Religious Right knows that when it comes to the big picture, their view of church-state relations is in the minority. In fact, they crow about it. During a November 1991 meeting of Pat Robertson's Christian Coalition, Guy Rodgers, the group's national field director, boasted that since only 30 percent of the eligible voters actually turn out on election day (half of the 60 percent of eligible adults who are registered), 15 percent of eligible voters determine elections. He urged the Coalition to exploit this apathy.

"We don't have to worry about convincing a majority of Americans to agree with us," Rodgers said. "Most of them are staying home and watching 'Falcon Crest.' "[3]

The message of such rhetoric is clear: Unless Americans wake up, the Religious Right and other anti-separationists will continue to consolidate power.

What can be done to bring about a reversal? Unfortunately, some of the solutions will be difficult to implement because they are tied to certain national trends that have nothing to do with separation of church and state or religious and civil rights.

For instance, one way to cut the Religious Right off at the knees would be to increase voter participation. Estimates vary, but the Religious Right probably accounts for less than 10 percent of the electorate. This small groups wields such power in politics—especially Republican Party politics—because, generally speaking, Religious Right activists are well disciplined and work together. They know how to get out the vote. If more Americans voted, the Religious Right's influence would be diluted. They might even be forced to moderate some of their extreme positions. Getting people to vote in this age of dirty politics and television-driven soundbite campaigns, however, is a challenge.

Another factor that works in favor of the Religious Right is its inordinate degree of influence over the Republican Party. Again, if the Religious Right were stopped here, separation would benefit. It won't be easy. Pat Robertson's political work has focused exclusively on the GOP. He and his forces are seeking to take over the party from the ground up, starting with precincts and moving up to state and national positions. So far, they have enjoyed great success.

In the past, the Republicans have been forced to accommodate the Religious Right because they thought they needed them to win elections. But the 1992 presidential election, in which Democrat Bill Clinton beat Republican incumbent George Bush, caused many GOP officials to reevaluate this strategy. The day after the election, some moderate Republicans began saying publicly that the presence of strident Religious Right activists, with their fire-toned rhetoric during the 1992 campaign, frightened away more votes than it brought in. At this writing, it is too early to tell what will happen, but some type of civil war in the Republican Party between the Religious Right and more moderate forces seems inevitable.

If this fight comes to pass, and if the moderates win, the outcome will go a long way toward boosting respect for church-state separation in America. In the past, the Religious Right has been able to cloak their extremism in the respectable clothing of the GOP. If they lose that cover, the Republicans are bound to become more separationist in the process. With luck, they may return to their roots and embrace separation fully, as many old-style conservatives still do.

A battle like this must obviously be waged by GOP partisans in the political trenches. Other strategies for boosting appreciation of church-state separation would affect Americans across the board. For example, enhancing the study of world and U.S. history in our public schools would help.

World history proves conclusively that unions of church and state are detrimental to freedom. But, tragically, many young people never read about the horrible persecution and tyranny that raged in colonial America and Europe of the Middle Ages. If they are exposed to this material at all, the presentation is often watered down or incomplete.

Educators must realize that history has to be taught "warts and all." It does not honor religion to exclude discussion of the excesses that have occurred in history when governments aligned themselves with religion. A frank assessment of our history as a people will help our youngsters understand and appreciate America's unique system.

And, as the last chapter pointed out, separationists must work with the religious community to boost support for church-state separation among the worshippers in the pews of America's churches, synagogues, and temples. In fundamentalist churches, ministers frequently rail against separation of church and state. Religious leaders in the so-called "liberal," "mainline," and right-thinking evangelical communities should tell their flocks the real story behind religious freedom. Religious groups have been the biggest beneficiaries of separation of church and state. Now that the concept is in trouble, it is up to the leaders of these groups to return the favor by standing up for the idea.

Separationist religious leaders must also keep in mind that it isn't enough to simply talk to their own congregations about the importance of separation. These leaders must be willing to undertake public relations campaigns on behalf of separation in their own communities so everyone can hear the message.

Religious Right activists do not limit their efforts to the already converted. They constantly attack separation on all fronts. They place anti-separation letters in secular newspapers and magazines. They produce videos giving a distorted view of U.S. history and pay to have them aired on local television stations. They buy time on radio stations to broadcast their far-right propaganda. They distribute anti-separationist pamphlets in public places. There is no reason why religious leaders who understand the value of separation should not adopt these strategies to defend church-state separation.

In any given town the evidence that a fundamentalist-inspired anti-separationist campaign is under way is usually obvious. Various types of anti-separationist material begin pouring out of a local church, most of it produced in the headquarters of national groups. As soon as this material begins to appear, moderate religious leaders must respond with an equally potent dose of the truth. If the Religious Right is left unanswered, they win by default.

Religious groups should form coalitions with secular organizations that favor separation—groups like the local Parent-Teacher Association, the Scottish-Rite Masons, area humanist organizations, and so on. The various groups must put their religious and political differences aside and work together toward the common goal of warding off the narrow views of the Religious Right. Anyone or any group willing to play a role should be welcomed as a full partner.

Religious leaders can clear up many common misconceptions about church-state separation. Somehow, separation of church and state has become too closely identified in the public mind with hostility toward religion. When religious figures take the lead in defending the principle, it proves to the public that separation works for everyone, from the deeply devout to the completely non-religious. No one group, religious or atheistic, can claim exclusive rights to benefits meant for all Americans to share. In other words, separation of church and state, like other great constitutional principles, is for everyone. Its protection extends equally to all Americans, regardless of sex, age, race, or creed.

Strategies for saving separation are important, but in the final analysis the concept will not survive unless the American people decide they want it. Right now, we as a nation are failing to make a positive assertion that we do.

Church-state separation has faced difficult tests before. In the early 1960s, when public hysteria over the Supreme Court's school prayer rulings was running high, misguided lawmakers tried to whip up enough outrage to convince Americans that altering the First Amendment was a smart thing to do. Thankfully, enough Americans looked at the situation without the color of fanaticism and brought that misguided drive to a halt. Cooler heads and calmer minds prevailed.

Separation's current test—the prolonged assault on it by the various forces of ignorance and extremism that constitute the Religious Right— may be its toughest. Certainly, this has been its longest test. But the fight is by no means over, and the fact that the concept has held up under such sustained and relentless attack is cause for optimism.

Americans are a people in transition, constantly working to improve their society and the way it treats all its members. Any effort at progress will always face stiff opposition from those who would drag our country back to false images of prior times of perfection. Although these times exist only in the minds of those who conjure them up, their hold on public consciousness can be powerful. The belief that vexing social problems can be solved through the imposition of a rigid code of morality and state-enforced orthodoxy seduces many Americans.

More enlightened Americans pierce through the haze of distortion and remind us of the hard truths. They tell us it's not that easy, that the difficulties we face in society today cannot be washed away with quick fixes like school prayer or a swift injection of church into state. Rather, these problems must be confronted, at the roots, one by one, with a lot of hard work and a spirit of cooperation from a people determined to make things right.

But the latter is not easy to conjure up. Despite our best efforts, it often exceeds our grasp. Unfortunately, the quest for the quick fix goes on. Separation of church and state continues to receive the blame for somehow creating a society that seems at times to be falling apart. Instead it should receive praise for holding together a diverse collection of immigrants and helping to sculpt them into the most successful society the world has ever known.

Will we lose separation of church and state? Maybe. Someday, if our luck runs out, America will keep the notion of church-state separation on parchment paper but stop respecting it in practice. That would be a tragedy.

But even in a disaster of that magnitude, one glimmer of hope can survive. As long as some Americans hold true to the idea and remember the value of church-state separation, the concept can never truly be taken from us. And in that memory—in that spark of hope—the promise of a brighter, freer tomorrow will always flicker.

Notes

1. Albert J. Menendez, "On The Fence About The Wall," *Church & State* 41(March 1988): 13-14.

2. Eugene H. Methvin, "Let Us Pray!" *Readers Digest* (November 1992): 75-78.v

3. Frederick Clarkson, "The Christian Coalition: On The Road To Victory?" *Church & State* 45(January 1992): 4-7.

Appendix 1

Common Myths About
Separation of Church and State

Much of what the Religious Right says about separation of church and state is a distortion of history or, in some cases, simply untrue. Despite the inaccuracy of many of the charges spread by the Religious Right, they frequently appear in the mass media—in letters to the editor, opinion columns, and other forums.

It is important that separationists debunk these myths wherever they appear. Don't think these untruths are harmless. If no one takes the time to set the record straight, well-intentioned Americans who normally have little sympathy for the Religious Right can swallow their propaganda.

Many of these myths are dealt with in other parts of this book. I thought it would be convenient, however, to list them all together in one place for the sake of convenience. Use these responses to challenge the Religious Right's myths wherever they appear. These myths and the responses to them are also available in pamphlet form from Americans United for Separation of Church and State, 8120 Fenton Street, Silver Spring, Maryland 20910.

Separation of church and state is not in the U.S. Constitution.

It is true that the literal phrase "separation of church and state" does not appear in the Constitution, but that does not mean the concept isn't there. The First Amendment says, "Congress shall make no law respecting an establishment of religion or prohibiting the free exercise thereof. . . ."

What does that mean? A little history is helpful: In an 1802 letter to the Danbury Baptist Association of Connecticut, Thomas Jefferson, then president, declared that the American people through the First Amendment had erected a "wall of separation between church and state." (Colonial religious liberty pioneer Roger Williams had used a similar phrase 150 years earlier.)

Jefferson, however, was not the only leading figure of the post-revolutionary period to use the phrase. James Madison, considered to be the father of the Constitution, said in an 1819 letter, "[T]he number, the industry and the morality of the priesthood, and the devotion of the people have been manifestly increased by the total separation of the church from the state." In an earlier, undated essay (probably early 1800s), Madison wrote, "Strongly guarded . . . is the separation between religion and government in the Constitution of the United States."

As the late eminent church-state scholar Leo Pfeffer notes in his book, *Church, State and Freedom,*

> It is true, of course, that the phrase "separation of church and state" does not appear in the Constitution. But it was inevitable that some convenient term should come into existence to verbalize a principle so clearly and widely held by the American people. . . . [T]he right to a fair trial is generally accepted to be a constitutional principle; yet the term "fair trial" is not found in the Constitution. To bring the point even closer home, who would deny that "religious liberty" is a constitutional principle? Yet that phrase too is not in the Constitution. The universal acceptance which all these terms, including "separation of church and state," have received in America would seem to confirm rather than disparage their reality as basic American democratic principles.

Thus, it is entirely appropriate to speak of the "constitutional principle of church-state separation" since that phrase summarizes what the First Amendment's religion clauses do—they separate church and state.

Thomas Jefferson's 1802 letter to the Danbury Baptists was a mere courtesy and should not be regarded as important.

Religious Right activists have tried for decades to make light of Jefferson's "wall of separation" response to the Danbury Baptists, attempting to dismiss it as a hastily written note designed to win the favor of a political constituency. But a glance at the history surrounding the letter shows they are simply wrong.

As church-state scholar Leo Pfeffer points out, Jefferson clearly saw the letter as an opportunity to make a major pronouncement on church and state. Before sending the missive, Jefferson had it reviewed by Levi Lincoln, his attorney general. Jefferson told Lincoln he viewed the response as a way of "sowing useful truths and principles among the people, which might germinate and become rooted among their political tenets."

At the time he wrote the letter, Jefferson was under fire from conservative religious elements who resented his strong stand for full religious liberty. Jefferson saw his response to the Danbury Baptists as an opportunity to clear up his views on church and state. Far from being a mere courtesy, the letter represented a summary of Jefferson's thinking on the purpose and effect of the First Amendment's religion clauses.

Jefferson's Danbury letter has been cited favorably by the Supreme Court many times. In its 1879 *Reynolds v. U.S.* decision the high court said Jefferson's observations "may be accepted almost as an authoritative declaration of the scope and effect of the [First] Amendment." In the court's 1947 *Everson v. Board of Education* decision, Justice Hugo Black wrote, "In the words of Jefferson, the clause against establishment of religion by law was intended to erect 'a wall of separation between church and state.'" It is only in recent times that separation has come under attack by judges in the federal court system who oppose separation of church and state.

Thomas Jefferson later said his "wall of separation" was meant to be "one-directional," meant only to protect the church from incursions by the state.

This statement is an example of one of the Religious Right's more blatant lies. It is impossible to determine where this myth originated, but we do know that it began appearing with increasing frequency in the early 1990s. The phrase "one-directional" often appears in quotation marks to make it appear as if it were lifted from a letter or personal writing of Jefferson's.

Of course, Jefferson said no such thing about his "wall," as any of his biographers or church-state historians will readily testify. Jefferson's writings indicate beyond a doubt that he believed separation would protect both church and state.

Separation of church and state is not an American principle but is found in Article 53 of the constitution of the Soviet Union.

This lie about separation of church and state—still frequently espoused by religious broadcaster Pat Robertson—is perhaps the most offensive to church-state separationists because it attempts to taint a vital American principle with the brush of Communism.

Even a brief review of the facts proves that this statement is nonsense. The modern Soviet state came into being after the Russian Revolution of 1917. The Soviet constitution was rewritten several times, and more recent versions included American-style guarantees of freedom of speech, press, religion, and assembly. These provisions, of course, were never obeyed by the Soviet government.

Article 124 of the country's 1947 constitution has been translated by some scholars to read, "In order to ensure to citizens freedom of conscience, the church in the USSR is separated from the state, and the school from the church. Freedom of religious worship and freedom of anti-religious propaganda is recognized for all citizens."

Since Jefferson coined the phrase "wall of separation between church and state" in 1802, a full *145 years* before the Soviet provision was written, it is obviously incorrect to suggest that the Soviets pioneered the separation principle. If anything, the Soviets stole the concept from the United States. In any case, what the Soviet constitution said about religious freedom has no bearing on U.S. constitutional provisions. The Soviet document also guaranteed free speech (at least on paper), but no one has labeled freedom of expression a Communist idea.

The United States was founded as a Christian nation.

Those who make this assertion confuse the founding of the United States as a political unit with the settlement of North America. It is true that a number of the first Europeans to arrive on our shores were religious dissenters who sought freedom to worship. Many of these people believed they were establishing some type of Christian utopia, and many supported religious liberty only for themselves. Most of the early colonies were theocracies where only those who worshipped according to state orthodoxy were welcome.

Following the Revolutionary War in America, political leaders began to construct the new U.S. government. Although a minority clung to European notions of church-state union, a general consensus emerged that the new country should steer clear of officially established religion. Over time, states with government-favored religions gradually began moving toward separation as well. Massachusetts, the last state to maintain an official religion, disestablished its state church in 1833.

During the Constitutional Convention, a minority faction favored some recognition of Christianity in the Constitution. In a report to Maryland lawmakers, delegate Luther Martin asserted that "in a Christian country, it would be at least decent to hold out some distinction between the professors of Christianity and downright infidelity or paganism." His views were rejected, and the Constitution was adopted as a secular document.

Incidentally, Benjamin Franklin did indeed urge the delegates of the Constitutional Convention of 1787 to open their sessions with morning prayers, as many Religious Right activists point out. However, the Convention, which had been meeting for a month without invocational prayers, did not concur. The Convention's records show that the delegates voted to adjourn rather than debate the issue. The matter was not brought up again when the Convention reconvened.

The Framers wrote the Constitution as a secular document not because they were hostile to Christianity but because they did not want to imply that the new federal government would have any authority to meddle in religion.

Further proof that the founders did not intend the government to be Christian is found in the Treaty of Tripoli, an agreement signed between the United States and the Muslim region of north Africa in 1797 after negotiations conducted under President George Washington. The document, which was approved by the Senate under John Adams, states flatly, "[T]he Government of the United States is not, in any sense, founded on the Christian religion." (The assertion remained a part of the trade agreement for eight years, until the treaty was renegotiated.)

The Supreme Court has declared that the United States is a Christian nation.

In the Supreme Court's 1892 *Holy Trinity Church v. United States* decision Justice David Brewer wrote that "this is a Christian nation." Brewer's statement occurred in *dicta*, a legal term meaning writing that reflects a judge's personal opinion, not an official court pronouncement that sets legally binding precedent.

Historians debate what Brewer meant by the statement, some claiming that he only intended to acknowledge that Christianity has always been a dominant force in American life. Research by Americans United for Separation of Church and State shows that five years after the Trinity ruling, Brewer himself seemed to step away from it in a case dealing with legalized prostitution in New Orleans.

The New Orleans dispute arose when a Methodist church sought an injunction to bar implementation of a city ordinance allowing prostitution in one zone in the city. The Methodists argued the measure would "destroy the morals, peace and good order of the neighborhood."

Citing the *Holy Trinity* decision, church officials insisted that the ordinance encouraged prostitution, an activity inconsistent with Christianity "which the Supreme Court of the United States says is the foundation of our government and the civilization which it has produced. . . ."

Writing for a unanimous court, Brewer completely ignored the church's religious argument and upheld the New Orleans law. Brewer's bypass suggests that he did not mean to assert in the *Holy Trinity* case that the United States should enforce Christianity through its laws.

Brewer himself clarified his views in a book he published on the "Christian nation" concept in 1905. In the volume, Brewer argues that the United States is "Christian" in the sense that many of its traditions are rooted in Christianity. He rejects the notion that the nation's laws should be based on Christianity.

In any case, the *Holy Trinity* decision is a legal anomaly that has been cited by the court only once since. And obviously the opinion of one obscure Supreme Court justice does not amount to an official decree that the United States is a Christian nation. If a Christian republic had been the goal of the Framers, that sentiment would have been included in the Constitution.

The First Amendment's religion clauses were intended only to prevent the establishment of a national church.

If all the Framers wanted to do was ban a national church, they had plenty of opportunities to state exactly that in the First Amendment. In fact, an early draft of the First Amendment read in part, "The civil rights of none shall be abridged on account of religious belief, nor shall any national religion be established. . . ." This draft was rejected. Following extensive debate, the language found in the First Amendment today was settled on.

The historical record indicates that the Framers wanted the First Amendment to ban not only establishment of a single church but also "multiple establishments," that is, a system by which the government funds many religions on an equal basis.

A good overview of the development of the language of the First Amendment is found in scholar John M. Swomley's 1987 book *Religious Liberty and the Secular State*. Swomley shows that during the House of Representatives' debate on the language of the religion clauses, members specifically rejected a version reading, "Congress shall make no law establishing any particular denomination in preference to another. . . ." The Framers wanted to bar *all* religious establishments; they left no room for "non-preferentialism," the view touted by today's accommodationists that government can aid religion as long as it assists all religions equally. (The Senate likewise rejected three versions of the First Amendment that would have permitted non-preferential support for religion.)

The First Amendment was intended to keep the state from interfering with the church, not to bar religious groups from co-opting the government.

Jefferson and Madison held an expansive view of the First Amendment, arguing that church-state separation would protect both religion and government.

Madison specifically feared that a small group of powerful churches would join together and seek establishment or special favors from the government. To prevent this from happening, Madison spoke of the desirability of a "multiplicity of sects" that would guard against government favoritism.

Jefferson and Madison did not see church-state separation as an either/or proposition or argue that one institution needed greater protection than the other. As historian Garry Wills points out in his 1990 book *Under God*, Jefferson believed that no worthy religion would seek the power of the state to coerce belief. In his notes he argued that disestablishment would strengthen religion, holding that it would "oblige its ministers to be industrious [and] exemplary." The state likewise was degraded by an established faith, Jefferson asserted, because establishment made it a partner in a system based on bribery of religion.

Madison also argued that establishment was no friend to religion or the state. He insisted that civil society would be hindered by establishment, charging that attempts to enforce religious belief by law would weaken government. In his 1785 "Memorial and Remonstrance," Madison stated flatly that, "Religion is not helped by establishment, but is hurt by it."

Madalyn Murray O'Hair, an atheist, single-handedly removed God, the Bible and prayer from public schools in 1962.

Atheist leader Madalyn Murray O'Hair played no role in the Supreme Court's school prayer decision of 1962. In the *Engel v. Vitale* case, the U.S. Supreme Court ruled 6-1 (one justice did not participate, and there was a vacancy on the court) against New York's "Regents' prayer," a "non-denominational" prayer state education officials had composed for public schoolchildren to recite. The government-sponsored religious devotion was challenged in court by a group of parents from New Hyde Park. Some were atheists, some believers. O'Hair was not involved in the case at all.

Murray O'Hair's case came one year later. It occurred simultaneously with a case originated by a Philadelphia-area man named Ed Schempp, who challenged mandatory Bible reading in Pennsylvania schools. The two cases reached the Supreme Court at the same time and were consolidated under the name *Abington Township School District v. Schempp.*

The cases were very similar. Like Schempp, Murray O'Hair, a Maryland resident, challenged Bible reading in public schools. She also challenged daily vocal recitation of the Lord's Prayer in schools. The Supreme Court in 1963 ruled 8-1 that devotional Bible reading or other government-sponsored religious activities in public schools are unconstitutional.

The *Engel* and *Schempp* cases were a result of the changing religious landscape of the United States. As religious minorities grew more confident of their rightful place in American society, they came to resent the de facto Protestant flavor in many public schools. Litigation was inevitable. Although Murray O'Hair did play an important role in this controversy, she did not "single-handedly" remove state-sponsored religious exercises from public schools. Other people were involved. Today the controversial Texas atheist serves as a convenient villain for Religious Right propagandists who hate religious liberty and church-state separation.

It is also important to remember that neither of these rulings removed prayer or Bible reading from public schools. Truly voluntary religious exercises in public schools have never been held illegal. The rulings of the early 1960s simply prevented the government, through the public schools, from intervening in sensitive religious matters. Voluntary student-initiated Bible study and prayer club meetings held at school after hours were reaffirmed by the Supreme Court in 1990, when the justices upheld the Equal Access Act, a federal law permitting the practices at public high schools under certain conditions.

The rulings from the 1960s are not hostile toward religion either, as the justices took pains to point out. In the *Abington* decision, Justice Tom Clark wrote for the court majority,

[I]t might well be said that one's education is not complete without a study of comparative religion or the history of religion and its relationship to the advancement of civilization. It certainly may be said that the Bible is worthy of study for its literary and historic qualities. Nothing we have said here indicates that such study of the Bible or of religion, when presented objectively as part of a secular program of education, may not be effected consistently with the First Amendment.

The school prayer rulings contain no references to prior cases or history, and the legal theory in them was invented by the justices on the spot.

This claim is simply false, as anyone who takes the time to read the *Engel* and *Abington* decisions can readily testify. Both decisions contain multiple references to earlier church-state cases as well as an ample review of history. *Abington* especially contains a lengthy (and interesting) review of church-state relations in the colonial period written by Justice William Brennan.

Ever since prayer was removed from schools, public school performance has declined and social ills have increased.

This argument is a common fallacy of logic known as *post hoc ergo propter hoc*, or the assumption that if two events occur in sequence that the first must have caused the second. (The phrase is Latin for "after this, therefore on account of this.")

It is true that some indices of school performance have decreased since 1962, but absolutely no evidence exists linking these developments to the school prayer issue. In fact, the drop has been caused by wholly unrelated factors. SAT scores, for example, are lower today simply because more students from a wider variety of socio-economic backgrounds take the test. In the years preceding 1962, the SAT was taken almost exclusively by upper-class, well-educated students from wealthy backgrounds.

The problems experienced in American society today are due to complex socio-economic factors. It is simplistic thinking to blame every societal problem, from the increase in teenage pregnancies to the escalating divorce rate, on a lack of required prayer in schools.

It should also be pointed out that not all indicators of American society have declined since 1962. Life expectancy, for instance, is up, as is the average standard of living. Impressive medical advances have occurred in the past thirty years, and labor-reducing technologies are commonplace. School prayer advocates are quick to blame every bad thing that has occurred since 1962 on the prayer ruling, but they never mention the positive developments, which, under their premise, must also be a result of the decisions.

The prayer and Bible reading decisions did cause two clear-cut results: Families gained greater religious liberty and the right to decide which religious exercises their children participate in, and church-state separation was strengthened.

School-sponsored prayer and Bible reading took place in all public schools before 1962.

By 1962 several state supreme courts had already removed government-sponsored school prayer and Bible reading from public schools. The Illinois Supreme Court, for example, declared mandatory public school religious exercises unconstitutional in 1910. By the time of the *Engel* decision, public school-sponsored religious exercises were most common in Northeastern and Southern states. Some Western and Midwestern states had already removed the practices.

A 1960 survey by Americans United for Separation of Church and State determined that only five states had required Bible reading laws on the books. Twenty-five states had laws authorizing "optional" Bible reading. Eleven states had declared the practice unconstitutional. The remaining states had no laws on the subject. The trend was clearly running in favor of a voluntary phase-out of these practices.

The Supreme Court has declared that secular humanism is a religion, and secular humanism is the established religion of the public schools.

In a footnote to the Supreme Court's 1961 *Torcaso v. Watkins* decision, Justice Hugo Black wrote, "Among religions in this country which do not teach what would generally be considered a belief in the existence of God is Buddhism, Taoism, Ethical Culture, Secular Humanism, and others." The *Torcaso* case dealt with religious tests for public office; it had nothing to do with public schools. The justice's comment is far from a finding that humanism is being taught in the schools.

The Supreme Court and lower federal courts have ruled repeatedly that public schools and other government agencies may not establish "a religion of secularism" any more than they can promote any other religious viewpoint. The courts have decreed that public schools must be religiously neutral. Government neutrality toward religion is not the same thing as government hostility toward religion. They are synonymous only in the view of Religious Right groups that label as hostility any action by government that does not favor their beliefs.

Furthermore, the percentage of Americans who call themselves secular humanists is very small. It is not possible that such a minuscule group could take control of an entire nation's public school system, one which is highly decentralized and controlled by local school boards chosen by the voters or their representatives. "Secular humanism" is merely a bogeyman the Religious Right uses to attack public education.

Appendix 2

A Short History of the Religious Right

The biggest threat to separation of church and state today comes from the activities of various groups affiliated with the Religious Right. The Religious Right is a political and theological movement that seeks to influence many aspects of American society. Religious Right activists work primarily through the Republican Party to achieve the movement's goals. Many separationists believe the Religious Right's ultimate goal is the establishment of a theocratic government in the United States.

To understand the threat the Religious Right poses to separation of church and state, it is necessary to know a little about the movement's history.

Conservative, politically active theological movements have always existed in American society. In the 19th century, a powerful religious coalition called the National Reform Association pushed a blatantly political agenda that called for mandatory Sunday closing laws, strict liquor control laws, and adding some type of acknowledgement of Christianity to the U.S. Constitution.

The modern incarnation of the Religious Right has its roots in the late 1970s with the rise of Jerry Falwell's Moral Majority. Falwell, a Lynchburg, Virginia, Baptist minister, first made headlines when he called for a moral renewal in America and encouraged born-again Christians of his stripe to become politically active.

These ideas did not originate with Falwell, however. In the 1960s he had preached sermons urging born-again Christians to keep out of politics and focus on winning souls for Christ.[1] Falwell's thinking changed as his national presence grew, however. During the 1976 presidential campaign, Falwell attacked Democrat Jimmy Carter for comments about adultery and lust that the future president had made in an interview with *Playboy* magazine. As the 1980 campaign approached and it became increasingly apparent that Carter was vulnerable, leaders of the New Right—a largely secular movement of conservatives held together by their fervent anti-Communism and belief in free-market economic theory—began casting around for a religious leader who could bring evangelicals into their camp. The man they chose was Jerry Falwell.

The New Right was spearheaded by a collection of Republican Party strategists: direct mail wizard Richard A. Vigeurie; Paul Weyrich, head of the Free Congress Research and Educational Foundation, a conservative think tank; the late Terry Dolan, a far-right fundraiser and media expert; and Howard Phillips, a former official in the Nixon administration.[2] The four, impressed by the power of the evangelical voting bloc in 1976 that helped Carter win, began plotting ways to bring those votes into the Republican column. Carter's liberal views on a variety of social issues such as abortion had angered evangelicals, making the task all the easier.

The nomination of Ronald Reagan, a candidate with New Right sympathies, consolidated the power of the conservative activists in the GOP. All that was needed was a religious leader to win over the evangelical vote.

Weyrich was already working with the Rev. Robert Billings, a former public school principal who by the late 1970s was traveling the country urging Christians to form private schools to escape the "humanism" of the public schools. Weyrich had brought Billings to Washington to do lobbying work but later set him up as the first executive director of the Moral Majority, a group Falwell was to form. It was Weyrich—not Falwell—who actually coined the phrase "Moral Majority."[3]

The group got its start after Weyrich and Phillips traveled to Lynchburg to pitch the concept to Falwell. Weyrich was put on to Falwell by Ed McAteer, a former salesman and Christian activist who knew Falwell from his days on the road.

Although Billings was the ostensible head of the Moral Majority, Falwell took most of the limelight as he conducted rallies and formed chapters in various states. The group set its goals high, focusing on Congress and hoping to exploit its close relationship with the Reagan Administration.

It was important that the movement have a clergyman in the leadership position. While Weyrich belongs to the conservative Eastern Rite Catholic denomination, he is a layman more known for economic policy than social activism. During the Reagan years the Free Congress Foundation and the Heritage Foundation, a separate group Weyrich also helped found, were known primarily for their economic ideas and emphasis on deregulation and tax-cutting to spur business growth. It would have been difficult and time-consuming for Weyrich to achieve credibility in the evangelical community. Falwell already had that credibility. In addition, Weyrich carried baggage in evangelical circles because he had founded Free Congress in 1973 with money from the Adolph Coors brewery fortune.

The early days of the Religious Right were heady ones. With Reagan in the White House and the GOP in control of the Senate, the movement's activists believed their agenda would be enacted. They were soon to grow disillusioned.

Reagan's first appointment to the Supreme Court, Sandra Day O'Connor, turned out to be a moderate on abortion and church-state issues, which infuriated the Religious Right. Worse from their perspective, the Senate in 1986 returned to Democratic control. As years went by with lots of talk but little action from the Reagan White House, Moral Majority leaders and other Religious Right activists came to believe they had been exploited for their votes. The GOP wanted their backing but seemed to have no intention of implementing the Religious Right's agenda. Years later in 1988 Reagan's Attorney General Edwin Meese admitted as much, telling a reporter that the "social issues" dear to the Religious Right had never been a priority of the Reagan administration.

By the end of Reagan's second term, the Religious Right—now represented by a plethora of new organizations other than the Moral Majority—shifted its focus away from Congress and began concentrating on local politics as the most effective way to bring about the changes it desired.

Alongside this development, a variety of Religious Right legal aid groups were formed to press for the groups' agenda in the nation's courts.

The Religious Right's mistake of focusing its energies on Congress and the White House nearly cost Falwell his livelihood. In 1989 he shut down the Moral Majority and announced that he would concentrate instead on Liberty University, the fundamentalist school he founded. Although Falwell remains on the fringes of the national scene today and threatened to reactivate the Moral Majority in the wake of Democrat Bill Clinton's election to the presidency in 1992, his stature and influence pales in comparison to other Religious Right figures who replaced him in the mid 1980s—leaders such as Pat Robertson and Beverly LaHaye of Concerned Women for America.

Today Robertson is the undisputed leader of the Religious Right. His sprawling, multi-faceted operation, based in Virginia Beach, is more sophisticated and high-tech than anything Falwell ever put together, including top-of-the-line television studios, a graduate university, a legal network of volunteer attorneys all over the country, and a formidable grassroots political machine in the form of the Christian Coalition. Although Robertson has great interest in Congress and the White House (as evidenced by his own unsuccessful 1988 run for the GOP nomination), his Christian Coalition spends most of its money and efforts on state and local politics. The group is seeking to take over the Republican Party from the ground up, and they have been extremely successful in some counties and states. The group is a continual headache for GOP moderates striving to return the party to a more centrist position.

Although they could not deliver the White House for George Bush in 1992, the Religious Right today is not to be dismissed. In the late 1980s many misguided journalists and political analysts were quick to proclaim the movement dead. They could not have been more wrong. The Religious Right never died, it simply shifted tactics. Today instead of trying to capture Congress, Religious Right groups, through networks of local chapters and church-based activists, seek to capture school boards and city councils. They are having much more success at the grassroots level than they ever did in the halls of Congress.

The Religious Right's growing strength is indicated by the escalating number of pressure groups the movement has spawned. No dead movement could support such a large number of organizations. Clearly, millions of Americans are still sending checks to these organizations and taking their advice on how to vote.

It is difficult to estimate how many Religious Right groups operate in the United States. If local, regional and single-issue groups are included, the number could run into the hundreds. Some organizations are more well known or active than others. Many of the smaller groups consist merely of a post office box, some letterhead, and a handful of members. But the larger organizations, which often claim hundreds of thousands of members as well as state and local chapters, have plush offices and are flush with cash. They easily have the means to create church-state conflict across the country. These groups are not forces to be taken lightly or simply written off as extremists.

Notes

1. Perry Deane Young, *God's Bullies* (New York: Holt, Rinehart & Winston, 1982), 310-317.
2. Flo Conway and Jim Siegelman, *Holy Terror* (New York: Dell Publishing, 1982), 110-121.
3. Ibid., 114.

Appendix 3

Major Religious Right
Organizations

What follows is a list of some of the larger Religious Right groups along with descriptions. Most of these groups will send literature for free to anyone who asks. However, most clean their mailing lists regularly and quickly drop anyone who does not contribute.

American Family Association
P.O. Drawer 2440
Tupelo, MS 38803

Founded by the Rev. Donald Wildmon, an ultra-conservative United Methodist minister, this group, originally named the National Federation for Decency, started out criticizing popular culture and calling for a clean-up of movies and television. In recent years the organization has stepped up its criticism of separation of church and state and has run several articles in its monthly magazine asserting that the concept is historically dubious.

Alongside these attacks on the wall of separation, the AFA has formed a legal arm and increased its criticism of the public schools, which the group says teach "humanism." The AFA sponsored litigation in the early 1990s challenging the use of the "Impressions" reading series in a public school in Woodlands, California. The AFA claims chapters across the country.

Catholic League for Religious and Civil Rights
1011 First Avenue
New York, NY 10022

Founded by the late Rev. Virgil Blum, the Catholic League exists ostensibly to counteract "anti-Catholic" bias in the media and popular culture. In reality, the group, with an estimated membership of about 30,000, is merely another conservative anti-separationist group that bashes public schools and pushes for various forms of parochiaid. The group has a small legal program that works primarily on the parochial school aid issue; it claims chapters in ten states and the District of Columbia. The Catholic League regularly attacks church-state separation in its monthly newsletter.

Chalcedon
P.O. Box 158
Vallecito, CA 95251

Chalcedon is the major Christian Reconstructionist organization functioning in the United States. It is headed by Rousas John Rushdoony, who is considered the movement's modern founder. The group publishes a newsletter and a variety of books that explore every aspect of the Reconstructionist philosophy.

Christian Advocates Serving Evangelism
P.O. Box 450349
Atlanta, GA 30345

This Religious Right legal aid group was founded by Jay Alan Sekulow, an attorney and born-again Christian. It focuses mainly on public school-centered litigation; Sekulow argued the equal access case before the Supreme Court in 1990. He has also argues for the rights of students to distribute religious literature at school.

In 1992 Pat Robertson announced on the "700 Club" that Sekulow was joining forces with Robertson's own legal aid group, the American Center for Law and Justice (see under Christian Coalition), leaving the future of CASE in doubt.

Christian Coalition
P.O. Box 1990
Chesapeake, VA 23327

One of Pat Robertson's most recent creations, the Christian Coalition claims 300,000 members in local chapters across the country. The group is incorporated as a 501 (c)(4) organization under Internal Revenue Service guidelines, which gives it greater latitude to get involved in politics. (Most Religious Right groups claim 501 (c)(3) status, meaning they may not get involved in partisan politics or endorse candidates for public office.) Although the Christian Coalition claims to be non-partisan, it functions more or less as an adjunct to the far-right wing of the Republican Party. Coalition supporters have been active in "taking over" local units of the Republican Party in many states and have achieved notable successes in California, Iowa, Minnesota, Colorado, Texas, Virginia and other states.

The Christian Coalition works closely with another Robertson project, the **American Center for Law and Justice**, a network of Religious Right attorneys who litigate church-state cases mostly on a free basis.

Citizens for Excellence in Education
Box 3200
Costa Mesa, CA 92628

CEE is headed by Robert L. Simonds, a former educator who stridently denounces separation of church and state as a "socialist myth" and attacks public education. Simonds says the group, which maintains chapters throughout the country, seeks simply to improve public education. Critics say Simonds really wants to abolish public schools and point to his harsh rhetoric against public education and support for vouchers.

CEE and its companion organization, the National Association of Christian Educators, work primarily to elect Religious Right activists to school boards across the country. They claim great success and say as many as 2,000 CEE supporters have been elected nationwide. The figure is impossible to verify, but known CEE backers currently sit on several school boards in Southern California. (Likewise, CEE's claim of 925 chapters nationwide is probably exaggerated.)

Coalition on Revival
89 Pioneer Way
Mountain View, CA 94041

Headed by Jay Grimstead, the Coalition on Revival is a Reconstructionist-style group that favors imposition of a government based on their understanding of the Bible. The organization is militantly anti-separationist and seeks to organize its followers at the local level.

Concerned Women for America
370 L'Enfant Promenade, S.W.
Suite 800
Washington, D.C. 20024

Headed by Beverly LaHaye, CWA claims 700,000 members and a network of chapters nationwide. Critics say the membership figure is inflated and that actual membership may only be half of that. CWA regularly bashes separation of church and state and public education; LaHaye portrays her organization as all that stands between the United States and a total capitulation to "secular humanism." Before the collapse of the Soviet Union, the group was stridently anti-Communist as well and supported the Nicaraguan *contras*. With Communism on the skids, the group today has stepped up its attack on "humanism" and feminism. LaHaye produces a daily radio program that is aired primarily on evangelical stations. Her husband is the Rev. Tim LaHaye, a well-known Religious Right figure who has written several books attacking "secular humanism" and promoting creationism.

Coral Ridge Ministries
P.O. Box 407137
Ft. Lauderdale, FL 33340-7137

Coral Ridge Ministries is headed by the Rev. D. James Kennedy, a vociferous opponent of separation of church and state. The group publishes a variety of anti-separationist literature and is probably responsible for many of the myths discussed in appendix 1.

Eagle Forum
P.O. Box 618
Alton, IL 62002

Headed by GOP anti-abortion activist Phyllis Schlafly, a conservative Roman Catholic, the Eagle Forum was founded in the early 1970s to oppose the Equal Rights Amendment. When that issue faded, the group took to attacking public education, homosexuality, and separation of church and state. Membership is estimated at under 100,000.

Focus on the Family
P.O. Box 35500
Colorado Springs, CO 80935-3550

Led by "Christian psychologist" James Dobson, Focus on the Family was launched in the late 1970s as a research center for Christian parents interesting in strengthening family ties. Dobson produced materials covering various aspects of child rearing. Dobson's books are mostly secular in approach, and a lot of the advice he gives is common sensical and not overtly sectarian. As a consequence, many people have used the books and become involved with the group, only to later find out that the organization is affiliated with the Religious Right.

At first apolitical, the group began drifting into the Religious Right during the 1980s. Today it still sells books on family life, but alongside that markets books and videos critical of church-state separation. Focus on the Family also works with conservative churches across the country to train activists for local political efforts, such as school board take overs.

The group publishes a slick magazine, *Focus on the Family*, and several other regular publications, including one aimed at teachers. (*Citizen* is FOF's political magazine.) Dobson also hosts a syndicated radio program that is carried on hundreds of mostly evangelical radio stations.

Family Research Council
700 13th St., N.W.
Suite 500
Washington, D.C. 20005

The Family Research Council is Focus on the Family's Washington affiliate. The group is headed by Gary Bauer, a former aide in Ronald Reagan's Education Department. It publishes the monthly newsletter *Washington Watch*. In 1992 the official ties between FRC and FOF were severed, though Dobson remains on FRC's board of directors.

National Legal Foundation
P.O. Box 100697
Ft. Lauderdale, FL 33310-0697

This Religious Right legal aid group was founded by Pat Robertson but was cut loose by him after some type of dispute in the late 1980s. Today the group is headed by Robert Skolrood. The organization attacks public education and was instrumental in defending the Equal Access Act in the federal courts. Its most recent stunt was a fundraising gambit during which Skolrood claimed he was going to single-handedly fend off a lawsuit by noted atheist Madalyn Murray O'Hair designed to remove "In God We Trust" from U.S. currency. Skolrood raised some cash, but no lawsuit was ever filed by O'Hair.

Rutherford Institute
P.O. Box 7482
Charlottesville, VA 22906

John Whitehead, the anti-separationist attorney who founded the Rutherford Institute in the early 1980s, insists that the group is not a Religious Right organization. The evidence indicates otherwise. Although the Institute has defended some non-Christians, the bulk of its work is aimed at helping evangelical Christians gain a foothold in the public schools. Whitehead is the author of several books that attack separation of church and state and the public schools. His first book is titled *The Separation Illusion* and contains an introduction by Christian Reconstructionist R. J. Rushdoony. Whitehead says he is not a Reconstructionist.

The Rutherford Institute is essentially a network of volunteer attorneys who litigate church-state cases on a *pro-bono* basis. Chapters exist in most states, and Whitehead produces a daily radio program, "Freedom Under Fire," for evangelical stations. The Institute is growing and even has chapters overseas.

Traditional Values Coalition
100 S. Anaheim Boulevard
Suite 350
Anaheim, CA 92805

Led by rabidly anti-homosexual minister the Rev. Louis Sheldon, this group promotes the standard Religious Right line: anti-public schools, pro-vouchers, pro-"biblical values," and so on. Although primarily active in California, the group has been working to achieve a nationwide presence. Lately, TVC has been active in promoting the voucher concept and other forms of parochial school aid.

WallBuilders, Inc.
P.O. Box 397
Aledo, TX 76008

WallBuilders was founded by David Barton, a Religious Right activist who attempts to prove that the United States was founded to be a "Christian" nation and that separation of church and state is a myth. Barton is the author of two books, *The Myth of Separation*, an attack on separation of church and state using distorted history, and *America: To Pray or Not to Pray*, which argues that recent American social problems were caused by the Supreme Court's school prayer rulings in the 1960s. WallBuilders, which is a business, not a non-profit group, also sells videos based on the books. In addition, Barton often speaks at sympathetic churches across the country.

Appendix 4

Suggestions for Further Reading

There are many excellent books that deal with separation of church and state. Some are general, while others cover specific topics of church-state relations. This list is by no means exhaustive, but it includes many books that are a good starting point for further research and learning.

Books

Church, State and Freedom (revised edition), by Leo Pfeffer (1967, Beacon Press, Boston). Unfortunately now out of print, this classic volume is well worth a trip to a used book store. Pfeffer thoroughly examines the history behind the religion clauses of the Constitution and looks at contemporary church-state issues. Well written and packed with information. Invaluable.

Toward Benevolent Neutrality: Church, State, and the Supreme Court (fourth edition), by Robert T. Miller and Ronald B. Flowers (1992, Markham Press Fund of Baylor University Press, Waco, Texas). This important reference tool contains the text of the Supreme Court's major church-state decisions from the late 19th century until 1992's *Lee v. Weisman.* Included are valuable interpretive essays on the scope and effect of the rulings.

Religious Liberty and the Secular State, by John Swomley (1987, Prometheus Books, Buffalo). A brief but thorough defense of the secular state as the best mechanism for safeguarding religious freedom for all Americans. Also contains valuable information about the historical development of the First Amendment's religious freedom clauses.

The Wall of Separation: A Primer on Church and State, by William M. Ramsay (1989, Westminster/John Knox Press, Louisville). A good overview of history and contemporary issues, written primarily from a Protestant perspective.

The Establishment Clause: Religion and the First Amendment, by Leonard W. Levy (1986, Macmillan Publishing, New York). This well-researched book demonstrates that there is no historical basis for the claim that the First Amendment was designed to allow for non-preferential aid to religion. A powerful corrective to much anti-separationist dogma.

James Madison on Religious Liberty, edited by Robert S. Alley (1985, Prometheus Books, Buffalo). Selections from some of Madison's most important writings on church and state. Blows apart arguments that Madison was not a separationist.

The Virginia Statute for Religious Freedom, edited by Merrill D. Peterson and Robert C. Vaughan (1988, Cambridge University Press, New York). A collection of notable essays on the development of religious liberty in the United States, with emphasis on the struggle in Virginia.

Original Intent: Chief Justice Rehnquist and the Course of American Church/State Relations, by Derek Davis (1991, Prometheus Books, Buffalo). A frightening but eye-opening look at the "accommodationist" church-state views of Chief Justice William Rehnquist and their consequences for religious freedom.

Lowering the Wall: Religion and the Supreme Court in the 1980s, by Gregg Ivers (1991, Anti-Defamation League, New York). This devastating critique examines the systematic attempt to undermine the wall of separation during the Reagan-Bush years.

Redefining the First Freedom: The Supreme Court and the Consolidation of State Power, 1980-1990, by Gregg Ivers (1992, Transaction Publications, Rutgers University, New Brunswick, New Jersey). Ivers's second book contains more valuable information about church-state law and the modern Supreme Court.

Caesar's Coin: Religion and Politics in America, by Richard P. McBrien (1987, Macmillian, New York). A thoughtful discussion on the interaction between religion and politics by a Catholic theologian. McBrien points out crucial differences between religious groups' use of the public forum to promote their views and misguided efforts to enforce sectarian doctrine through civil power.

Jews, Turks, and Infidels, by Morton Borden (1984, University of North Carolina Press, Chapel Hill). Interesting study of the struggle for religious freedom by American Jews. Contains much good information about the "Christian nation" view of the United States common in the 19th century.

Challenging the Christian Right: The Activist's Handbook, by Frederick Clarkson and Skipp Porteous (1992, Institute for First Amendment Studies, Inc., Great Barrington, Massachusetts). A useful handbook for anyone looking for practical suggestions on ways to combat the Religious Right at the local level. The book contains useful information about various Religious Right groups.

The Great Victorian Sacrilege: Preachers, Politics and the Passion, 1879-1884, by Alan Nielsen (1991, McFarland & Company, Inc., Jefferson, North Carolina). Looks at efforts by religious leaders and municipal authorities to squelch a theatrical performance of the passion of Jesus Christ in late-19th century America. A good example of the dangers of church-state union. Well written and entertaining.

Blue Laws: The History, Economics, and Politics of Sunday-Closing Laws, by David N. Laband and Deborah Hendry Heinbuch (1987, D.C. Heath and Company, Lexington, Massachusetts). Extensive examination of the history, scope and effect of Sunday-closing laws on business, religion and society.

Dominion Theology: Blessing or Curse? An Analysis of Christian Reconstructionism, by H. Wayne House and Thomas D. Ice (1989, Multnomah Press, Portland, Oregon). An analysis of the goals of the Christian Reconstructionist movement from a critical perspective. The book is aimed at a religious audience and contains a thorough refutation of Reconstructionism from a biblical perspective.

Periodicals

Church & State. A monthly journal of news and analysis of church-state developments from around the country. Contains much news unavailable elsewhere. Provides powerful arguments in favor of separation of church and state. Published by Americans United for Separation of Church and State, 8120 Fenton St., Silver Spring, Maryland, 20910, (301) 589-3707. $25 per year.

Liberty. A magazine of religious freedom. Emphasizes theory and philosophy of church-state relations more than hard news. Strongly contends for separation. Published by the Seventh-day Adventist General Conference, 12501 Old Columbia Pike, Silver Spring, Maryland, 20904, (301) 680-6000. $6.95 per year.

Religious Freedom Reporter. An excellent tool for attorneys and academics interested in church-state law, this monthly publication gives summaries of church-state cases from state and federal courts across the United States. Published by the Church-State Resource Center, Norman Adrian Wiggins School of Law, Campbell University, Box 505, Buies Creek, North Carolina, 27506, (800) 334-4111, ext. 4301. $95 per year.

Report From The Capital. A publication of the Baptist Joint Committee on Public Affairs that contains news updates on church-state issues and opinion columns that speak in favor of religious liberty through separation of church and state. BJC, 200 Maryland Avenue, N.E., Washington, D.C., 20002. $8 per year.

The Freedom Writer. A hard-hitting newsletter that takes on the Religious Right. Published bimonthly by the Institute for First Amendment Studies, Inc., P.O. Box 589, Great Barrington, Massachusetts, 01230, (413) 274-3786. $25 per year.

Index